Occupy D.C.:
A Photo Essay In Black & White

John B. Parks

ISBN: 1484859227
ISBN-13: 9781484859223

DEDICATION

This book is dedicated to all persons engaged in peaceful protest for positive change throughout the world, past, present and future.

CONTENTS

INTRODUCTION

Occupy D.C. was one of over 90 protest movements that spread throughout the United States in the fall of 2011. It was inspired by the Occupy Wall Street Movement in New York at Zuccotti Park. Occupy Wall Street began on September 17, 2011 as a protest against social and economic inequality in response to the fallout from the 2008 global financial crisis, the subprime mortgage crisis and the Arab Spring. The Occupy slogan "We are the 99%" underscored the widening gap between the wealth of the top 1% and everyone else. But the movement also included protest against U.S. militarism, support for universal healthcare and more government account ability. Although Occupy was a peaceful movement it had staunch detractors embedded in national news coverage as its message grew and permeated national dialogues across party lines and other social demographics.

Occupy D.C. began on October 1, 2011, several weeks after Occupy Wall Street. Headquartered at McPherson Square, between 14th & I Streets, N.W. at the corner of Vermont Ave and I Streets within the vicinity of the White House, the secondary location was at Freedom Plaza, located between 14th and 13th streets on Pennsylvania Ave in N.W. D.C. directly in view of the U.S. Capitol. From these locations protesters joined by other participants from around the city marched to the National Air & Space Museum to stage a protest of the growth of the U.S. military presence around the globe in the use of drones. The protest ended with at least one arrest after an attempt had been made to enter the museum for an anti-drone demonstration.

Although the Joint Terrorism Task Force had labeled Occupy movement a peaceful one the movement came to a violent end as its encampments became an issue of contention between the right to protest verses trespassing and public safety. The New York Police Department provided the precedent for evicting the occupy encampments in cities nationwide. Occupy Wall Street was evicted just after 1:00 AM on November 15, 2011. The Occupy D.C. encampments, Freedom Plaza and McPherson Square, faced a January 30, 2012 deadline, but D.C. police and the National Park service police took a slightly softer approach than their NYPD counterparts. The D.C. Occupiers were finally removed on June 10, 2012.

The collection of photographs in this book were taken on October 8, 2011, the day the Occupy D.C. march began from Freedom Plaza to the National Air & Space Museum. Two years after the Occupy Movement disappeared from the streets it has also disappeared from the national dialogue, but its organizers maintain an active online presence through its website, Occupy.com. Thousands of images of the movement, mostly in color, proliferate the internet from media organizations and individuals illustrating the diversity of interrelated issues and enthusiastic participants. Very few if any were recorded the movement in black and white. The four chapters of this photo essay represent a part of one day in the life of the Occupy D.C. Movement. "We The People" set the stage for the march and included a Bill of Rights pep talk from Adbusters. "Signage" represents the language of the movement. "The March" documents the march from Freedom Plaza to the National Air & Space Museum. It was joined by protesters coming from McPherson Square. During the march the protesters chanted "We Are The 99%". The designated route from Freedom Plaza turned left on 13th Street the right onto E Street then right onto 7th Street crossing Pennsylvania Ave. then making their way to the National Air & Space Museum. "At The National Air & Space Museum" Occupy D.C. drew larger crowds as it was joined by the McPherson group. Emotions became more intense especially after police prevented the Occupy organizers from staging a demonstration inside the museum. This essentially marked the end of protests for the day.

Protesters assembling at Freedom Plaza prior to the march to the National Air & Space Museum listening to a presentation from Adbusters.com one of the principle organizing bodies of the Occupy movement.

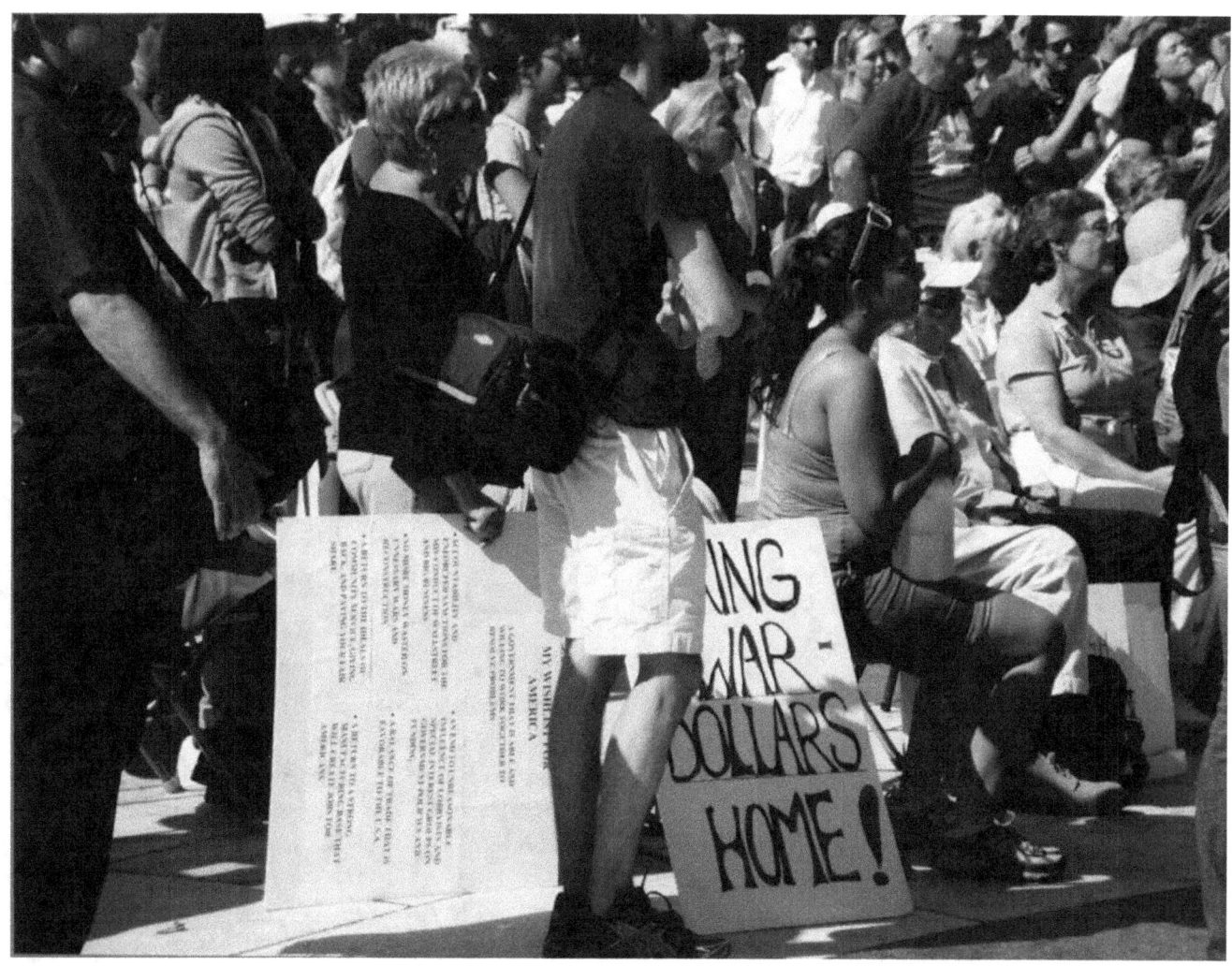

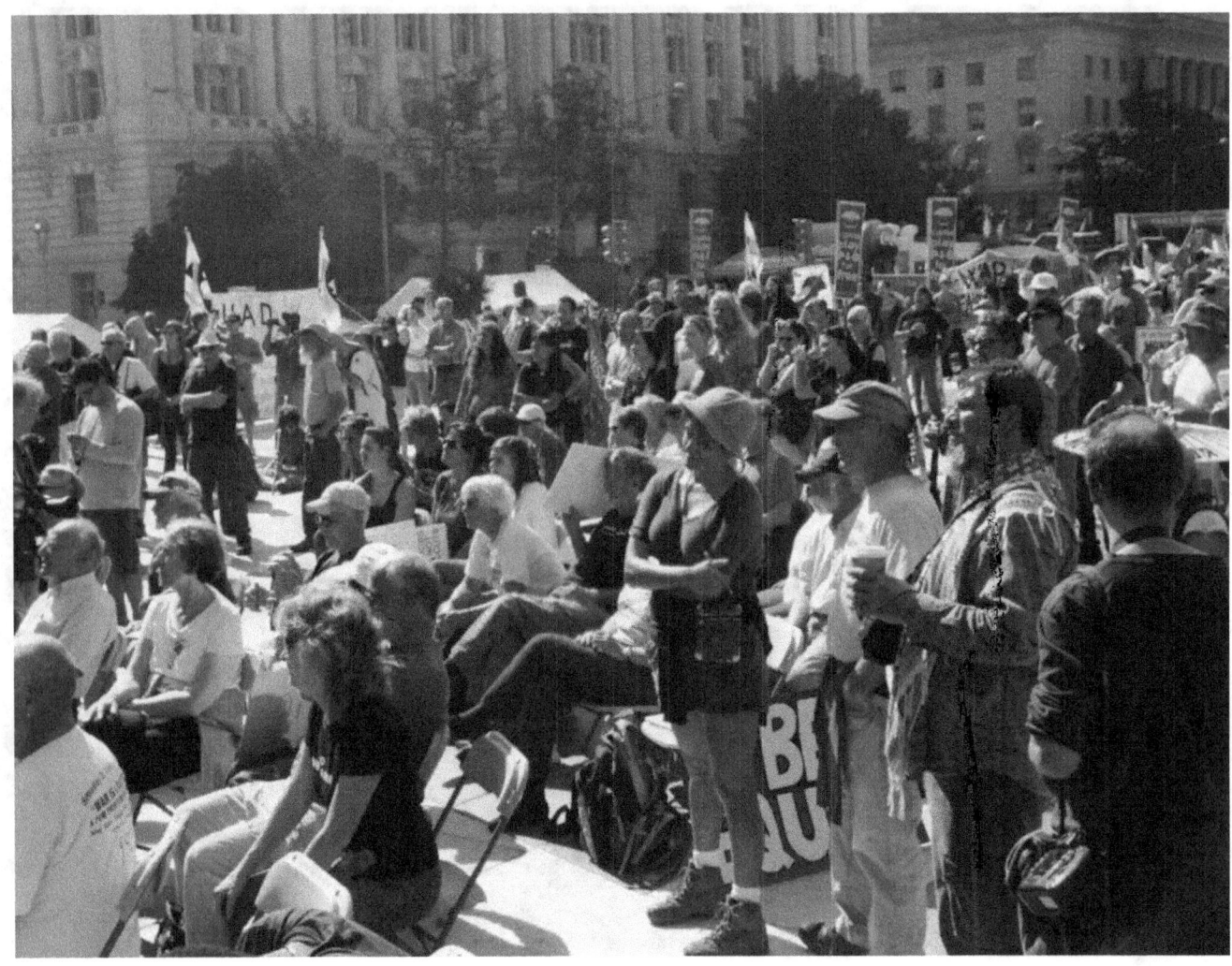

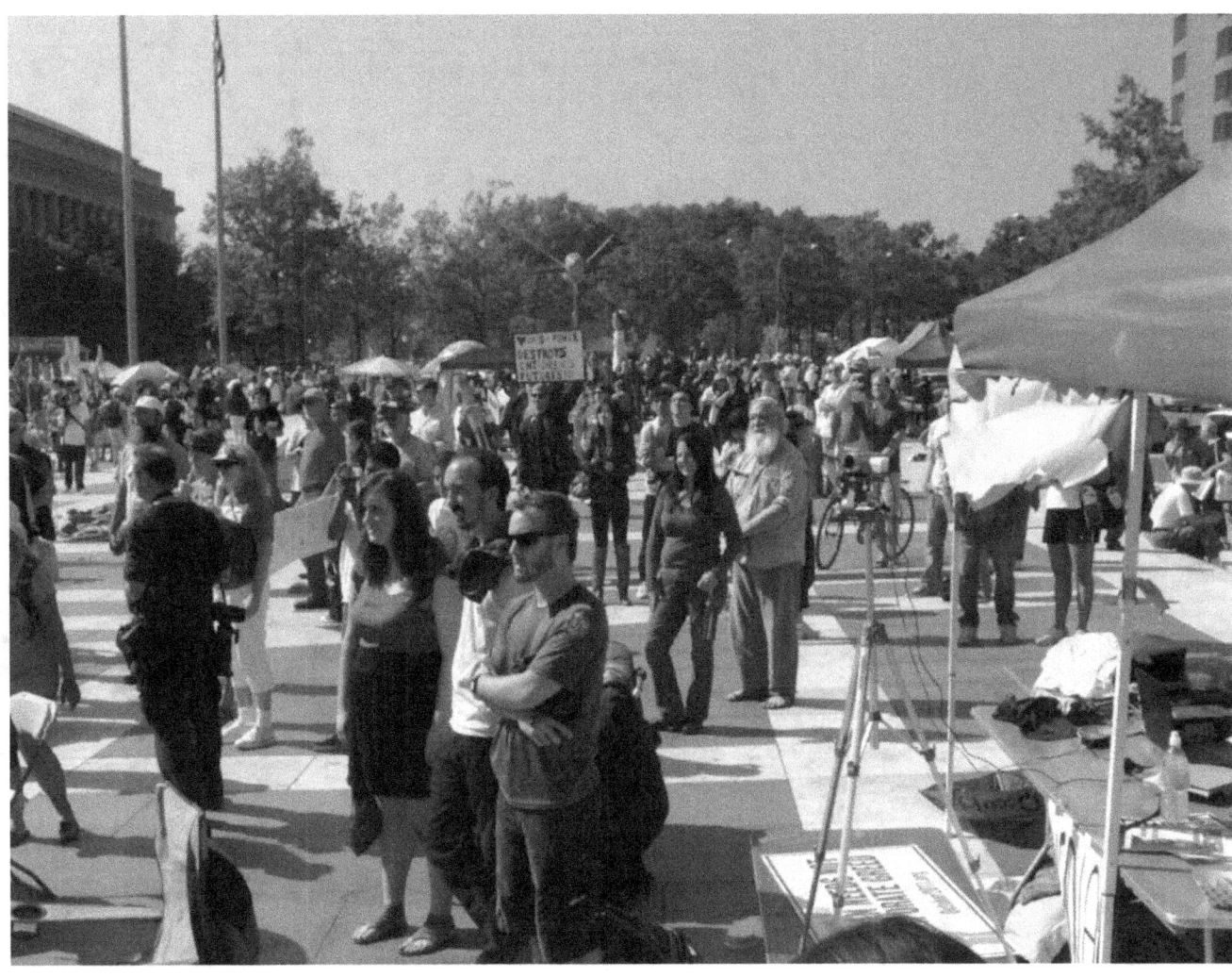

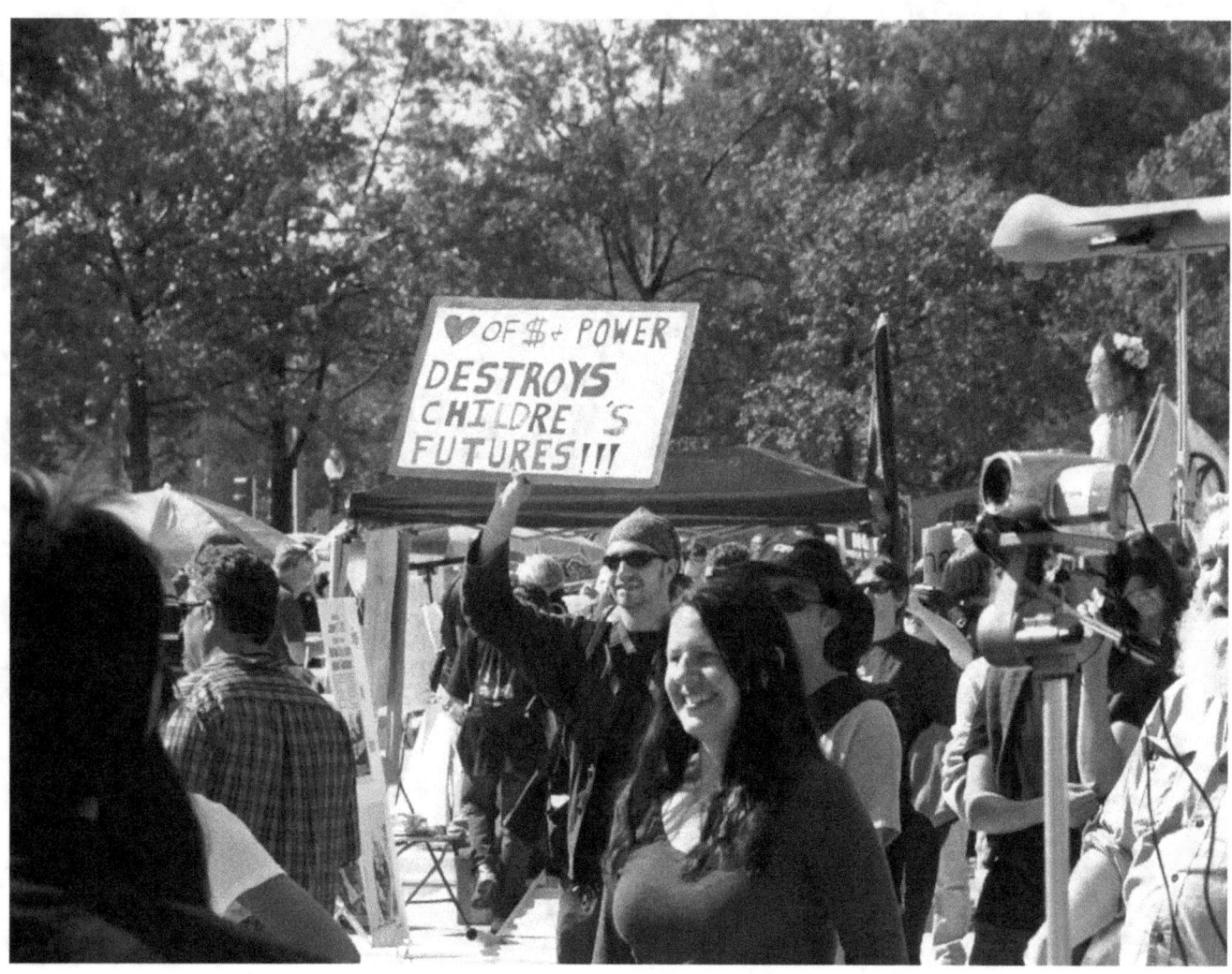

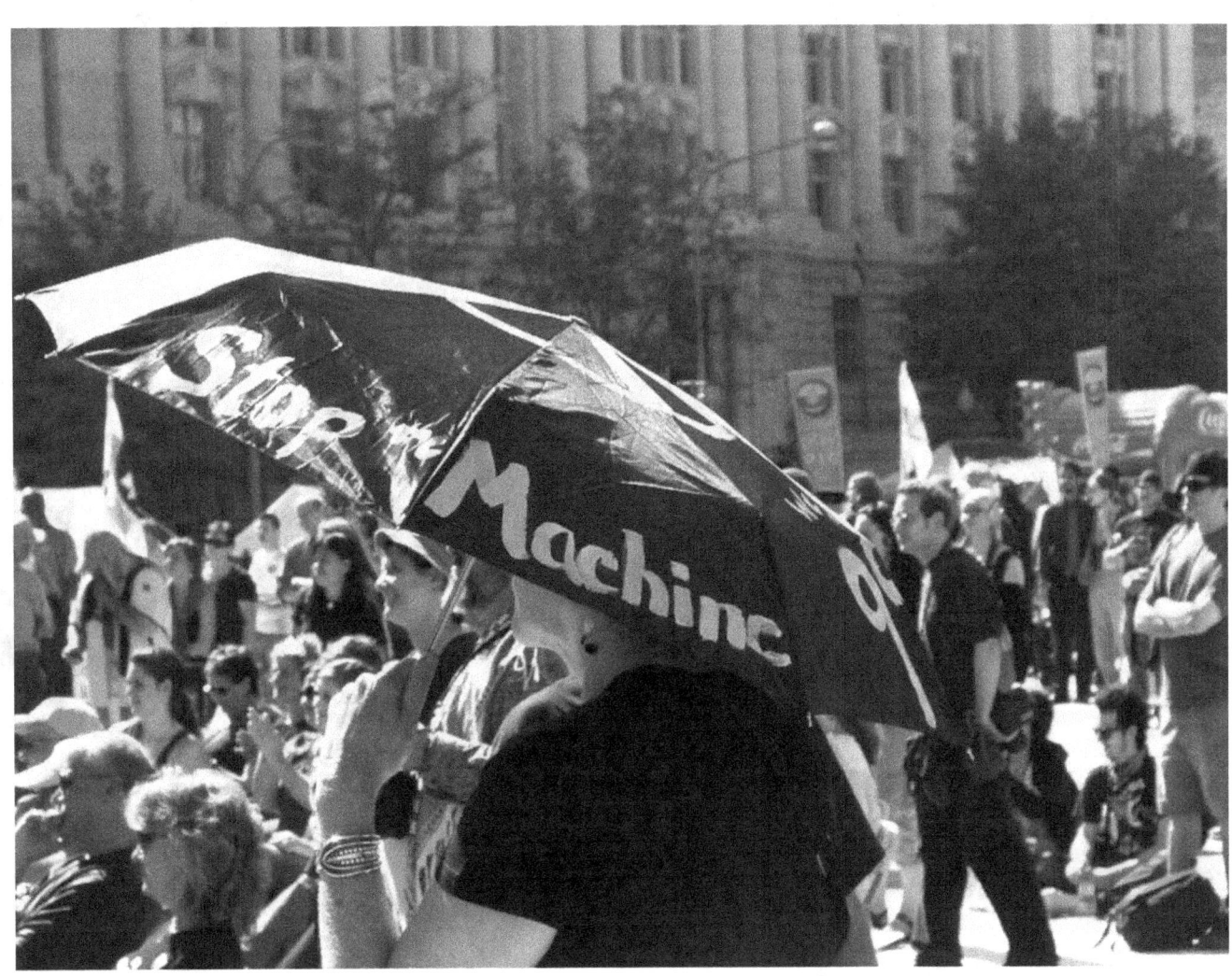

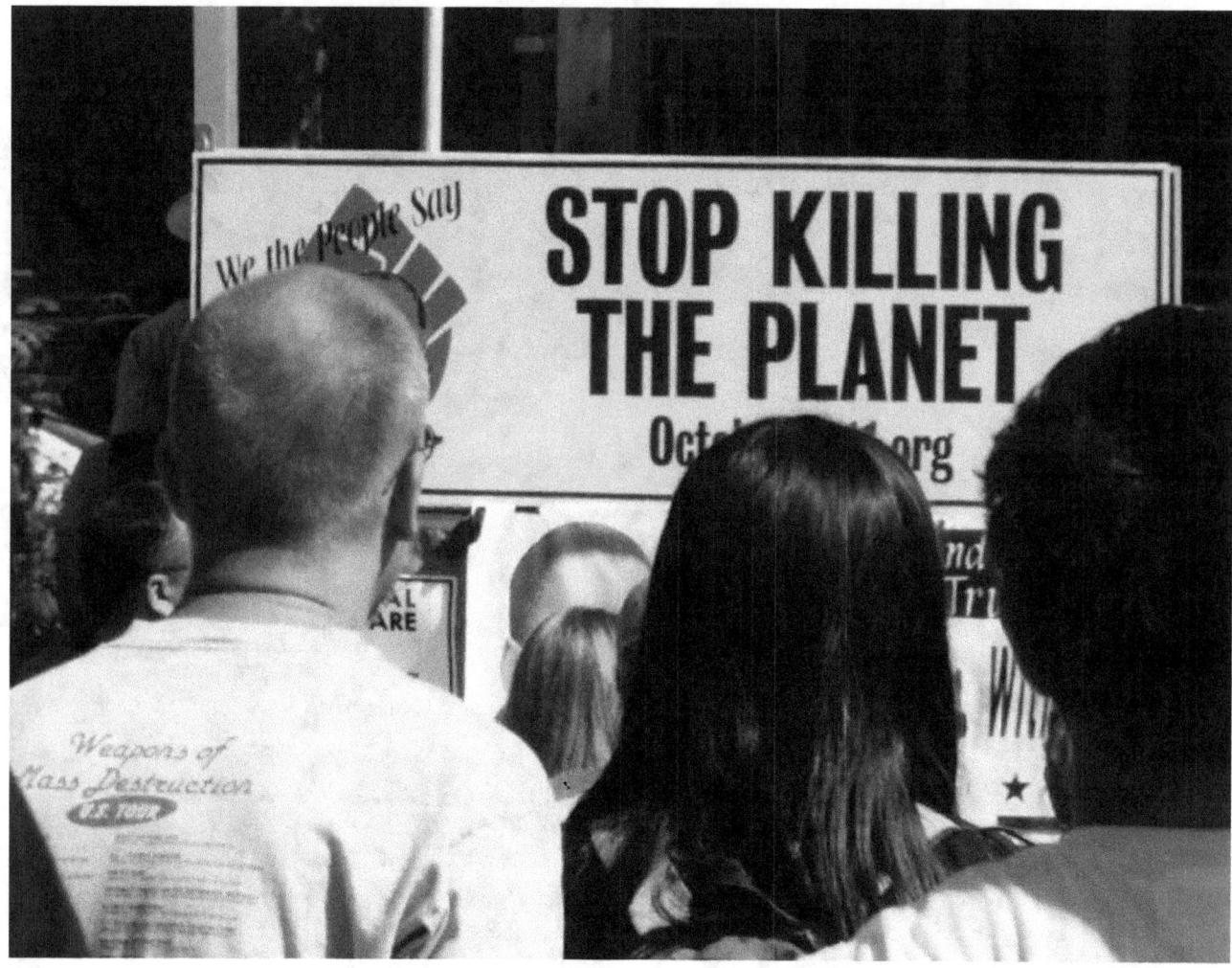

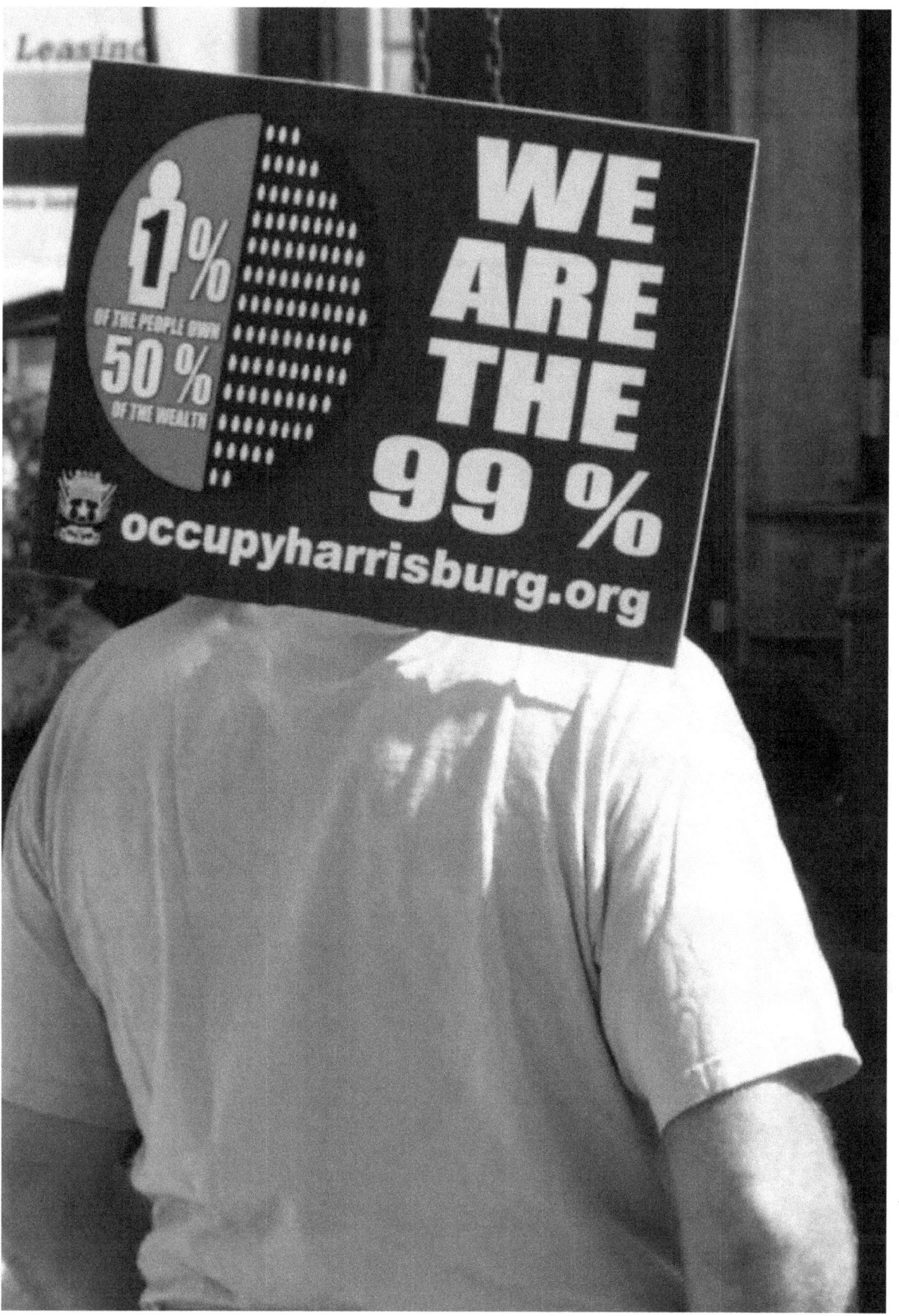

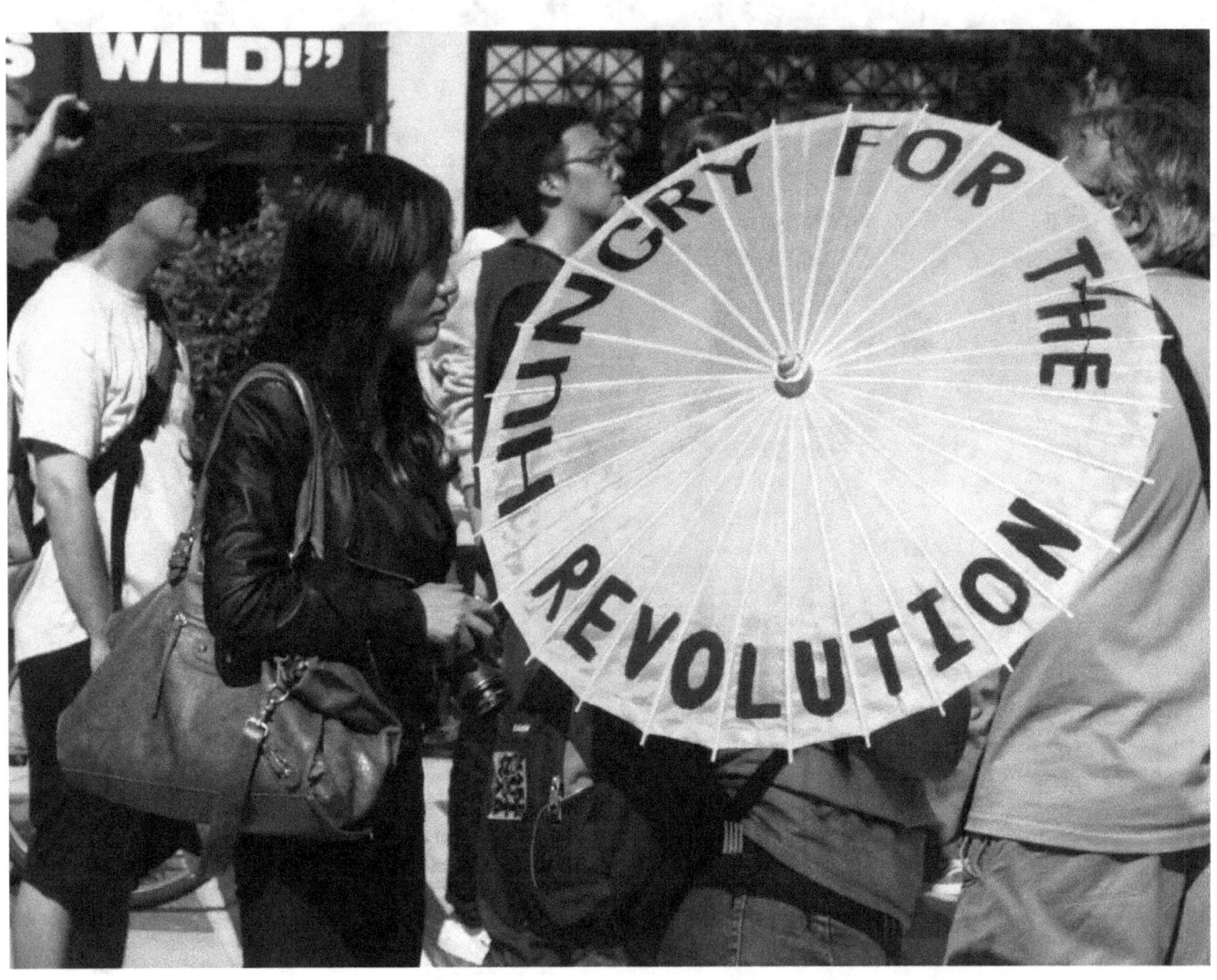

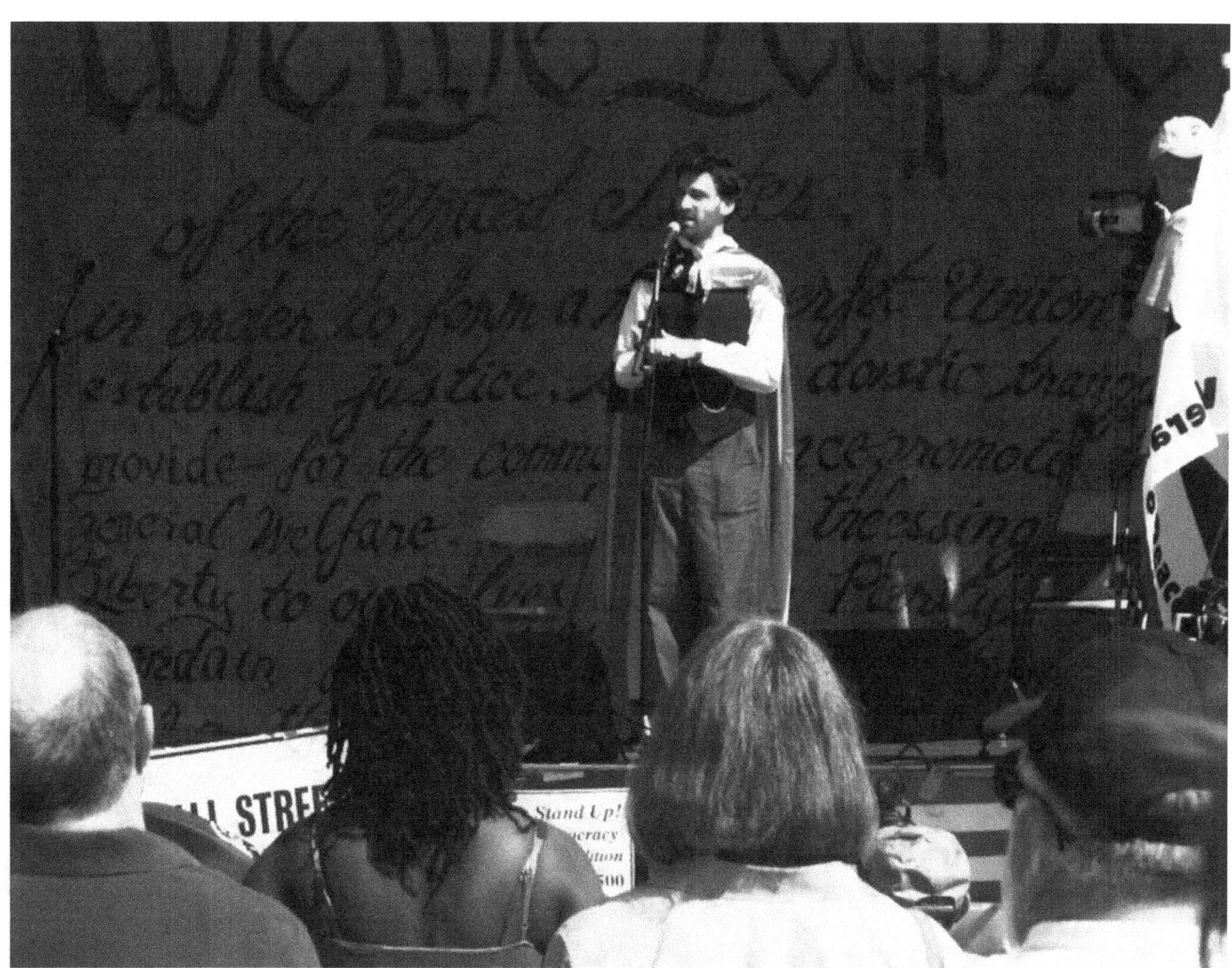

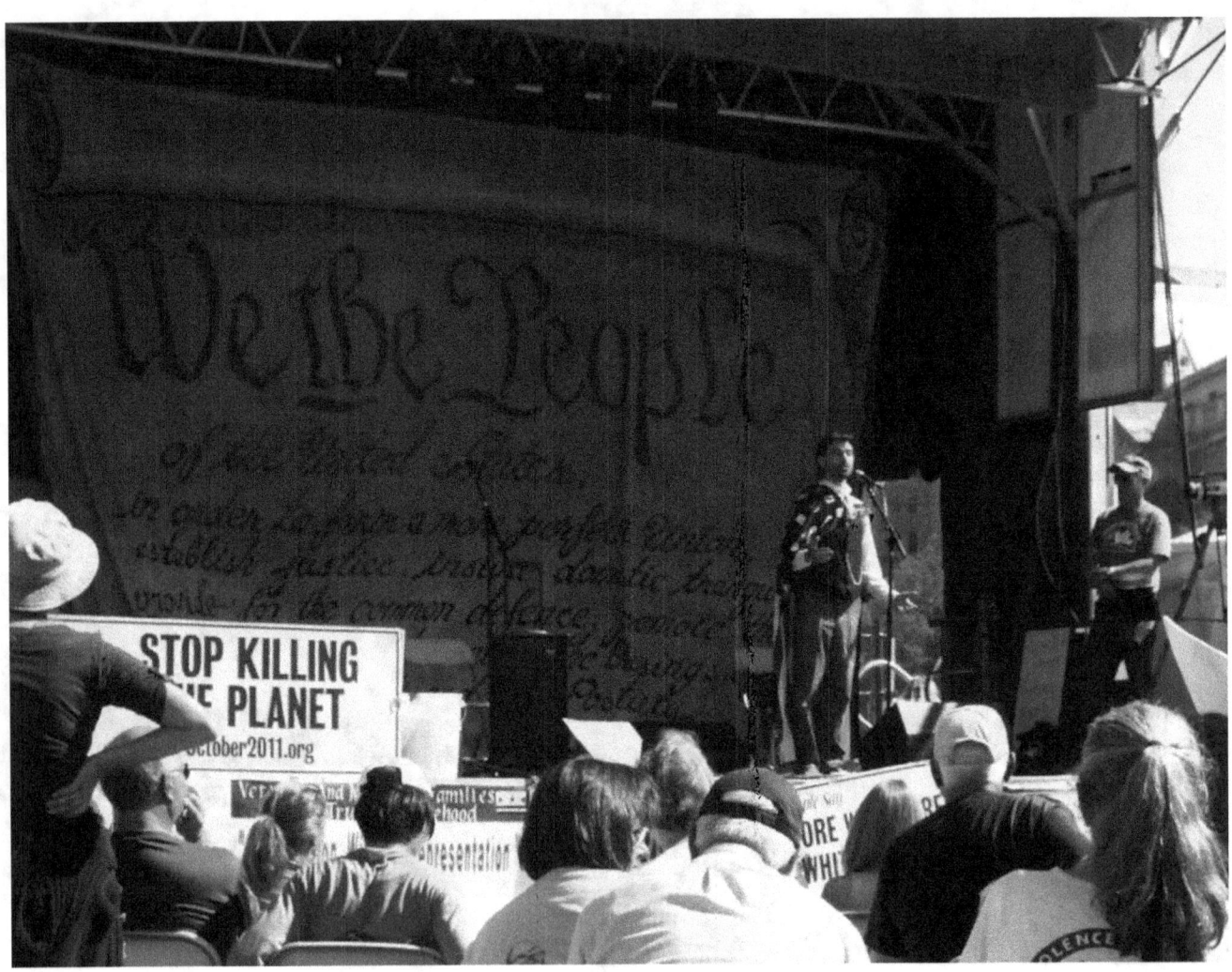

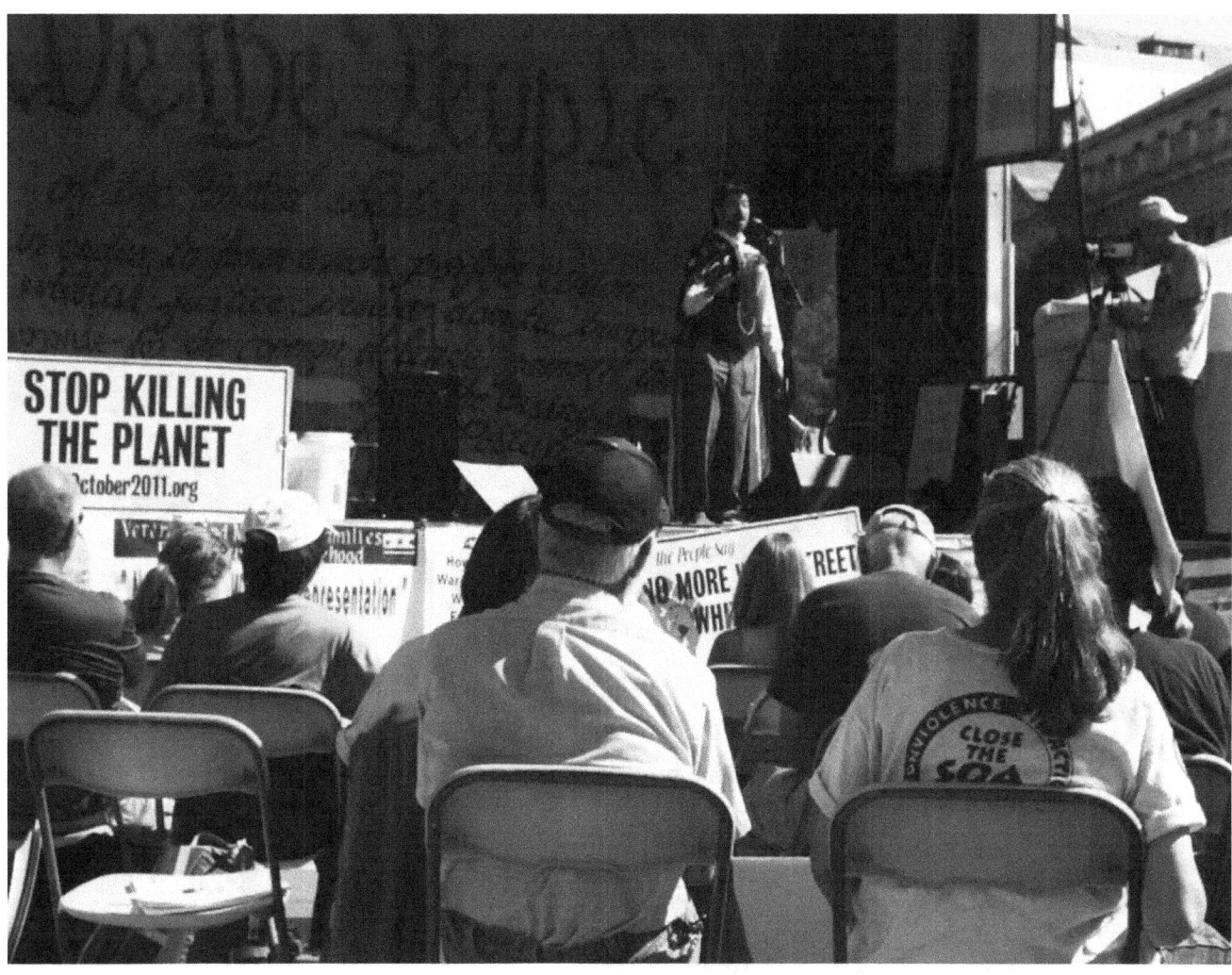

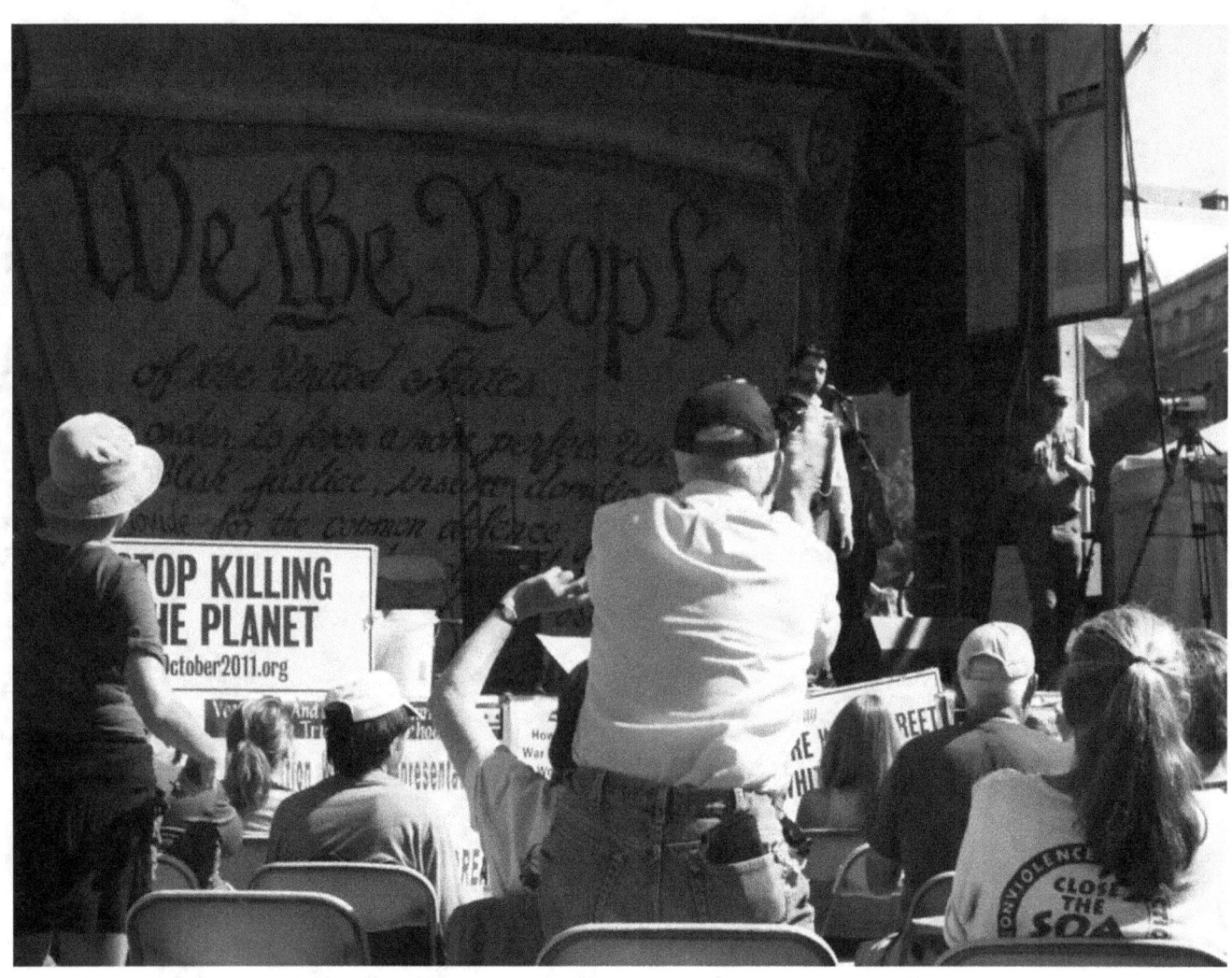

2 SIGNAGE

Signs! The language of the Occupy movement.

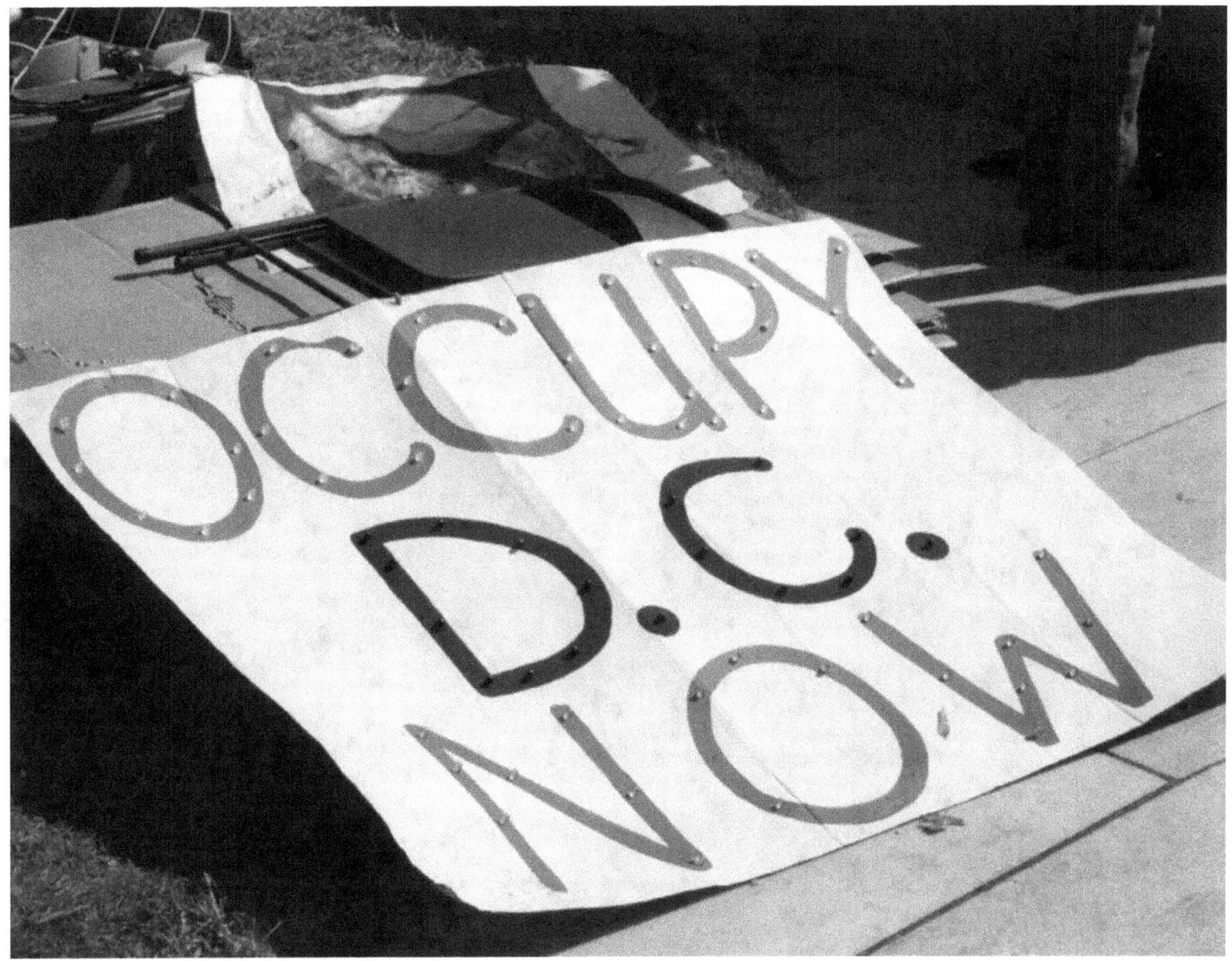

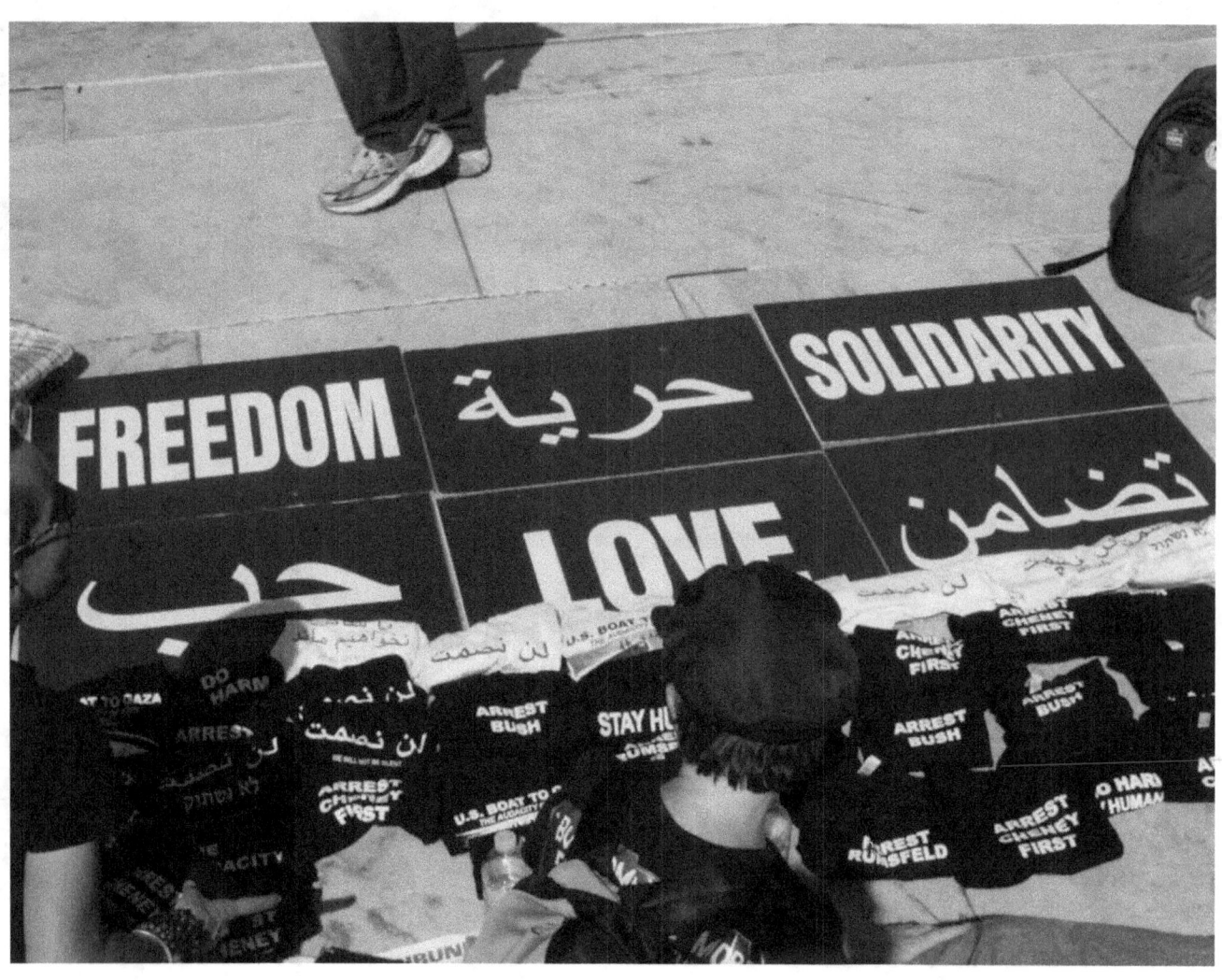

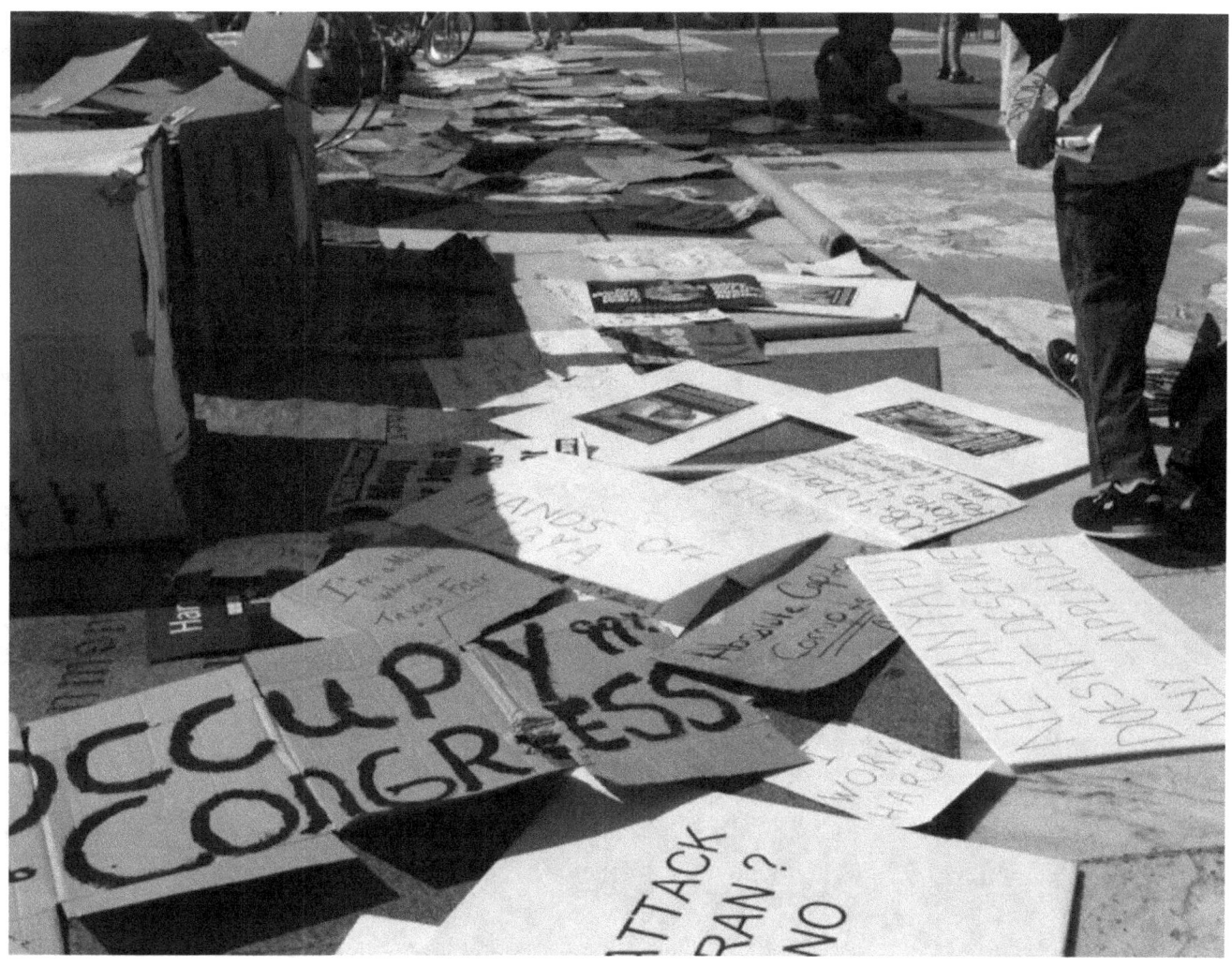

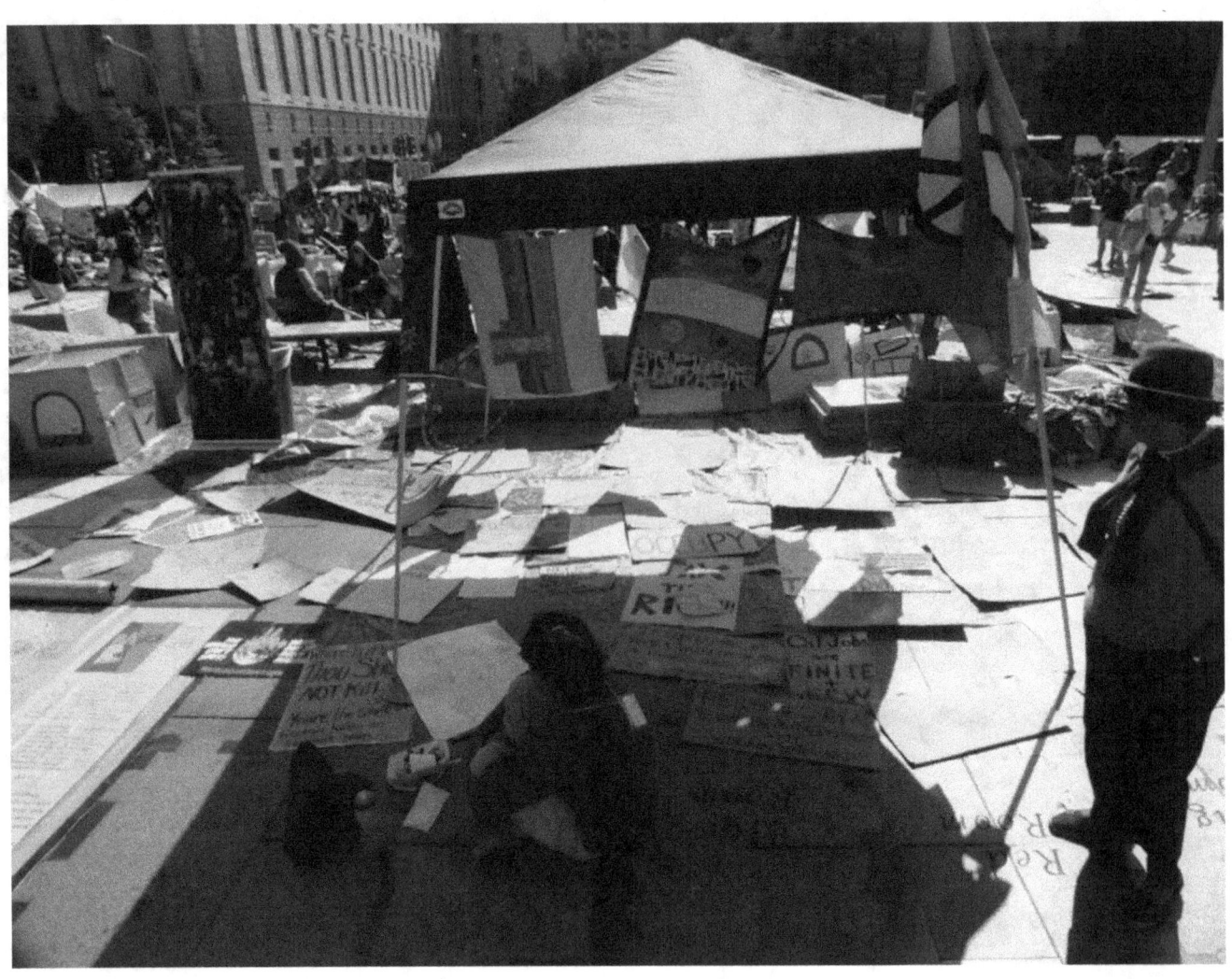

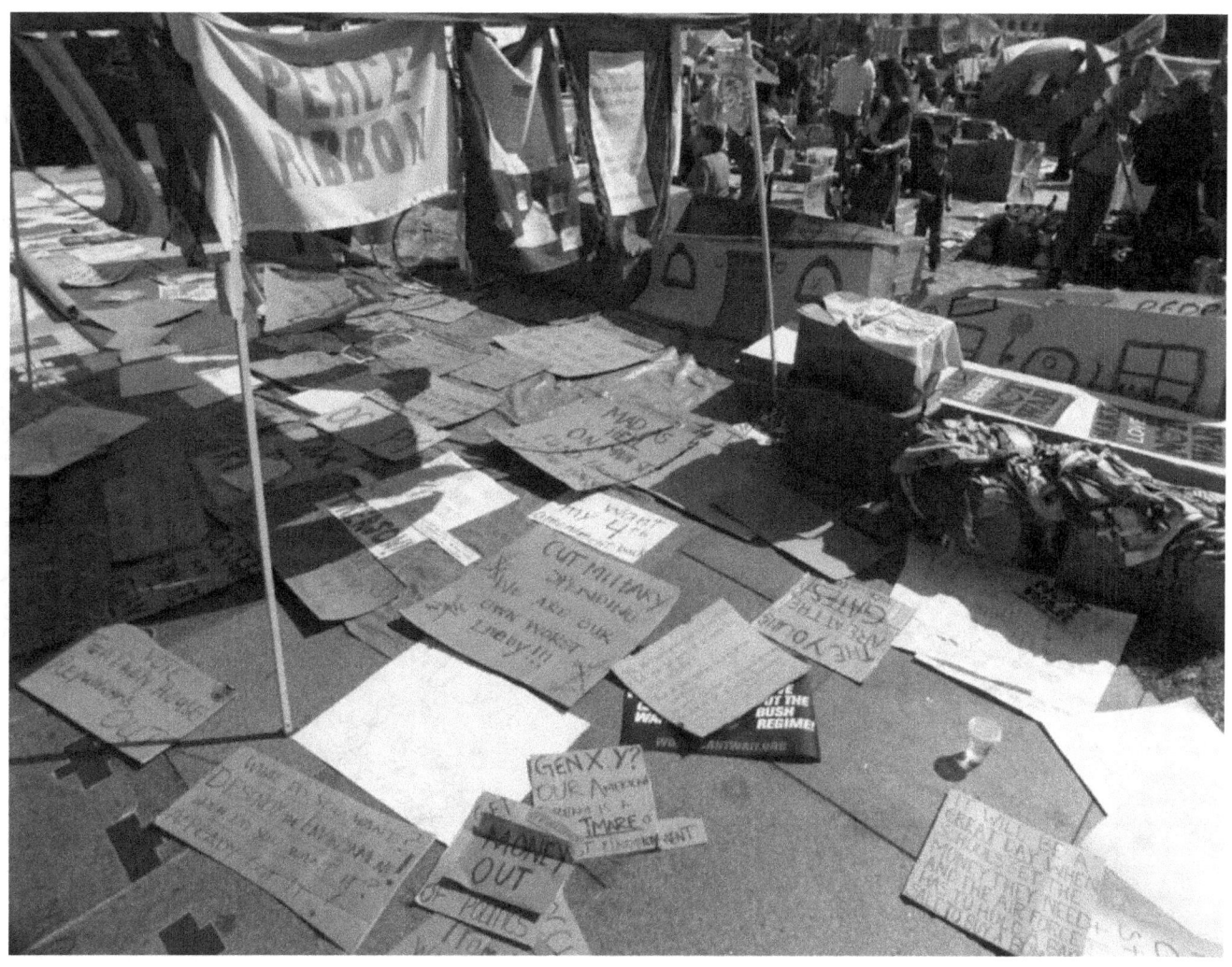

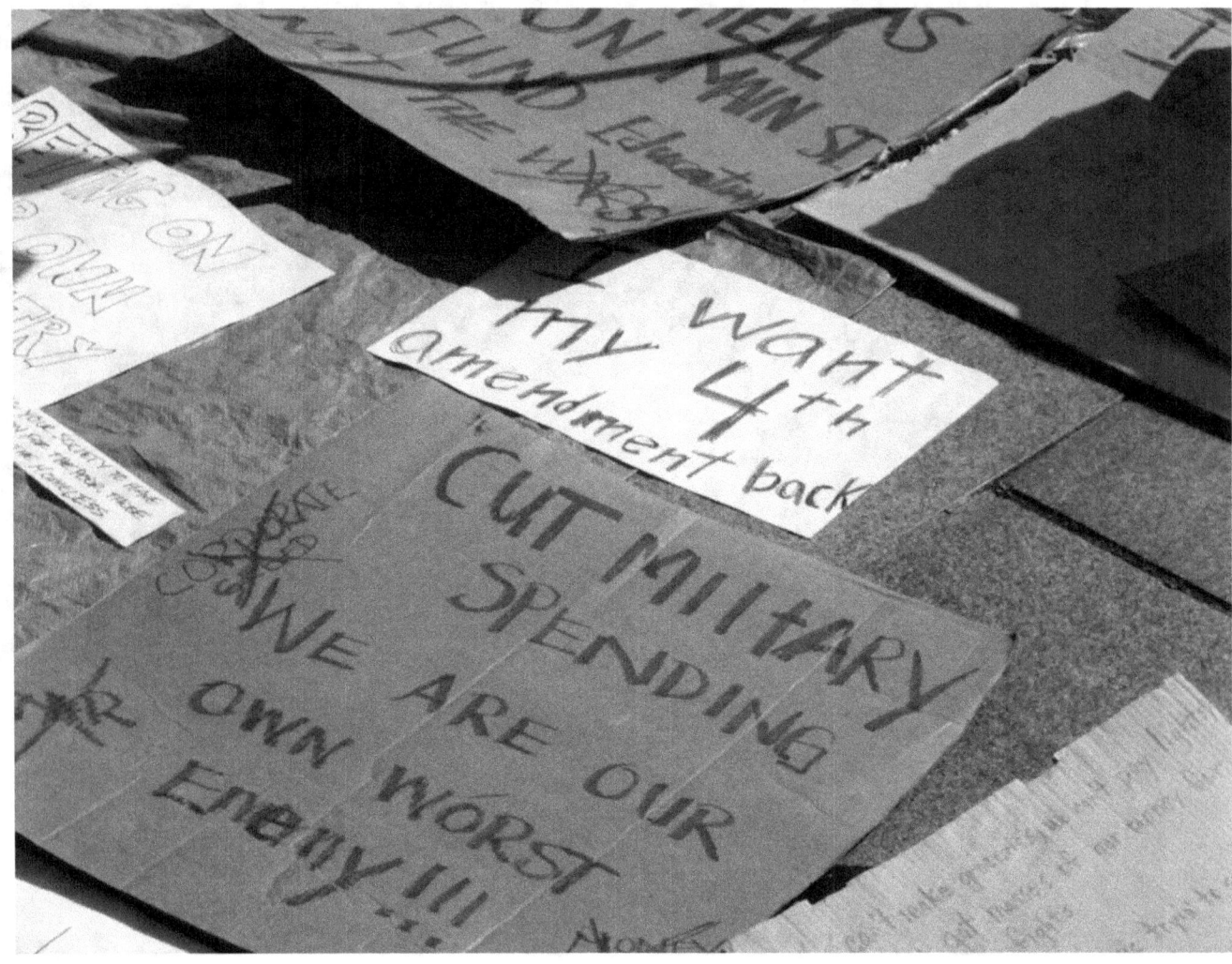

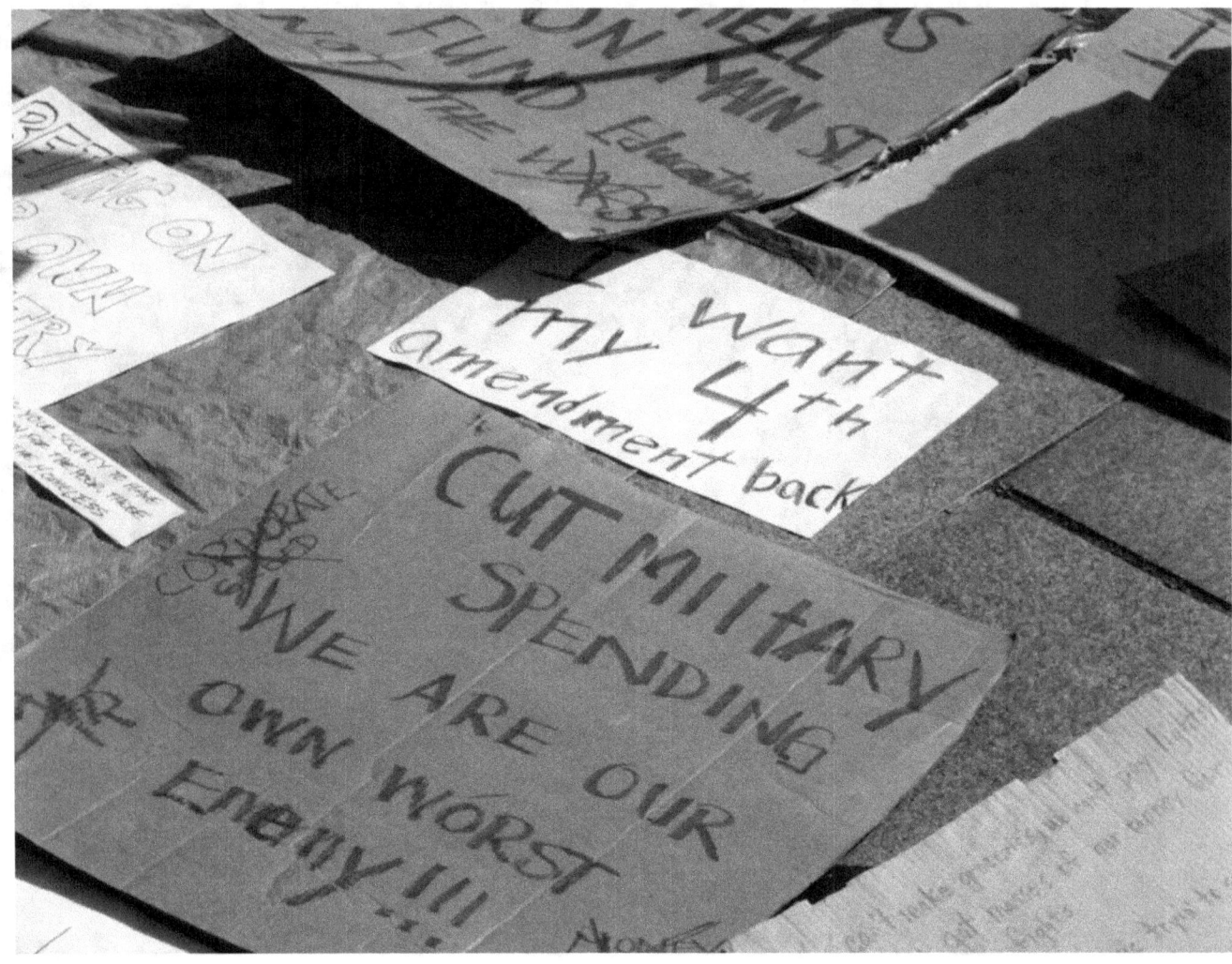

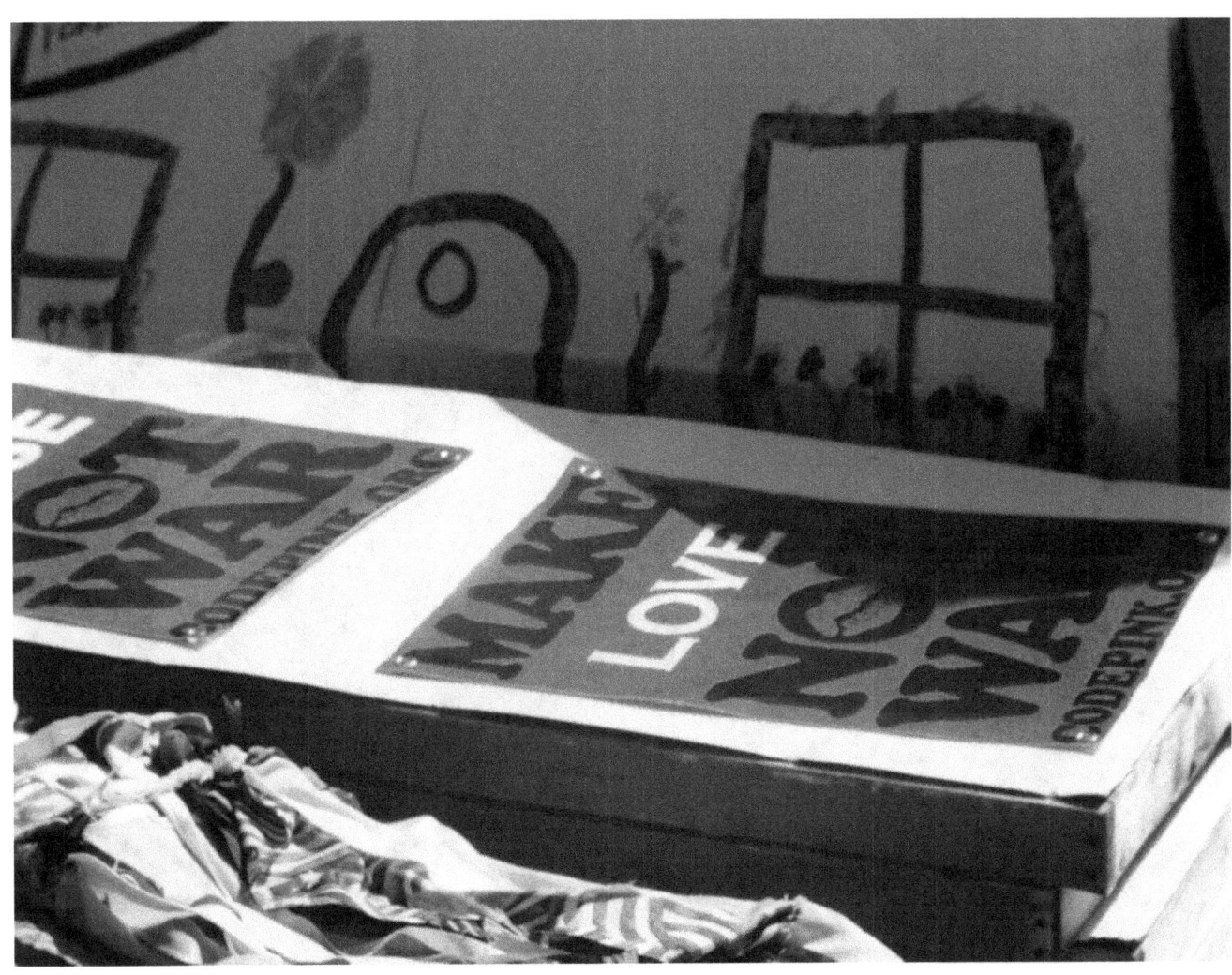

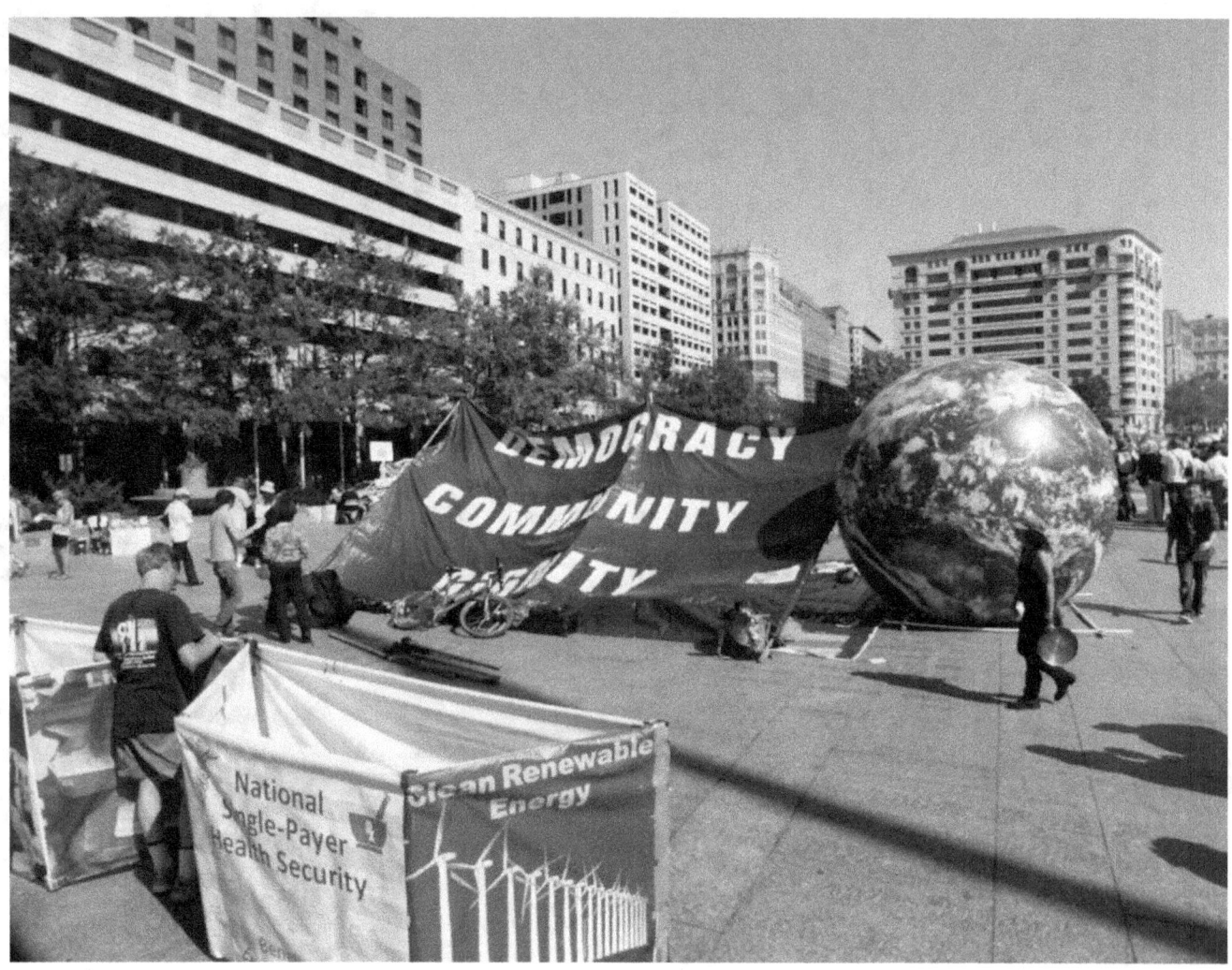

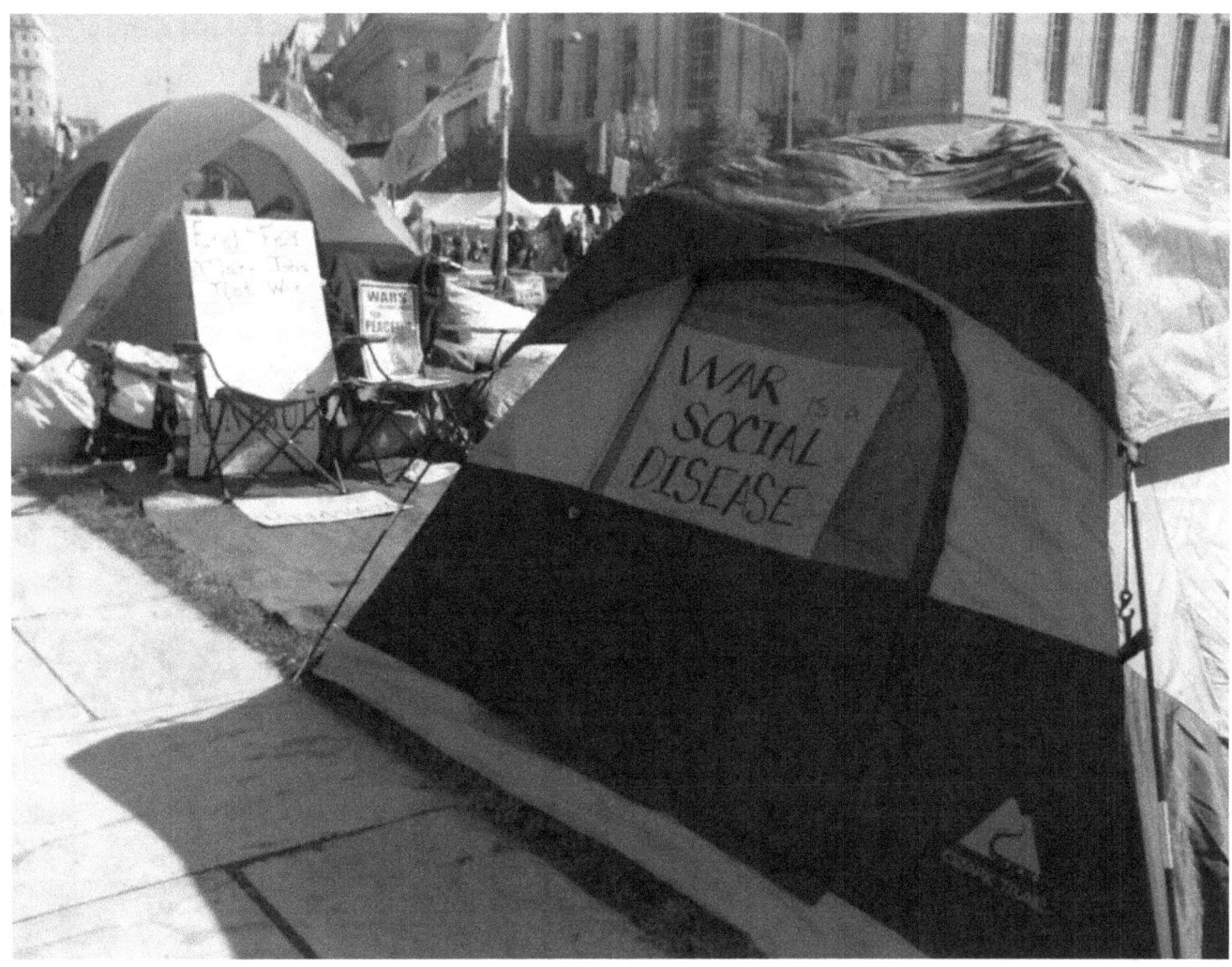

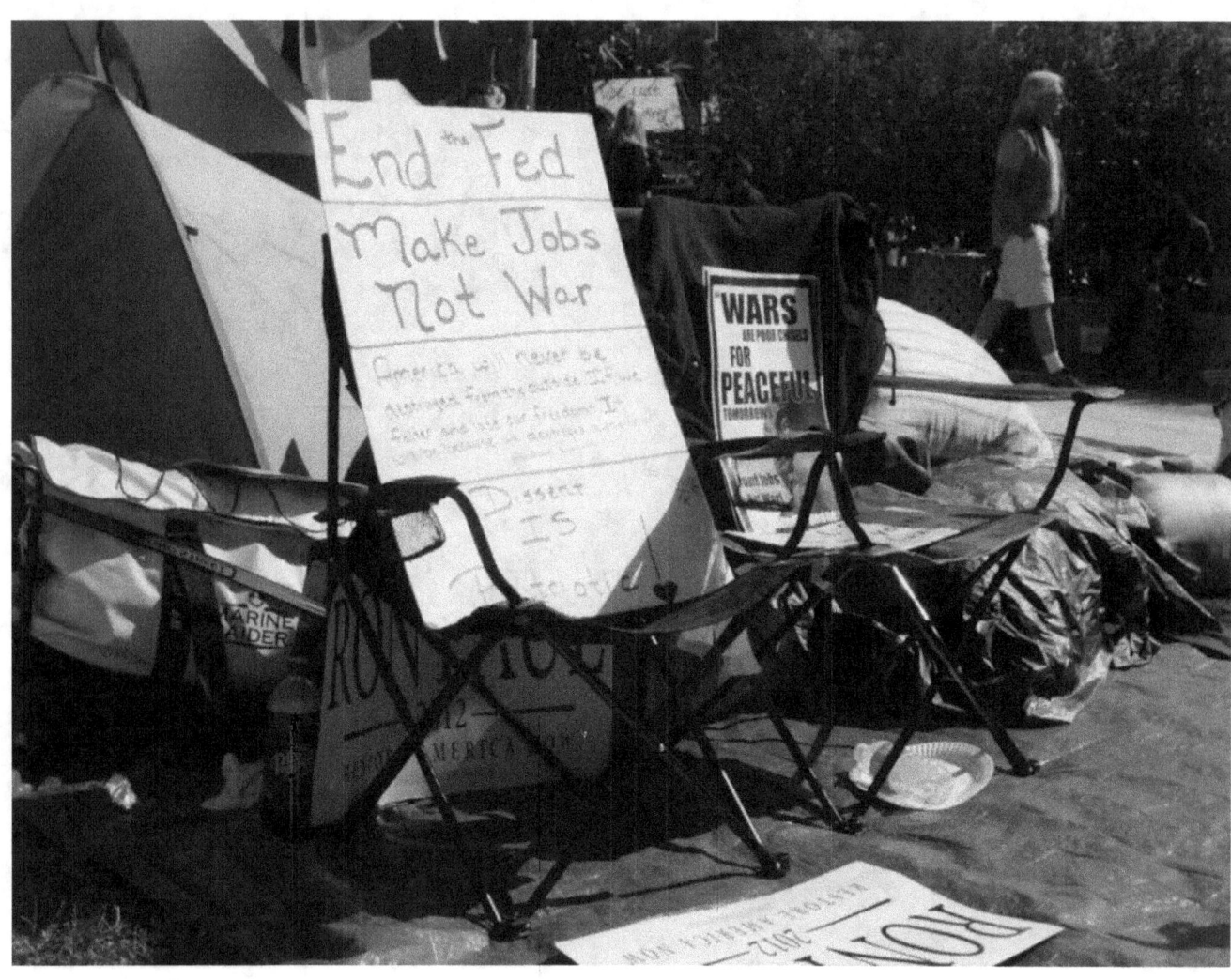

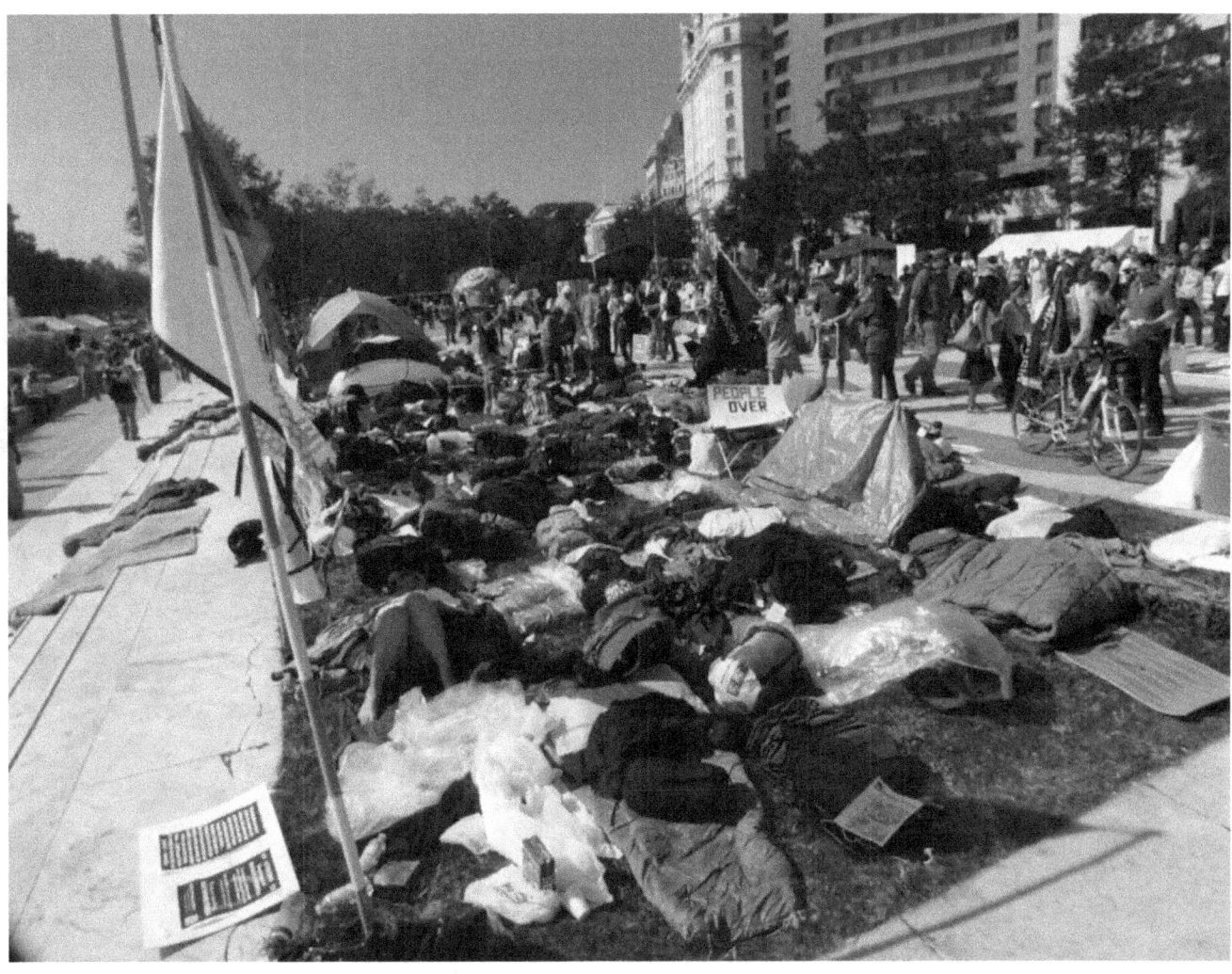

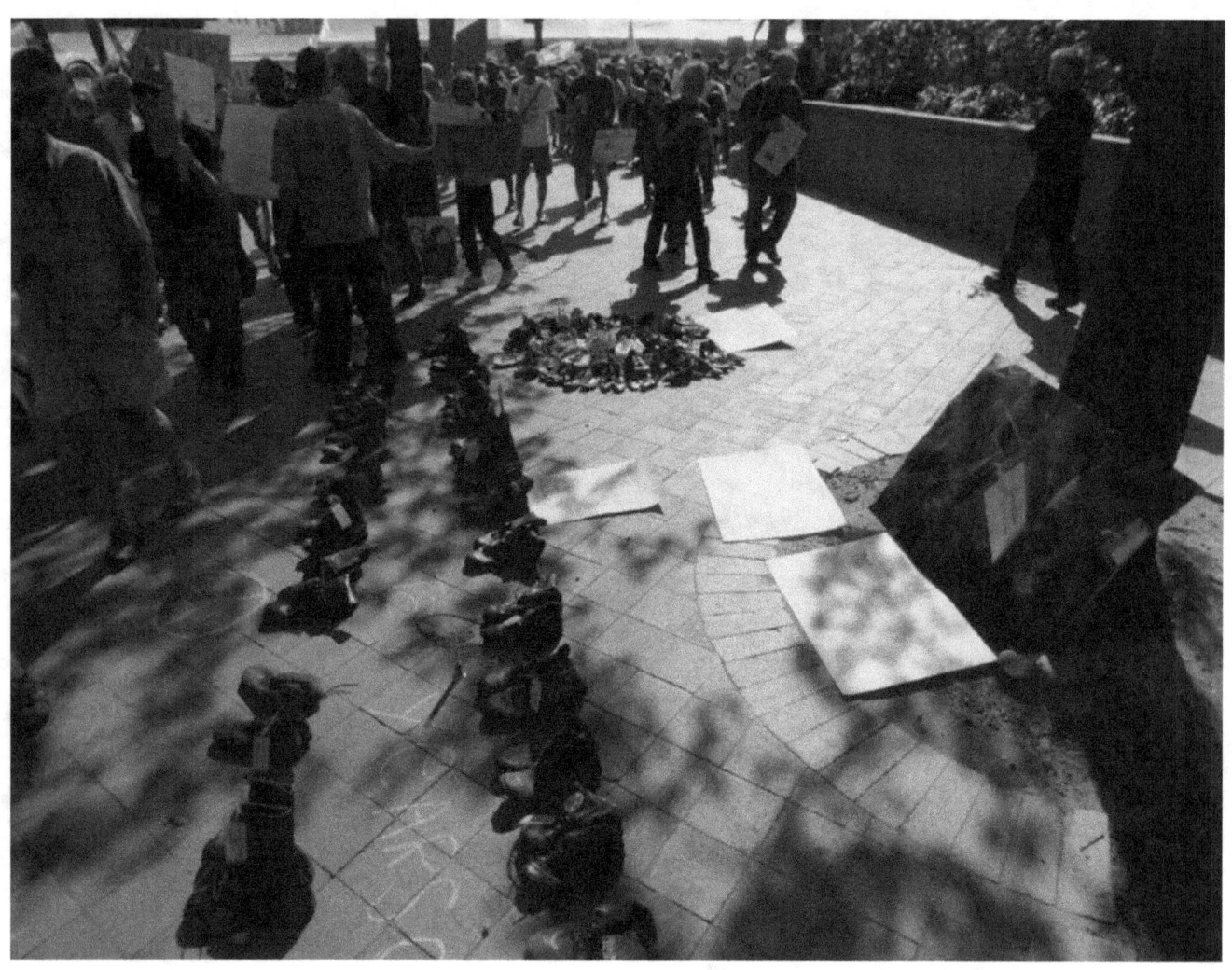

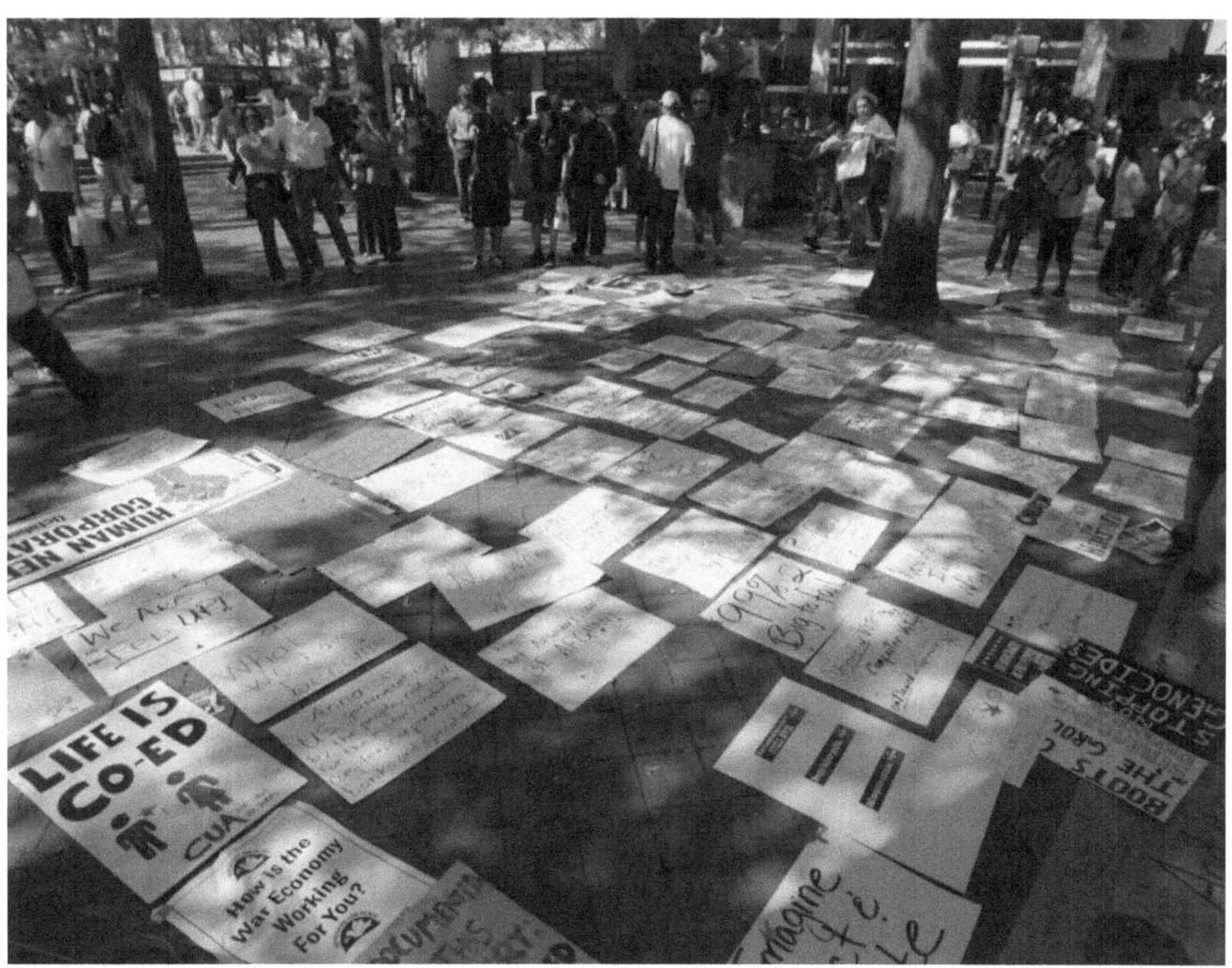

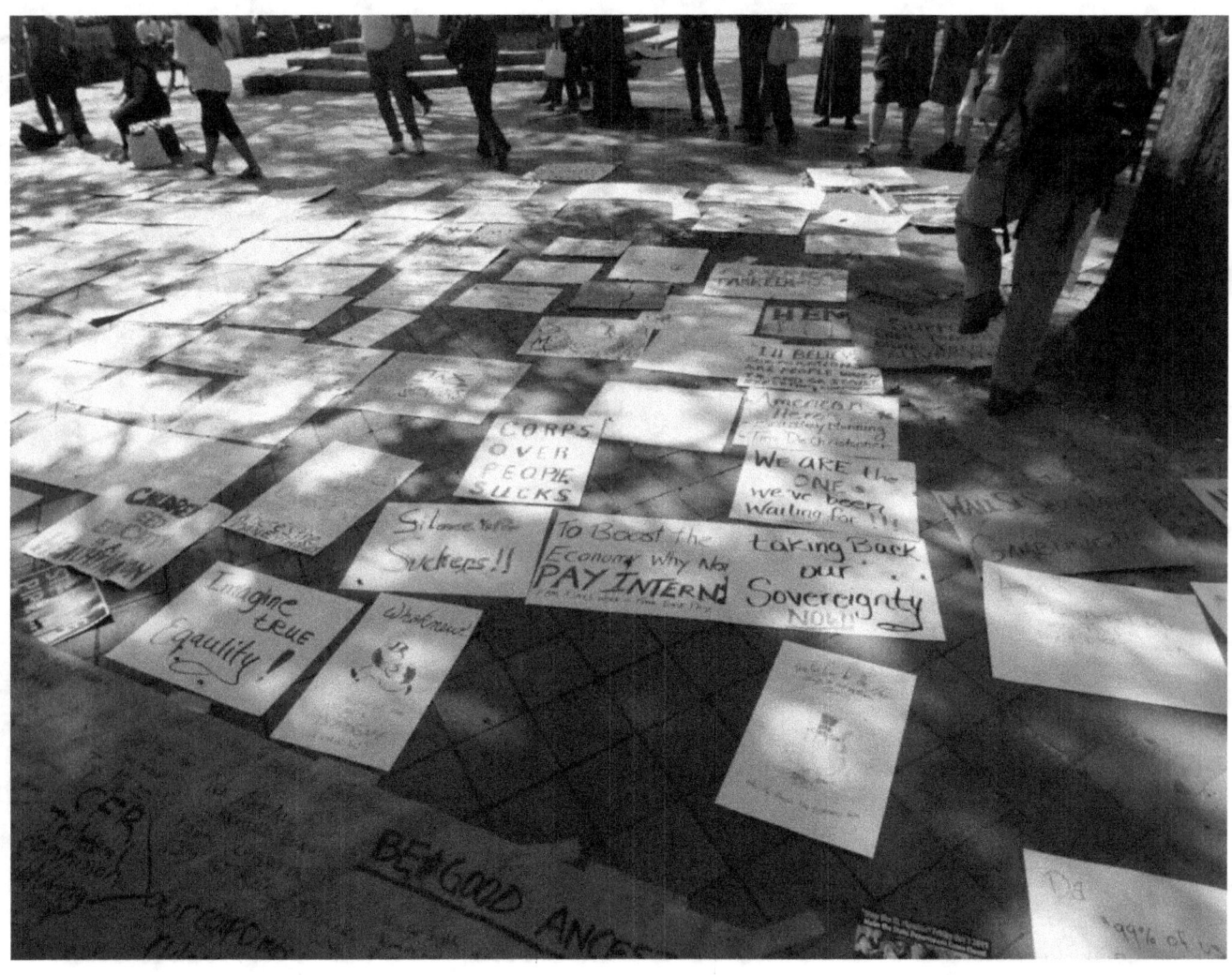

3 THE MARCH

The march to the National Air & Space Museums gets under way.

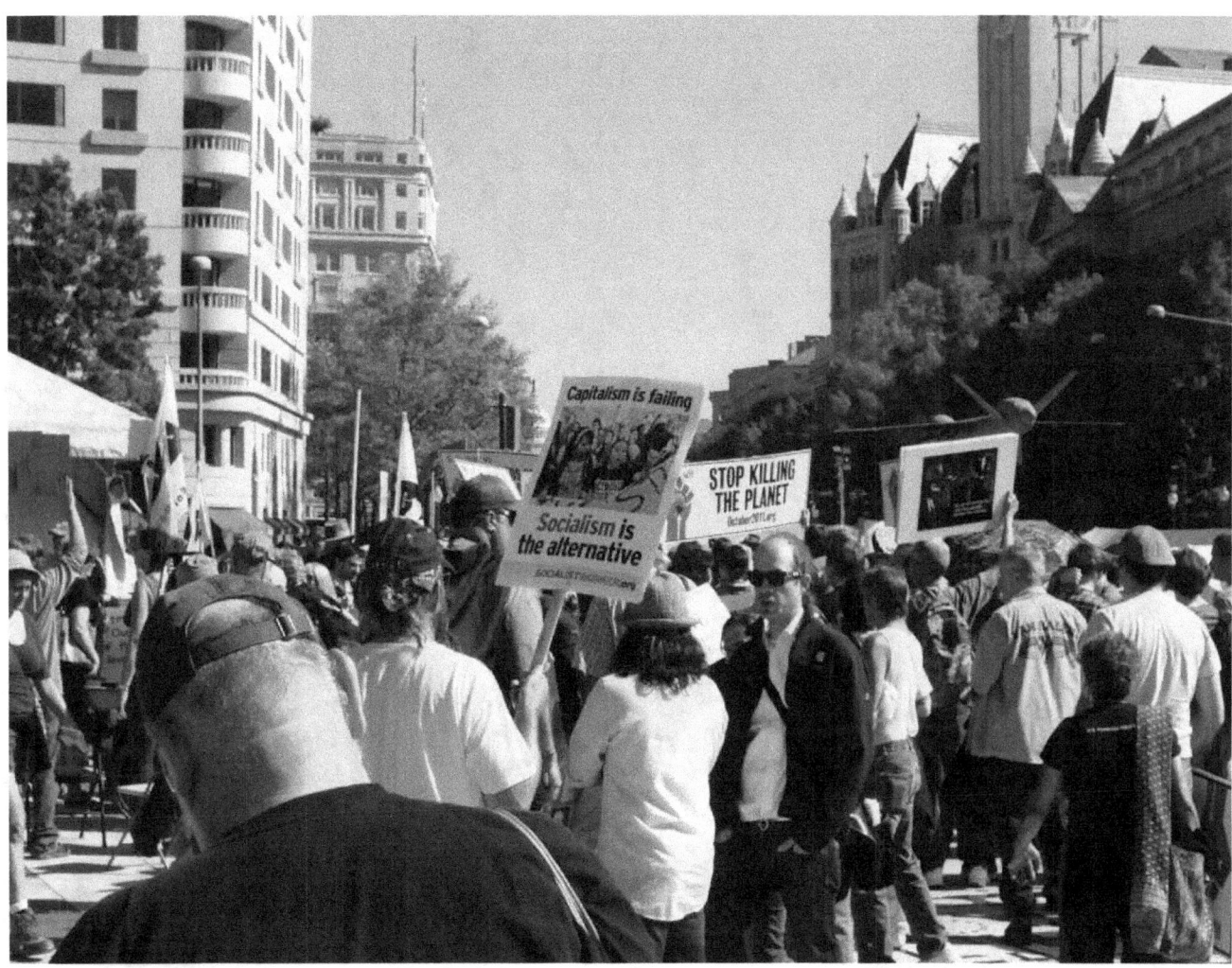

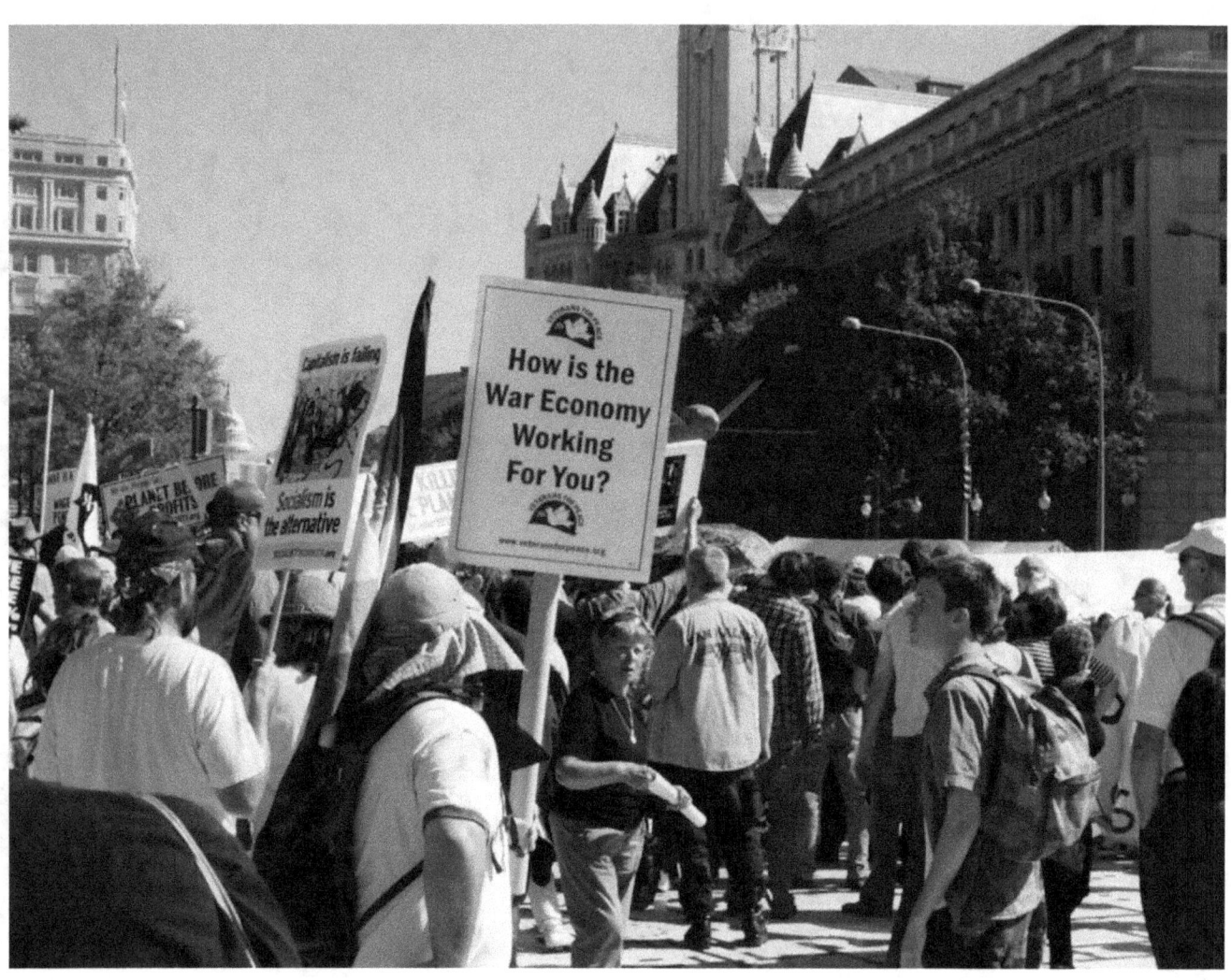

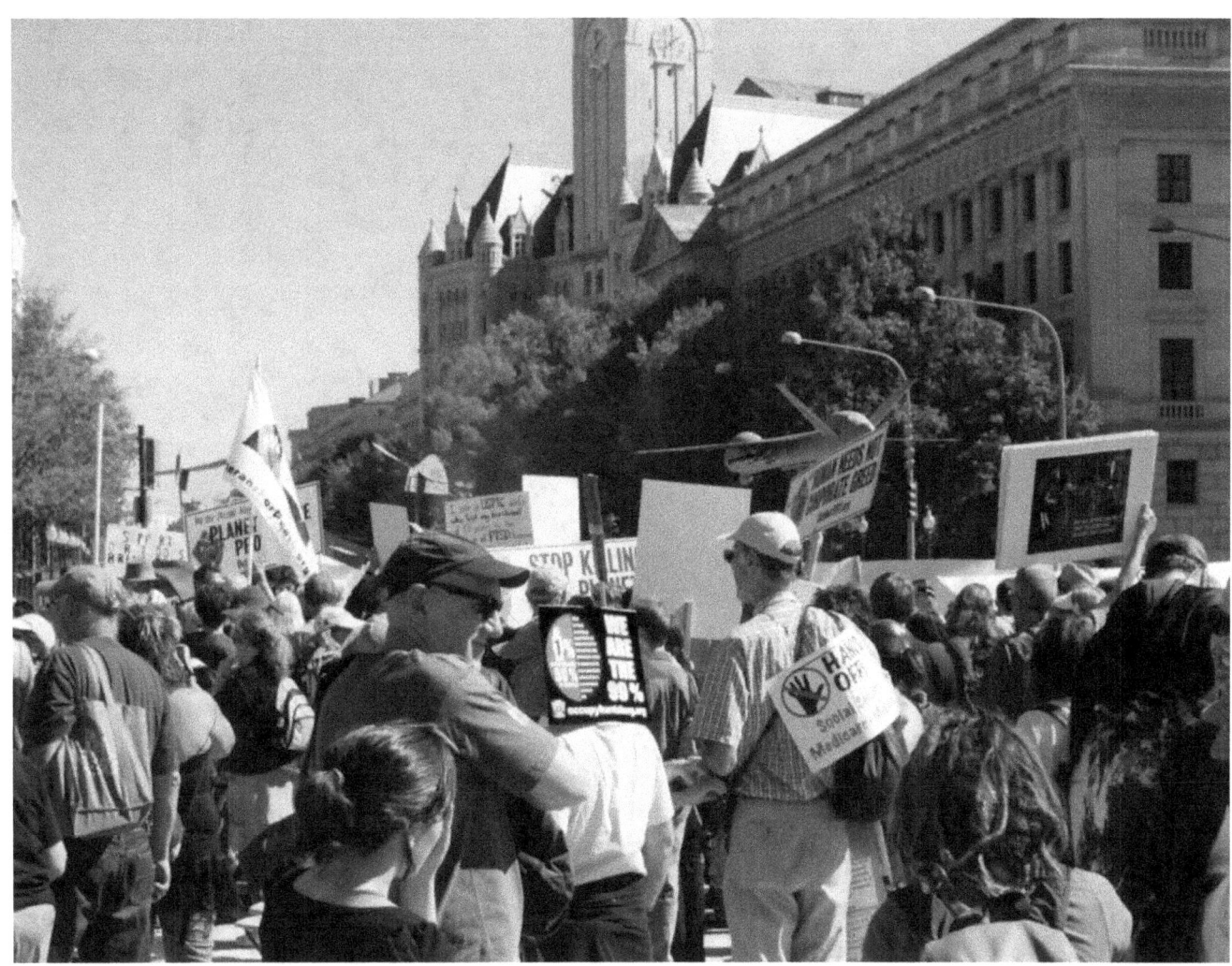

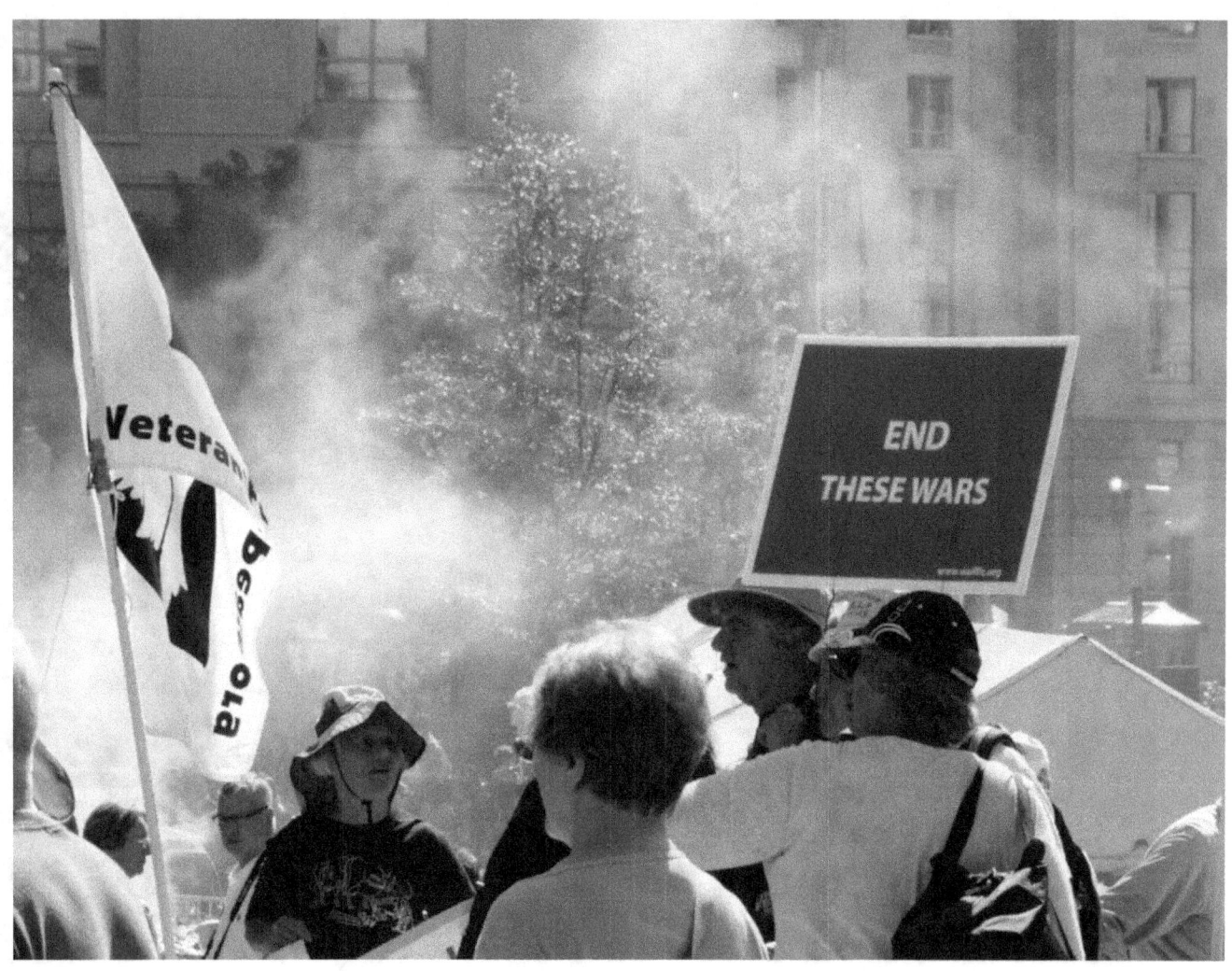

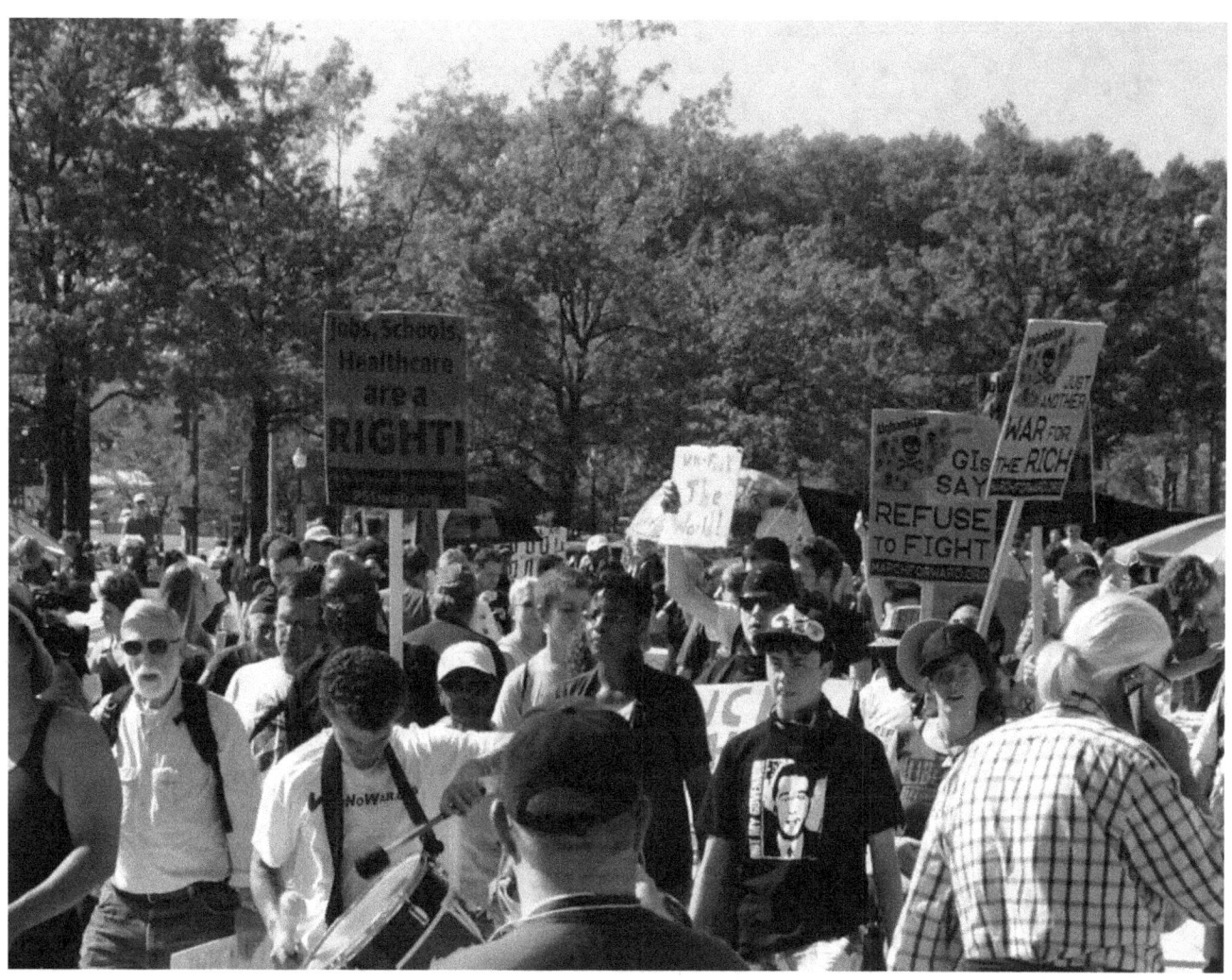

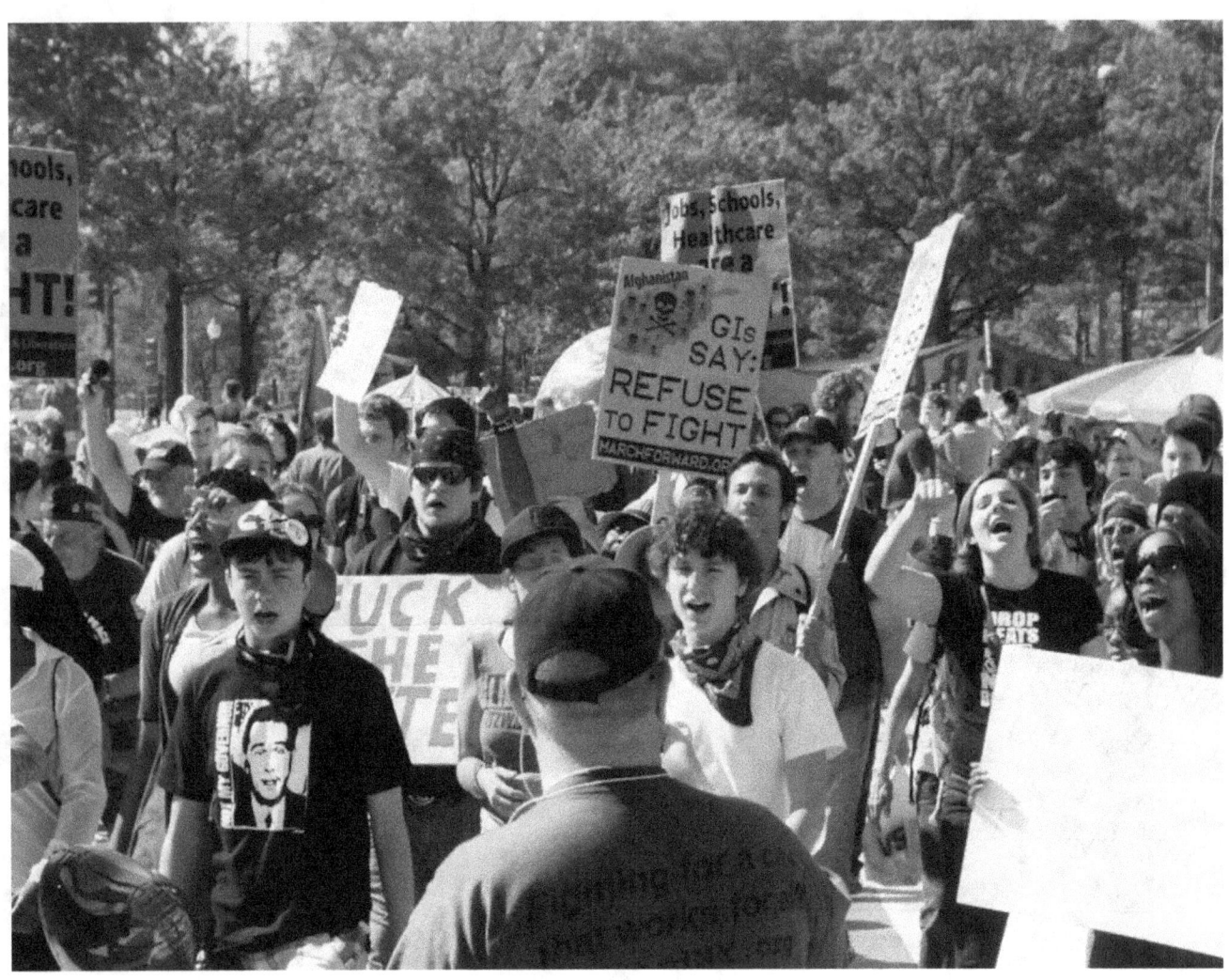

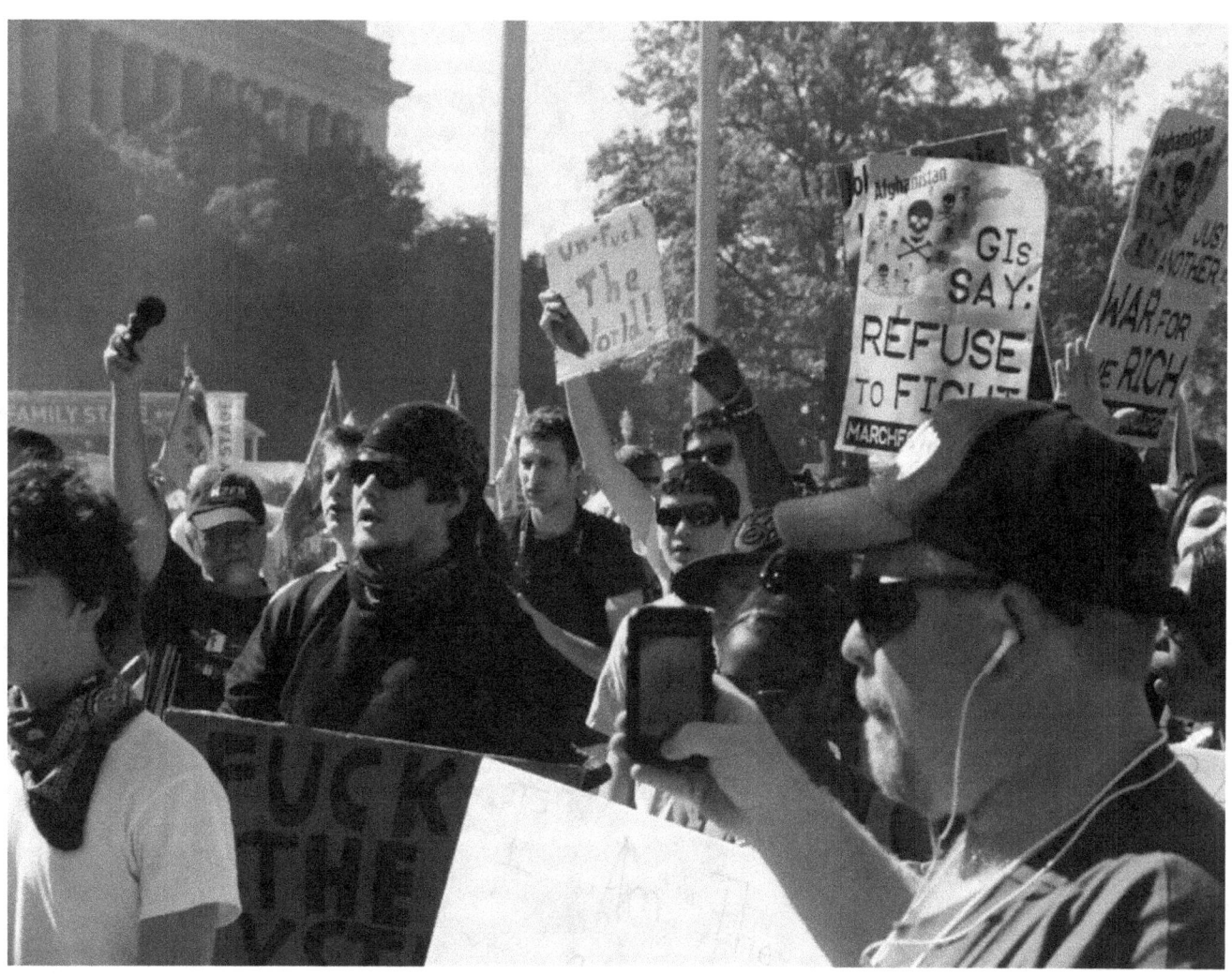

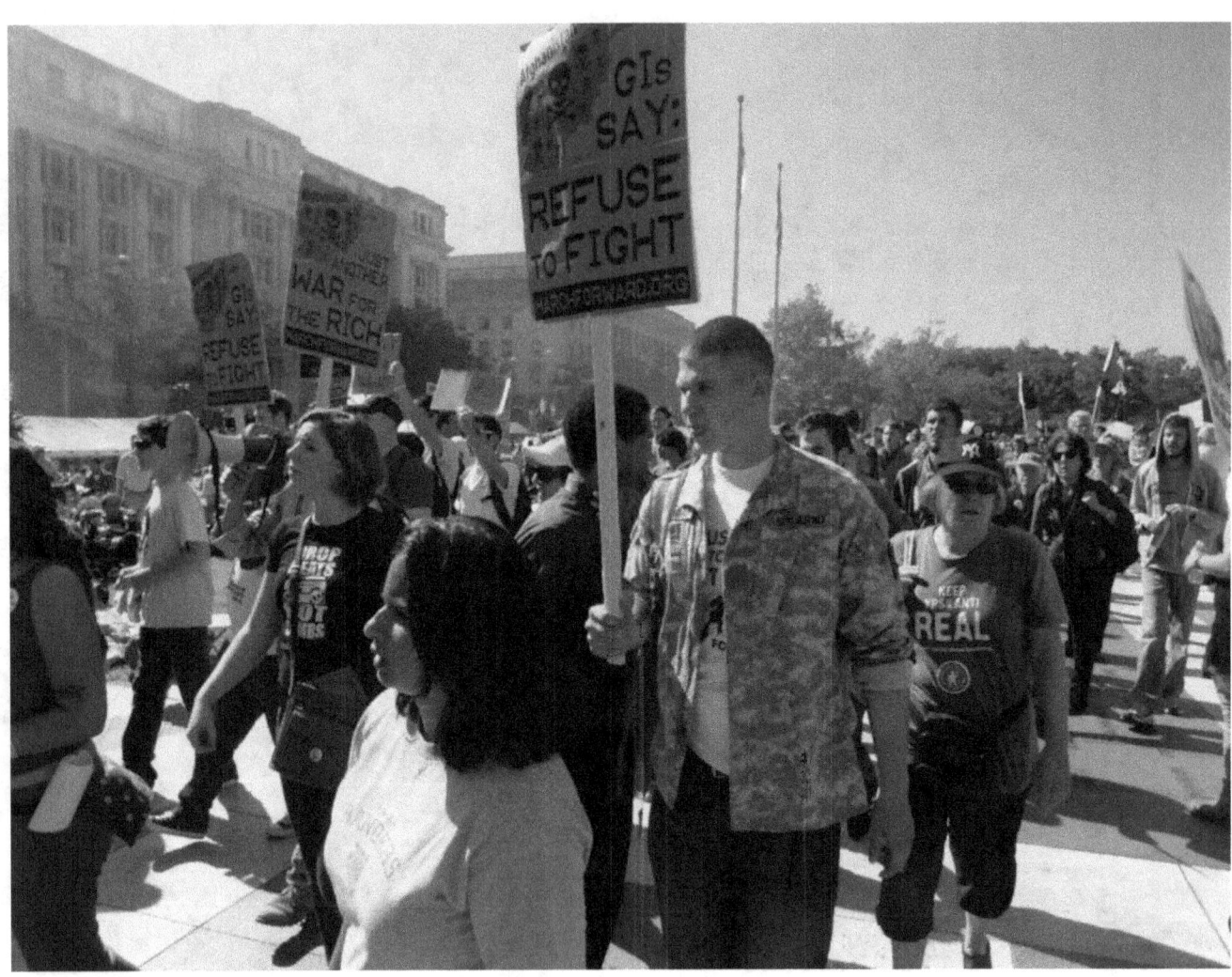

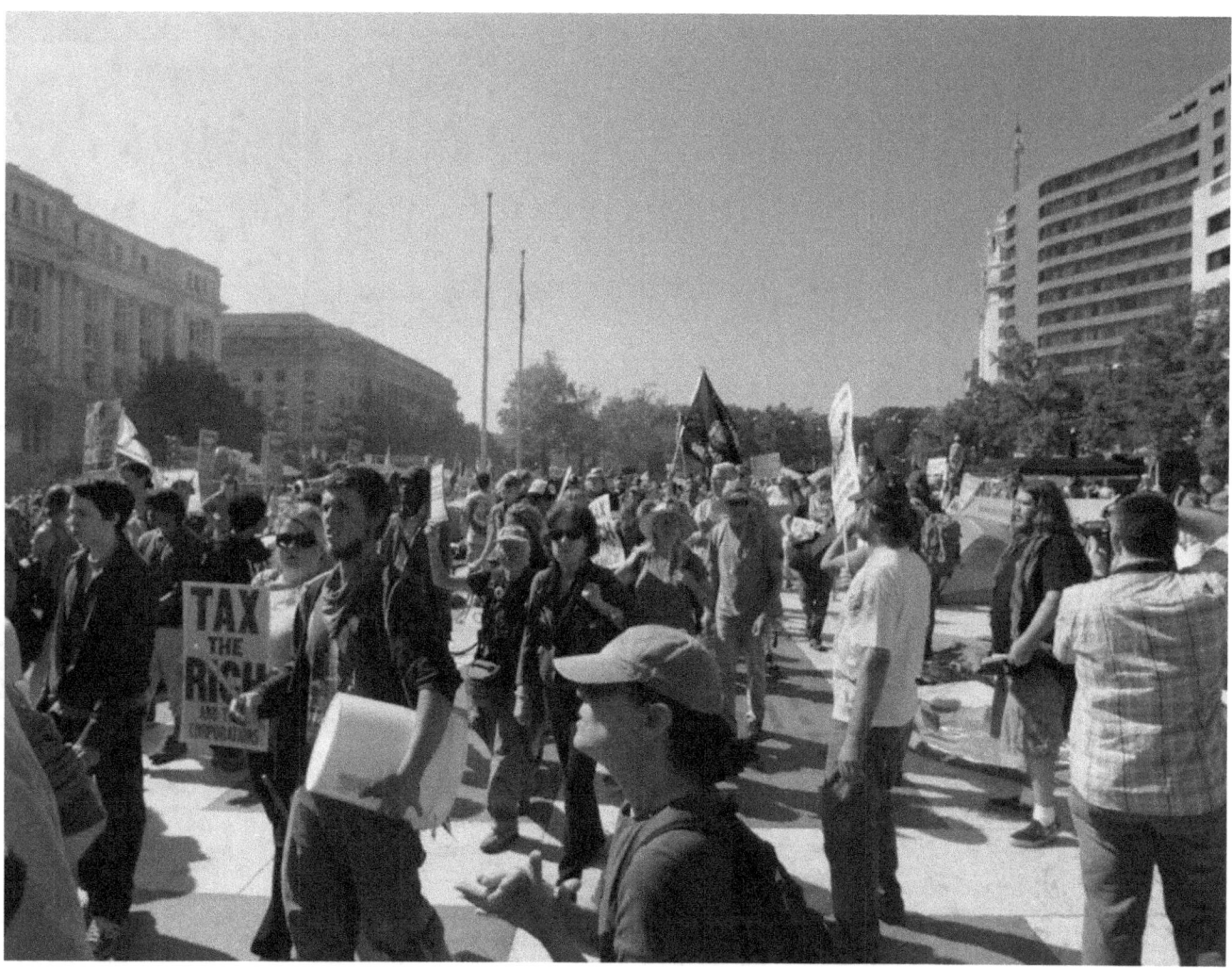

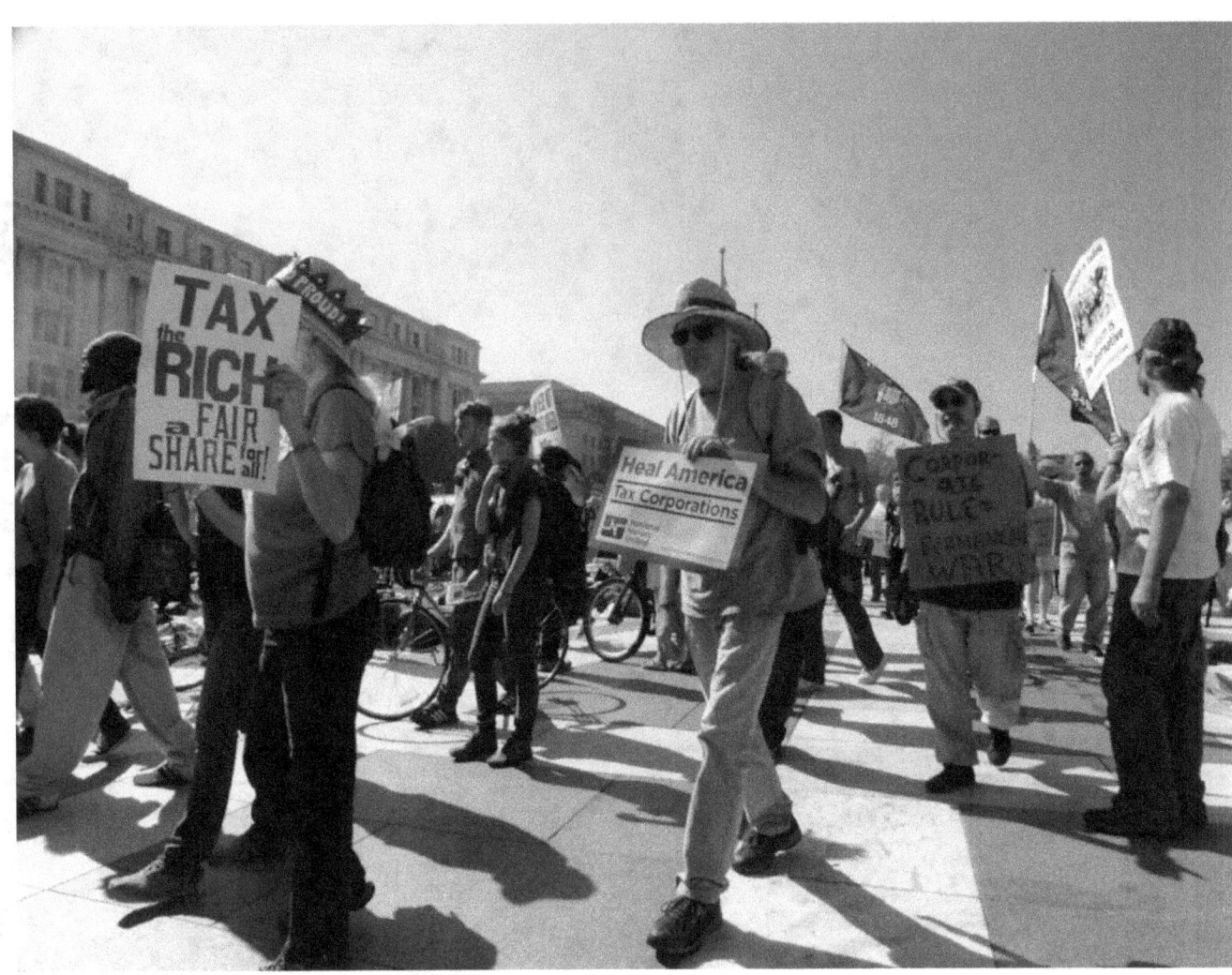

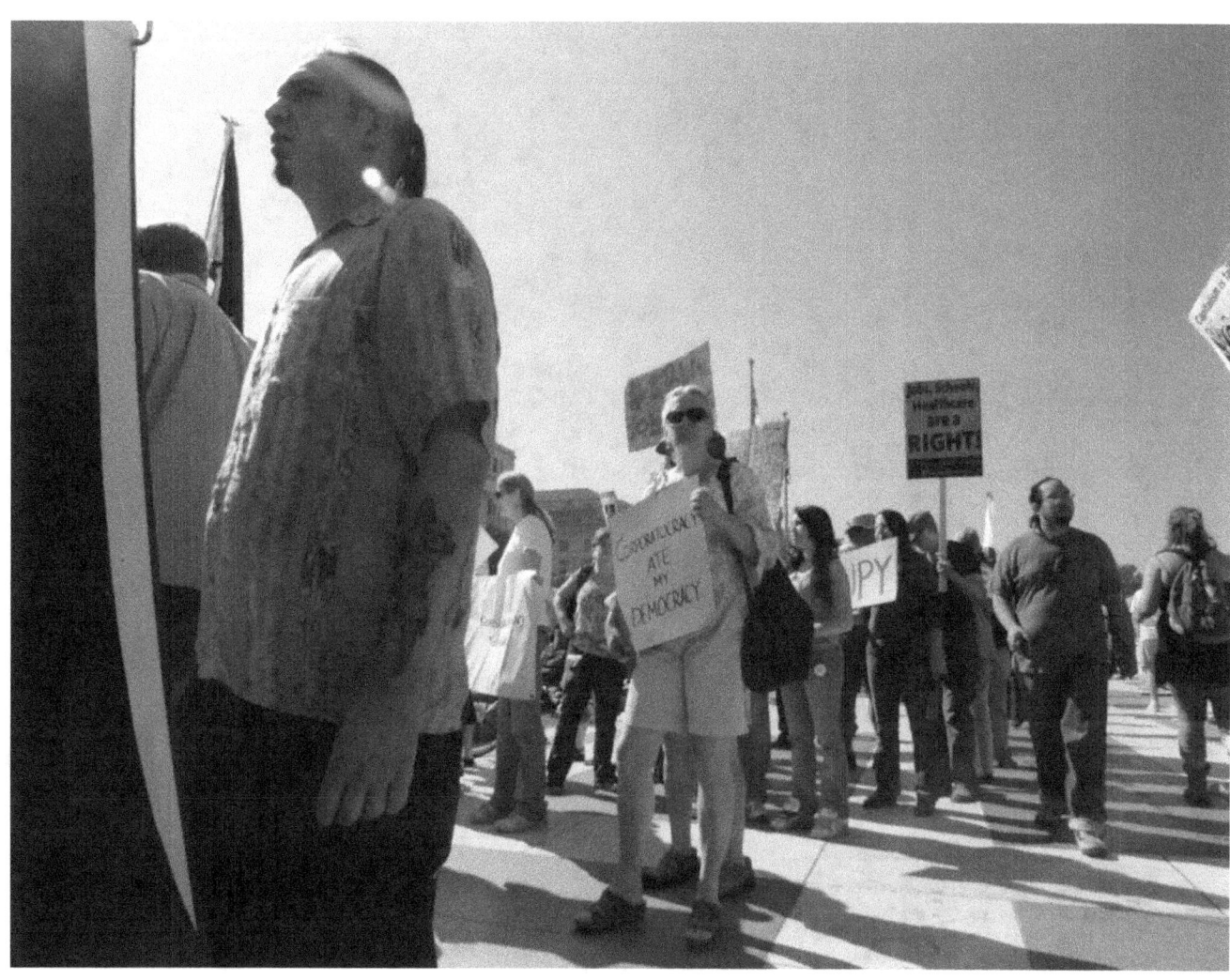

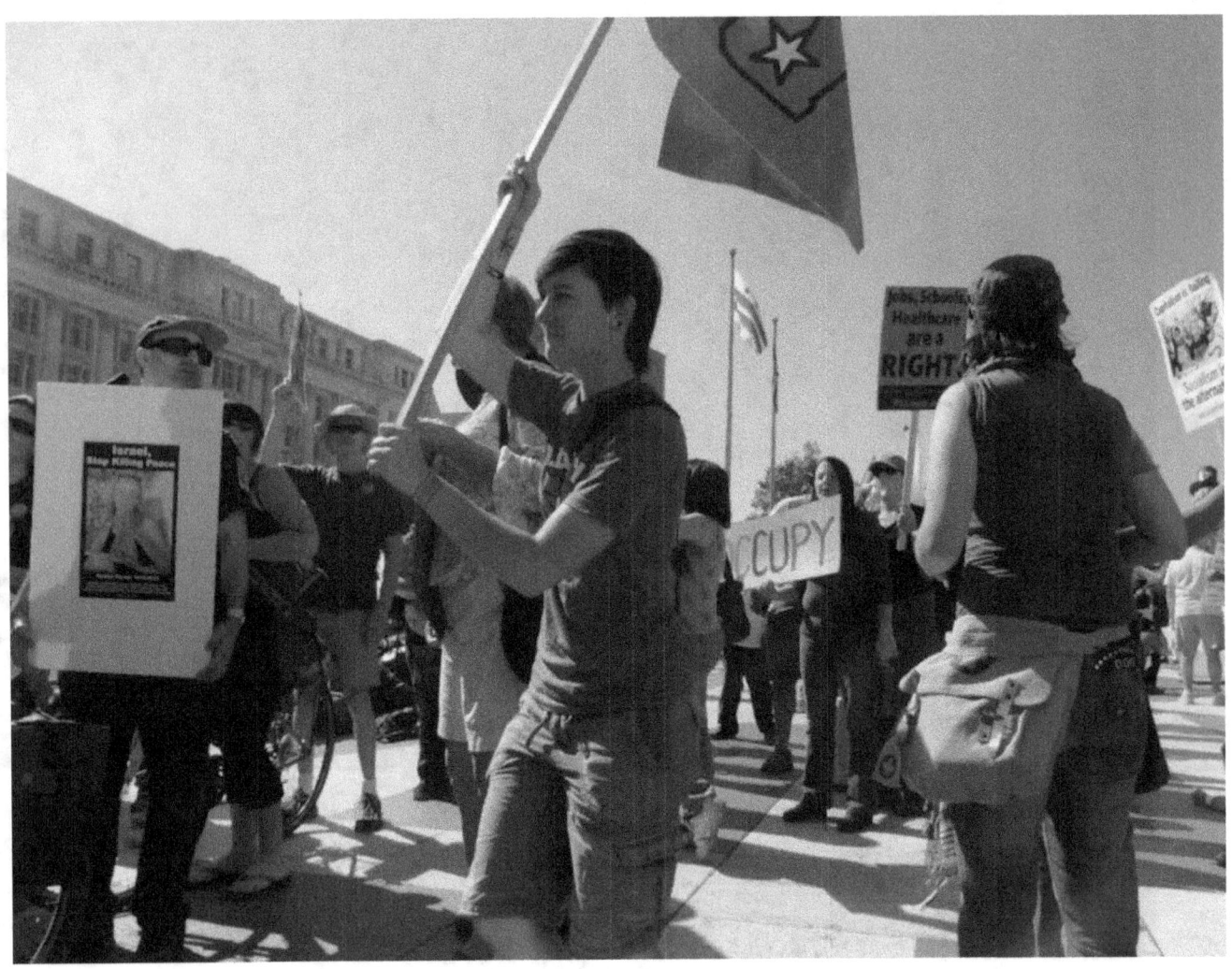

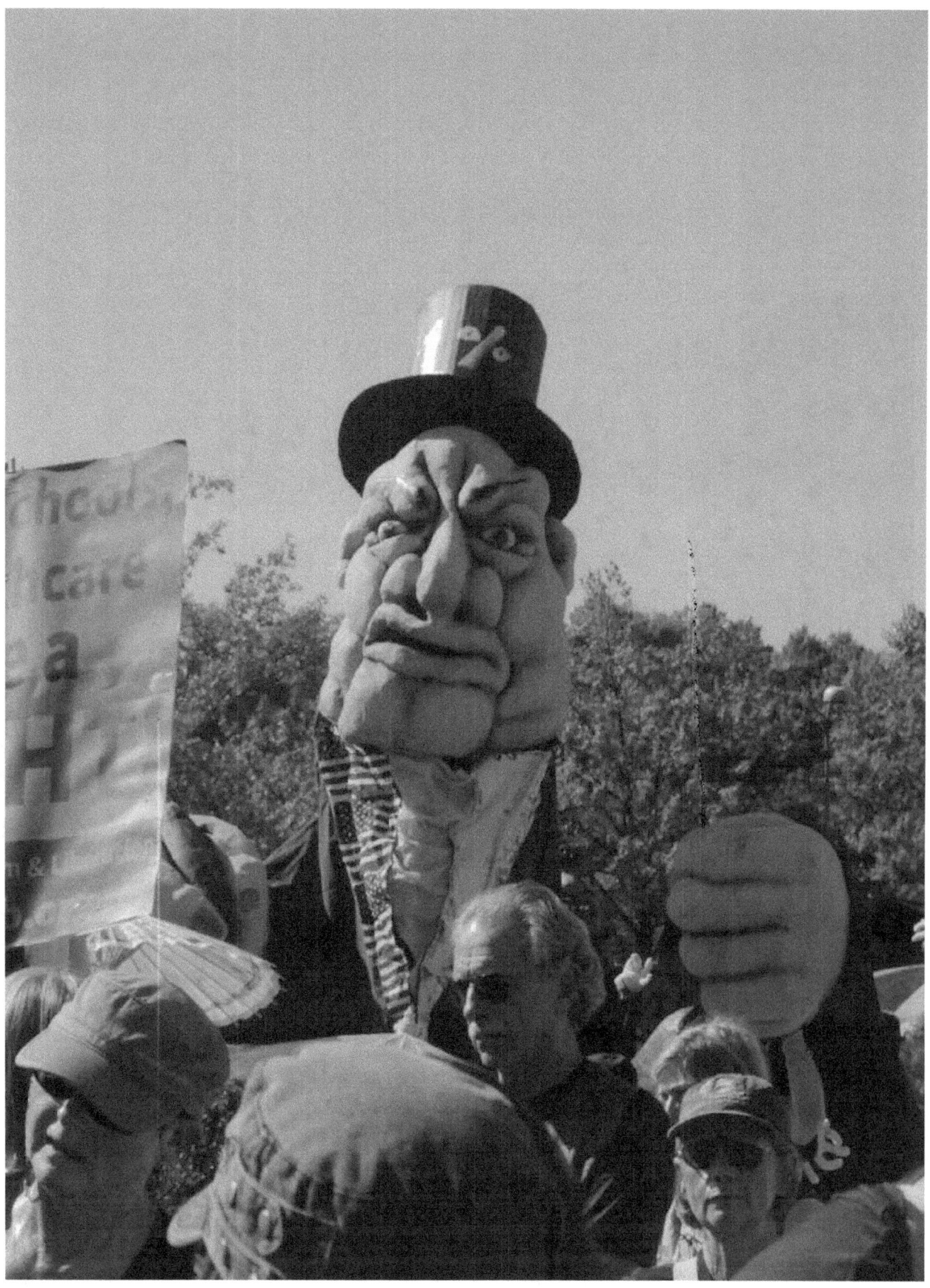

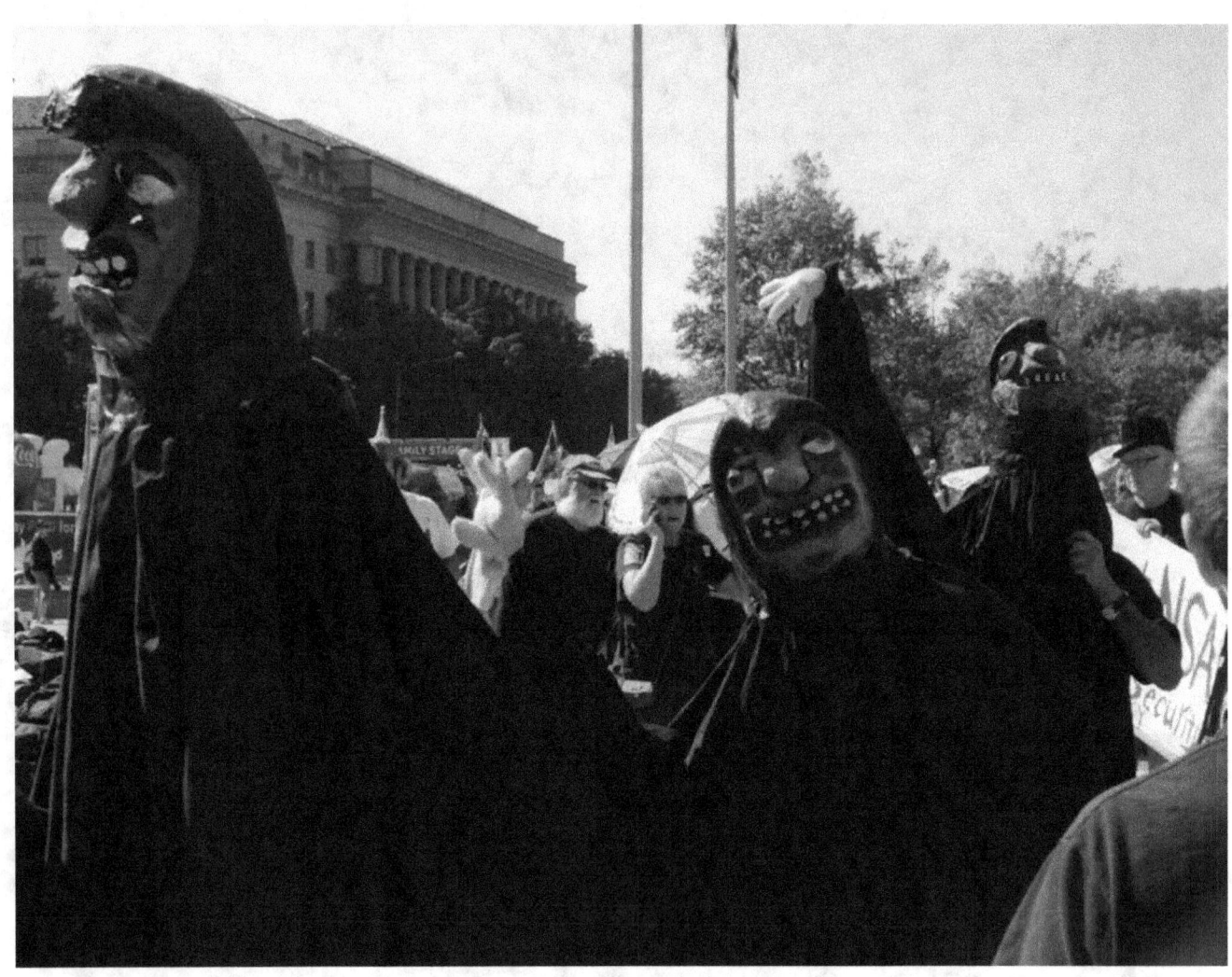

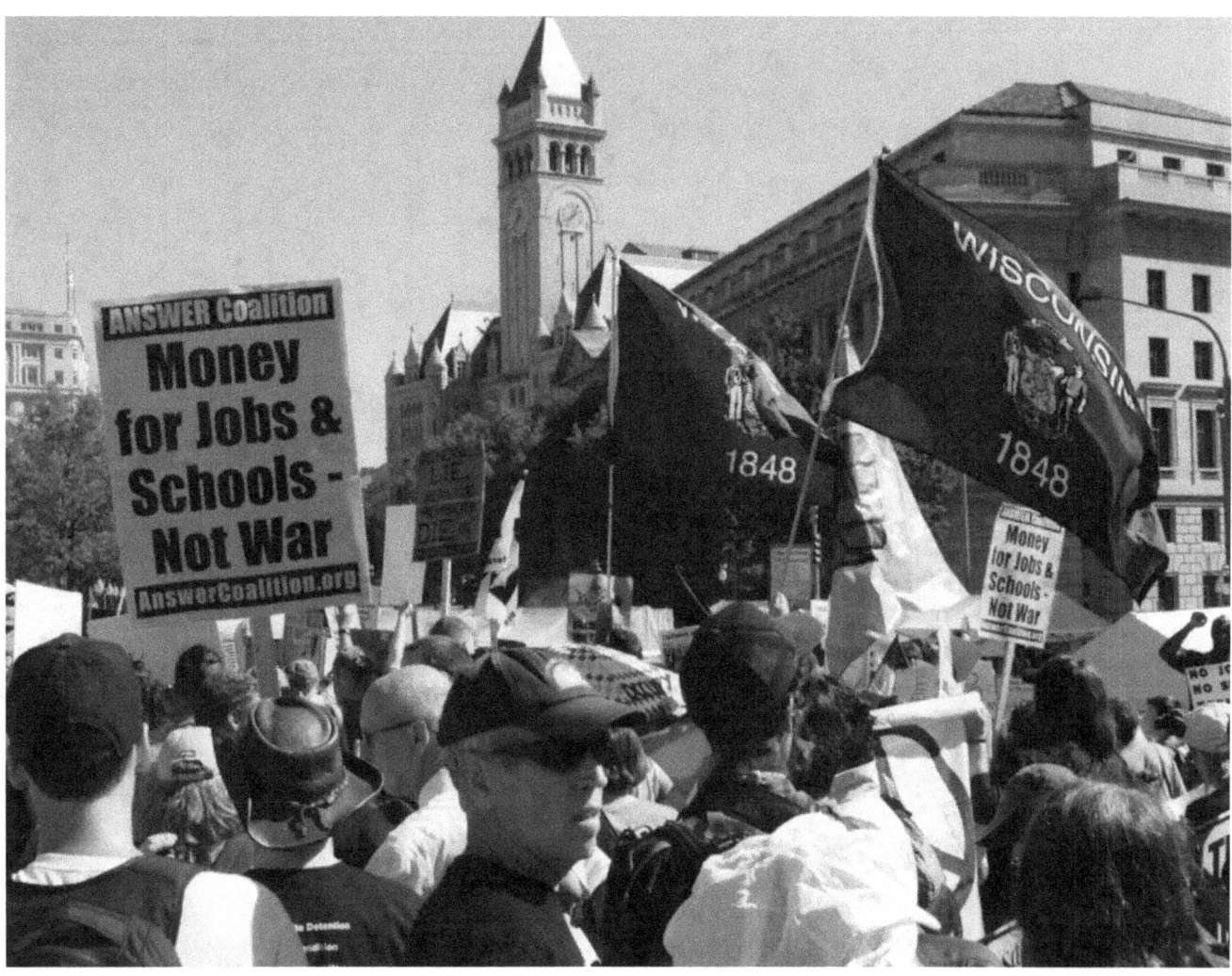

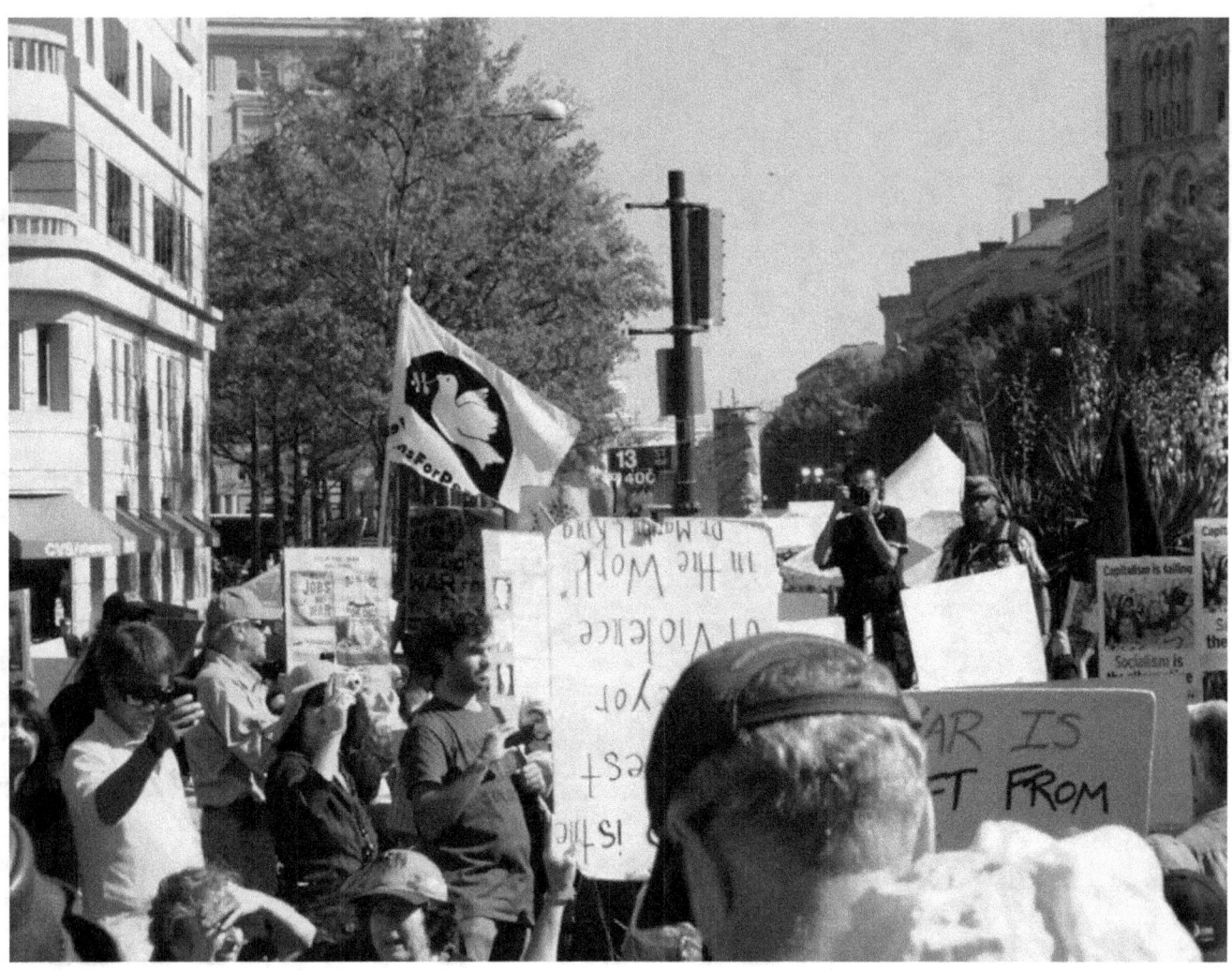

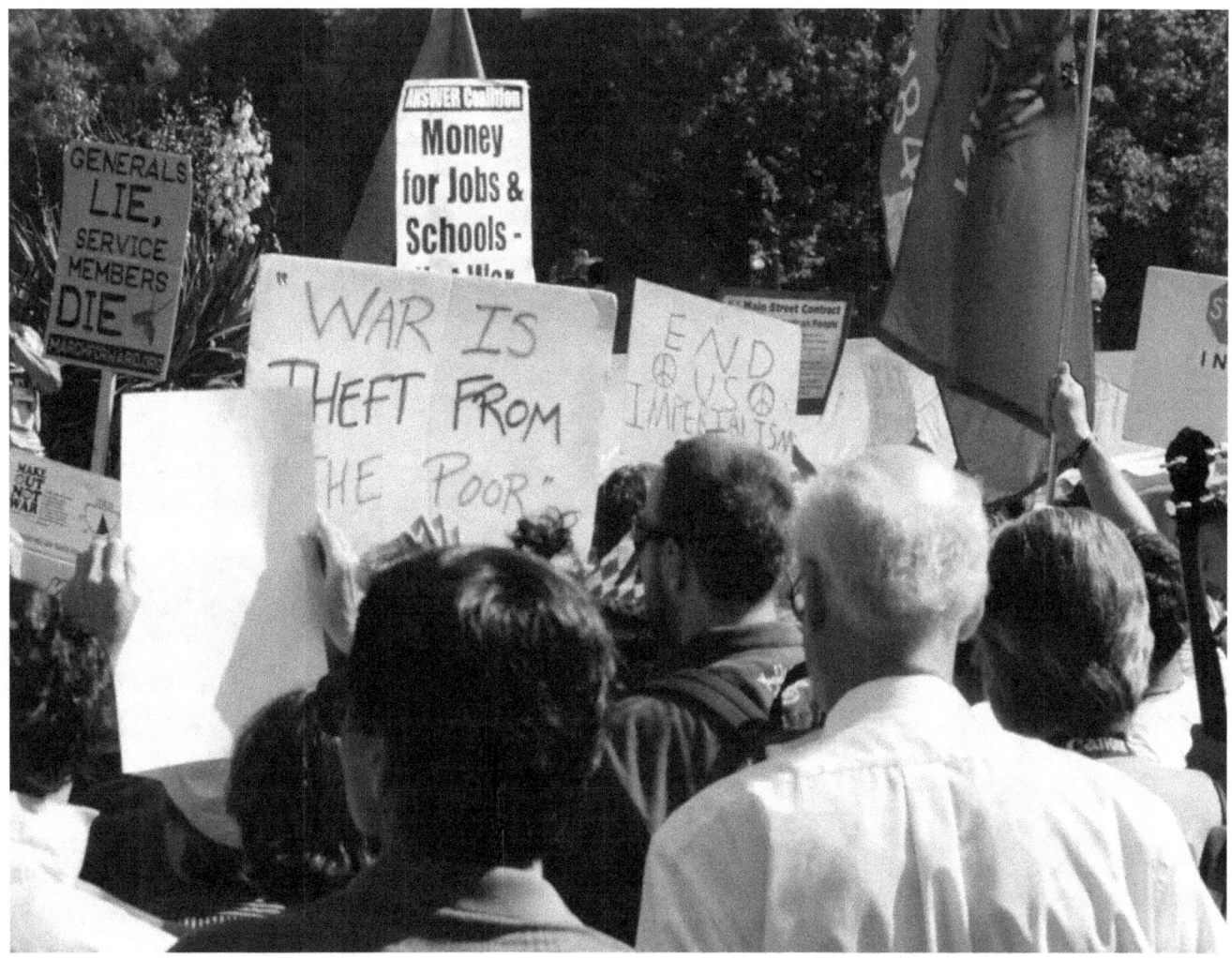

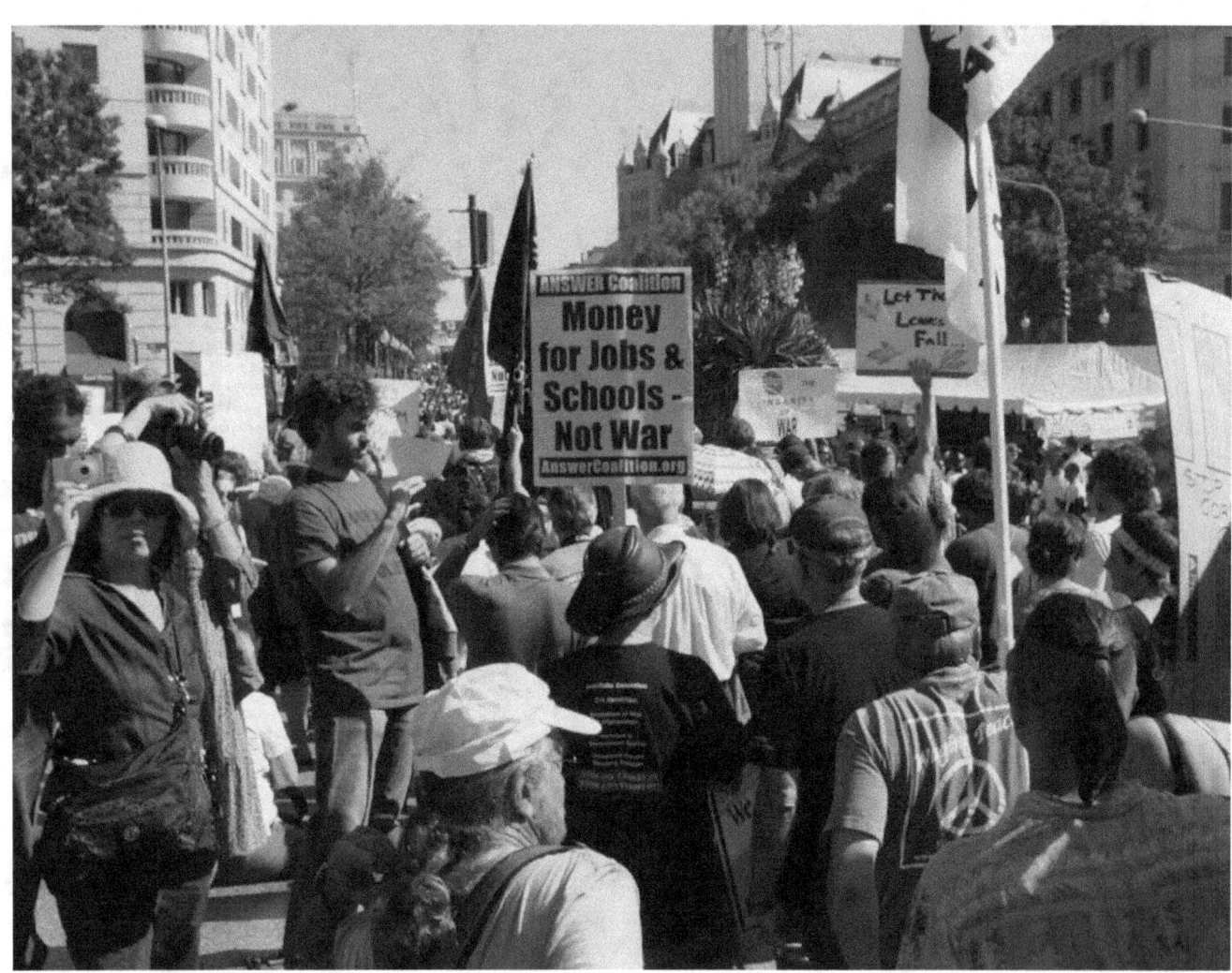

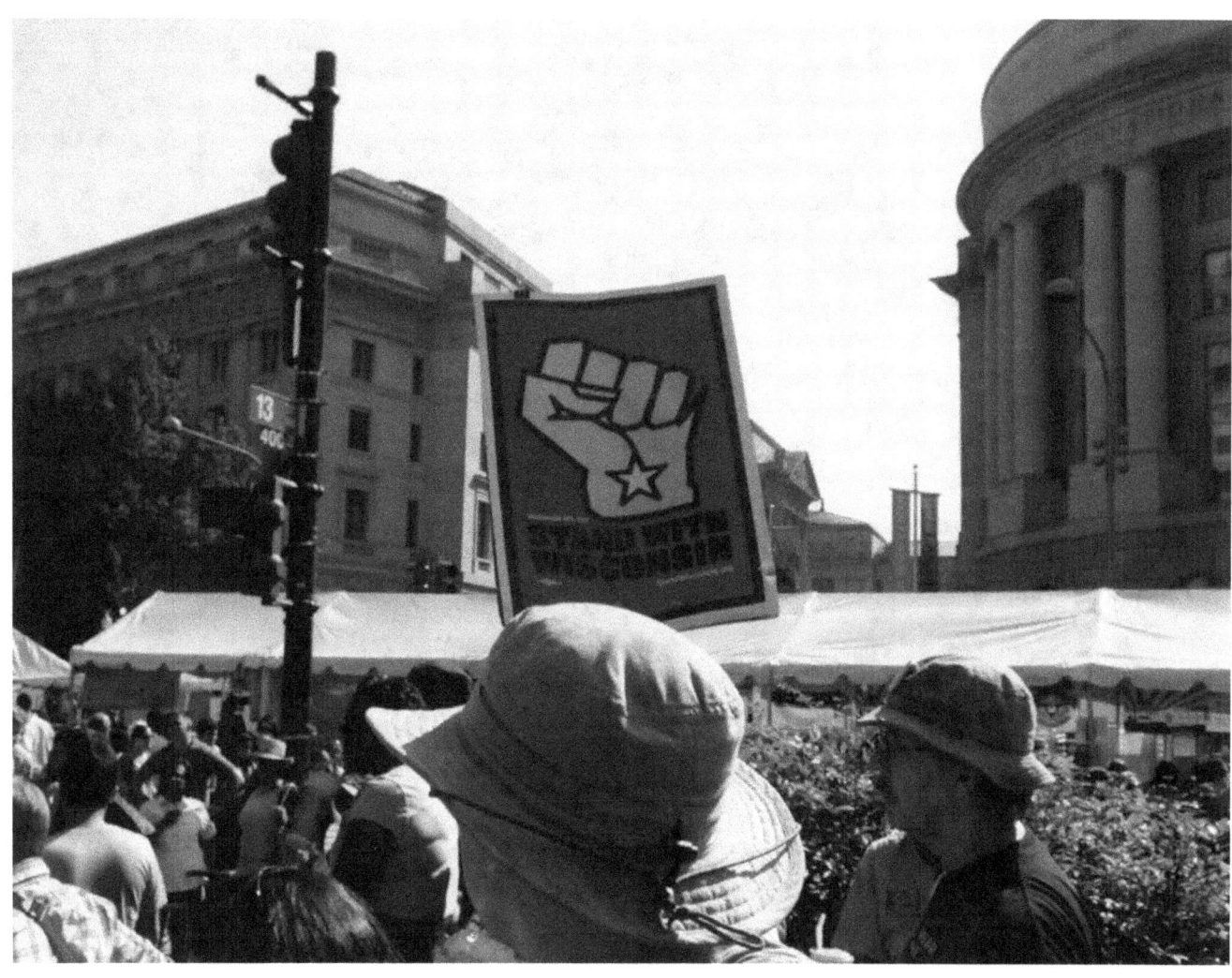

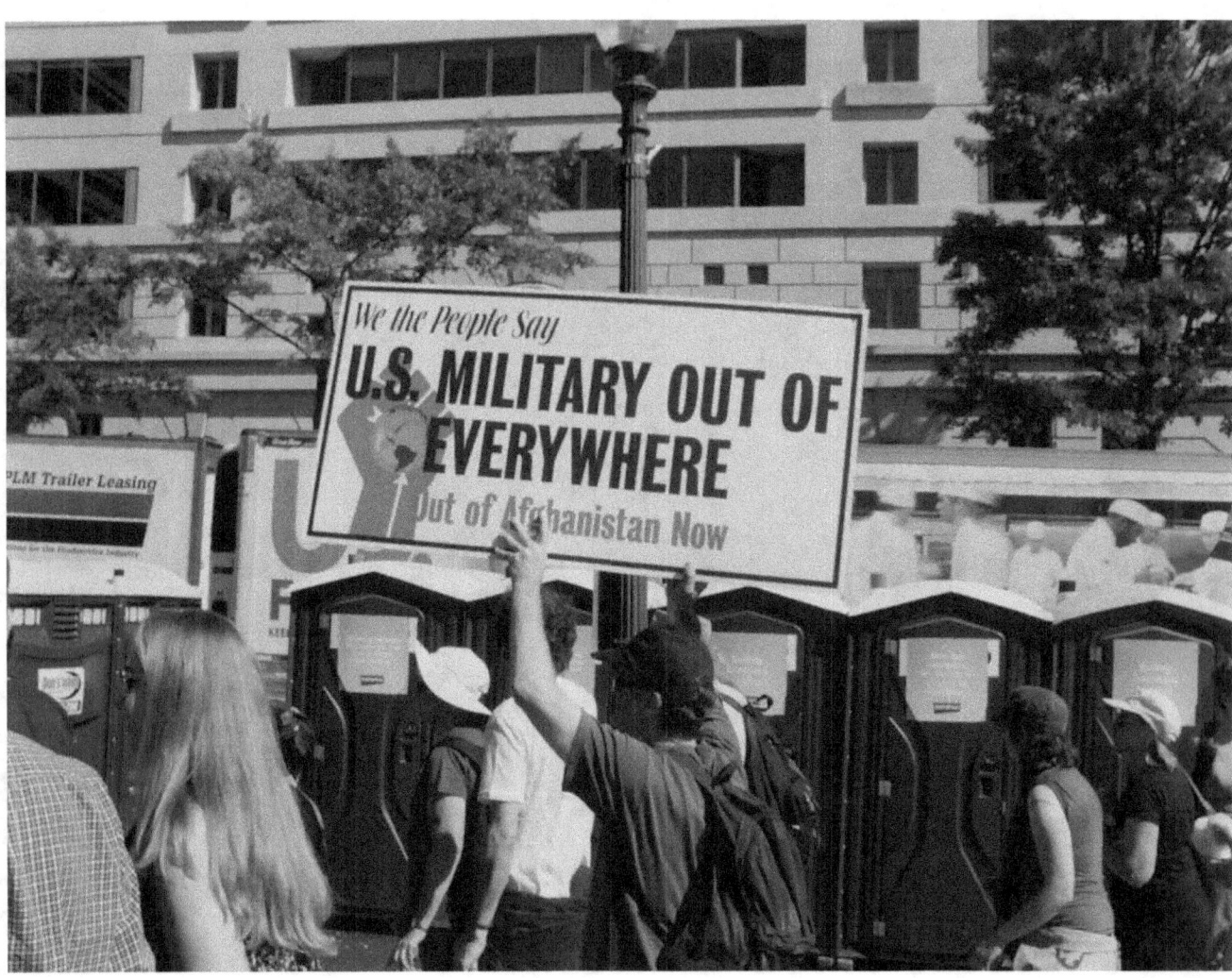

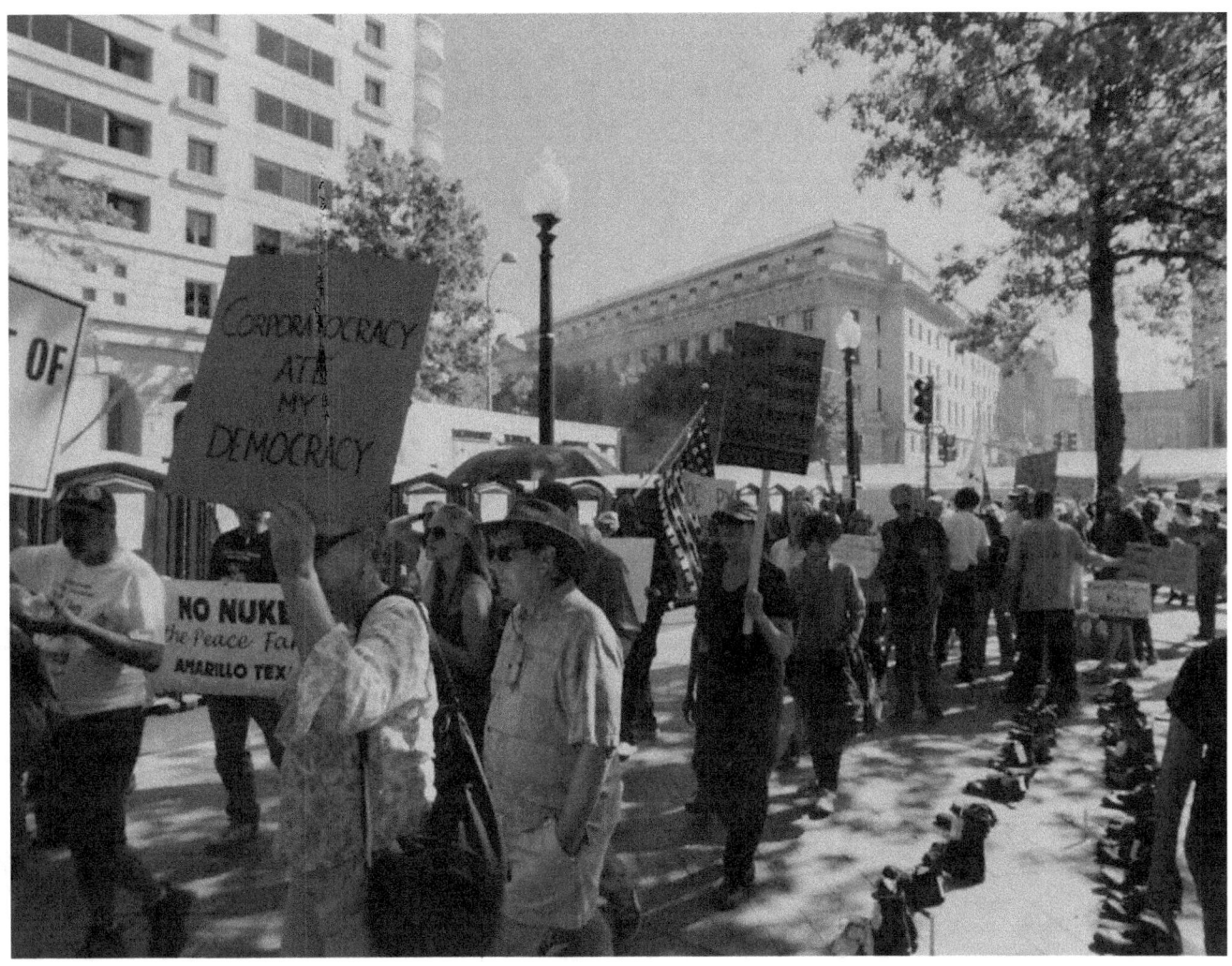

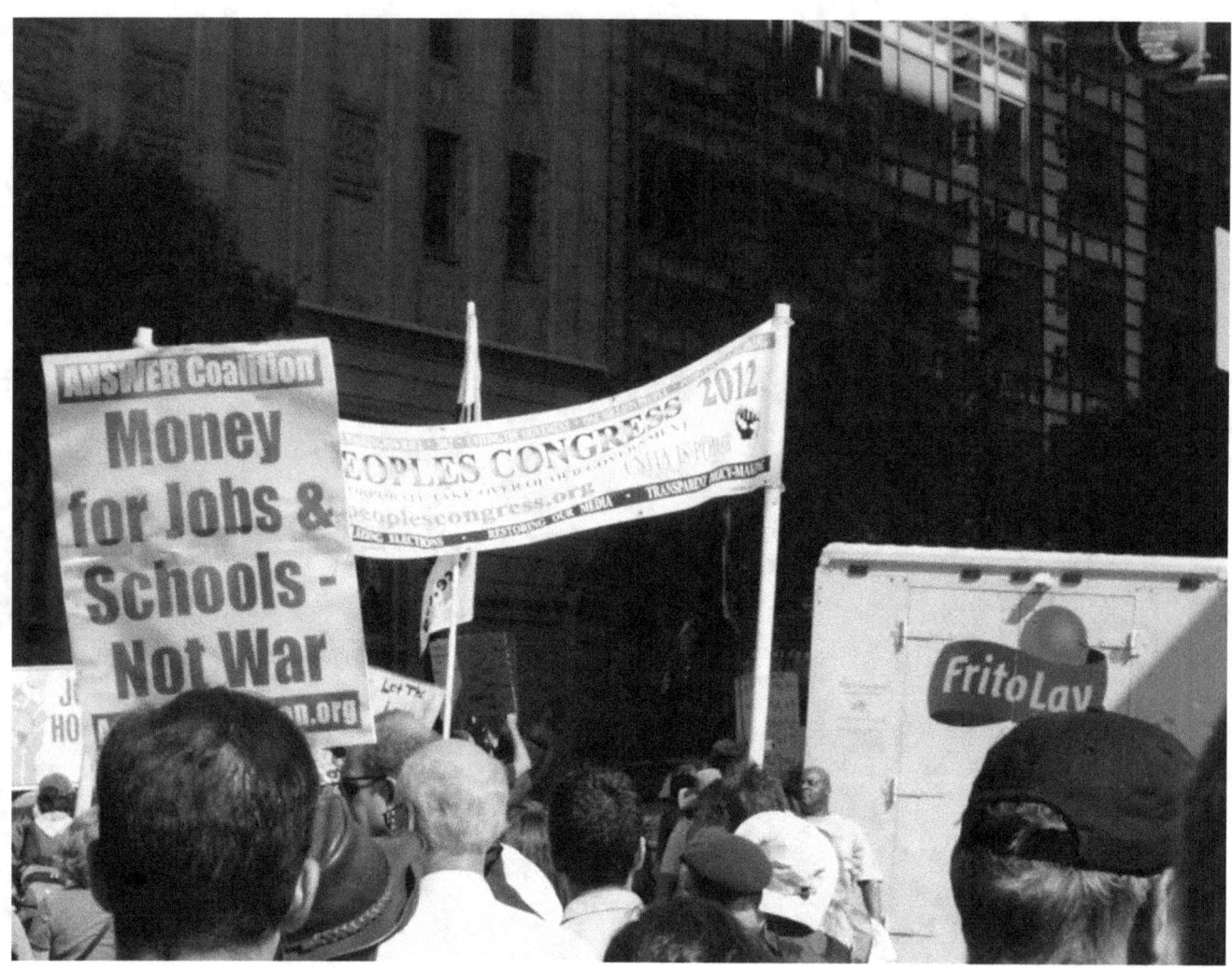

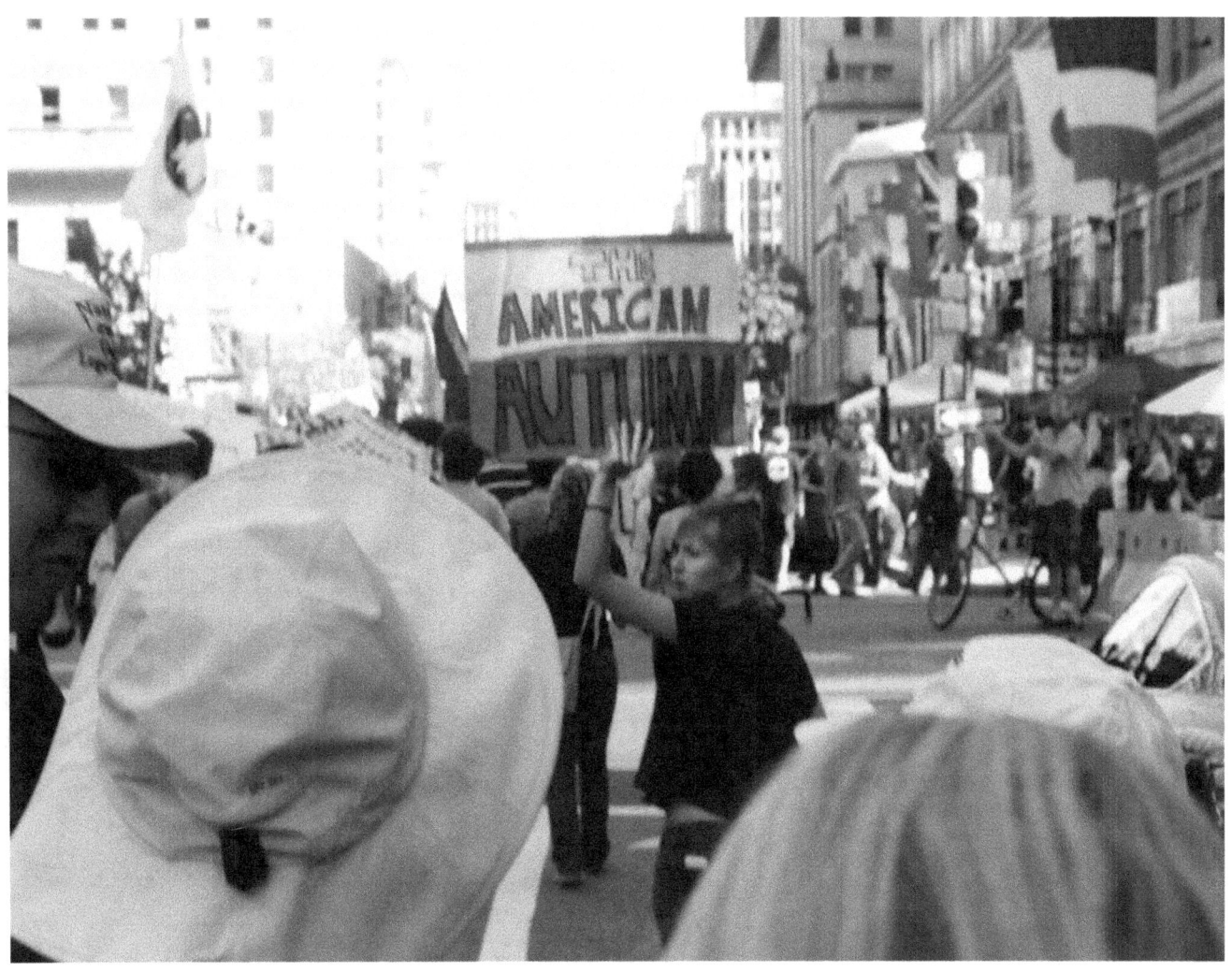

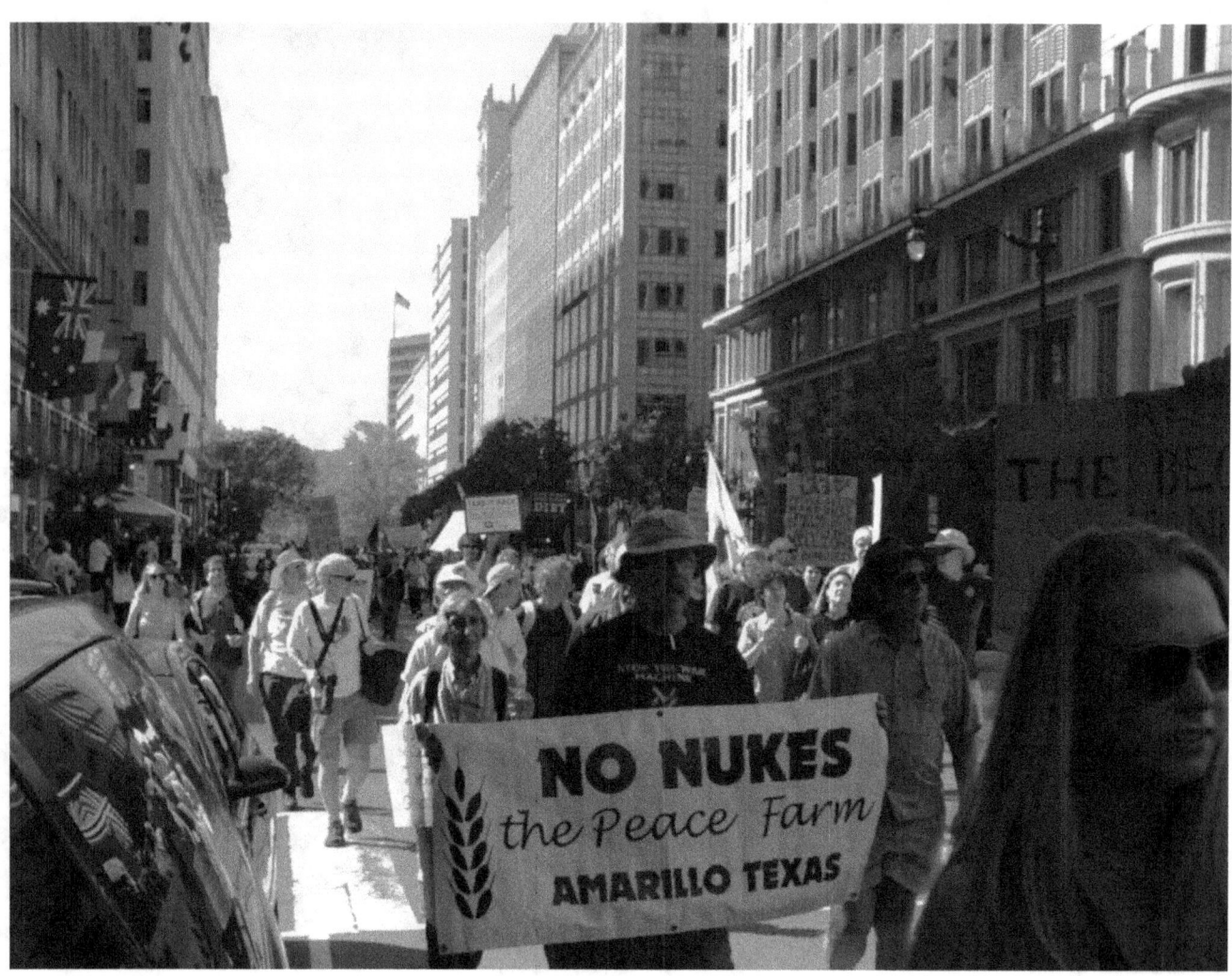

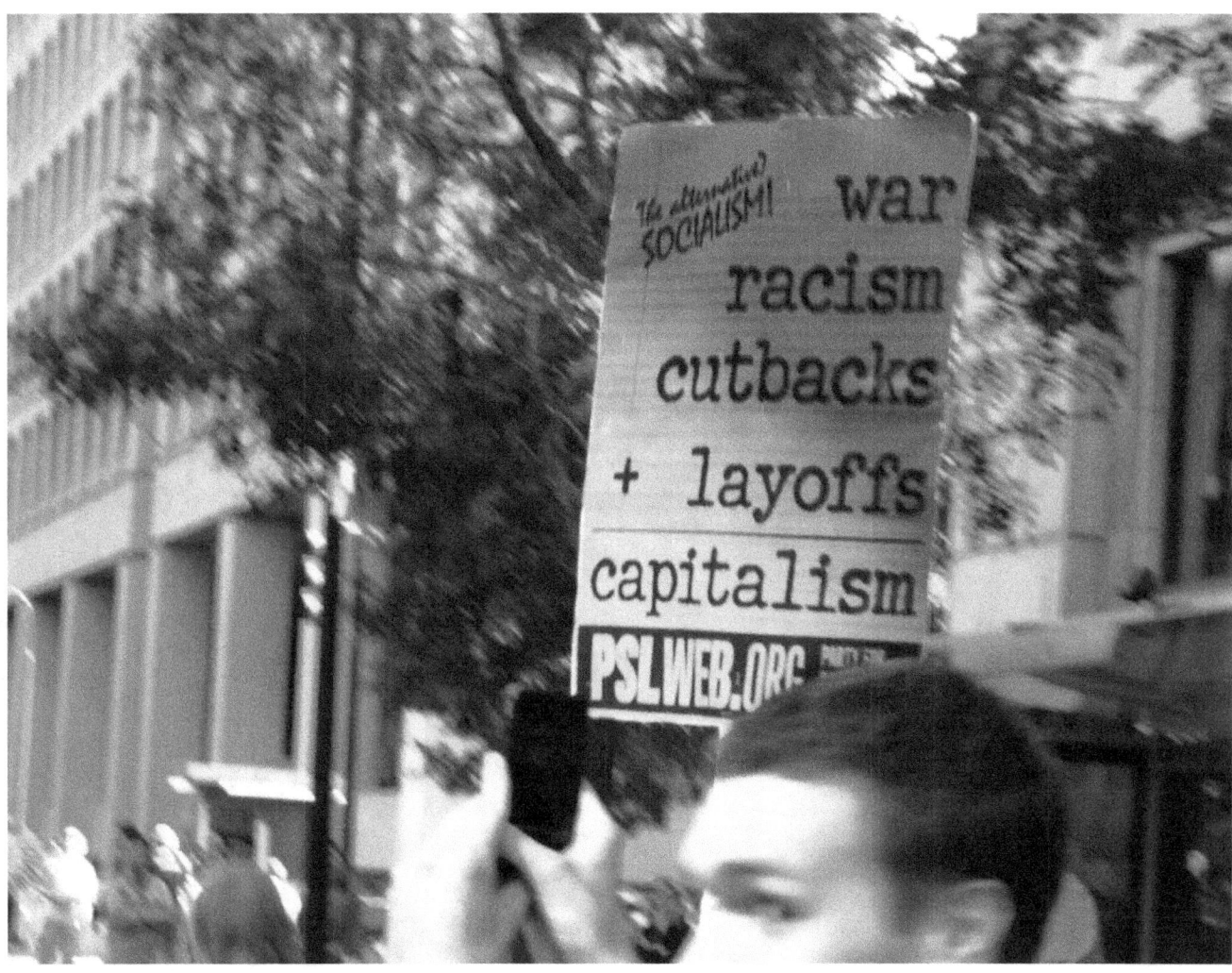

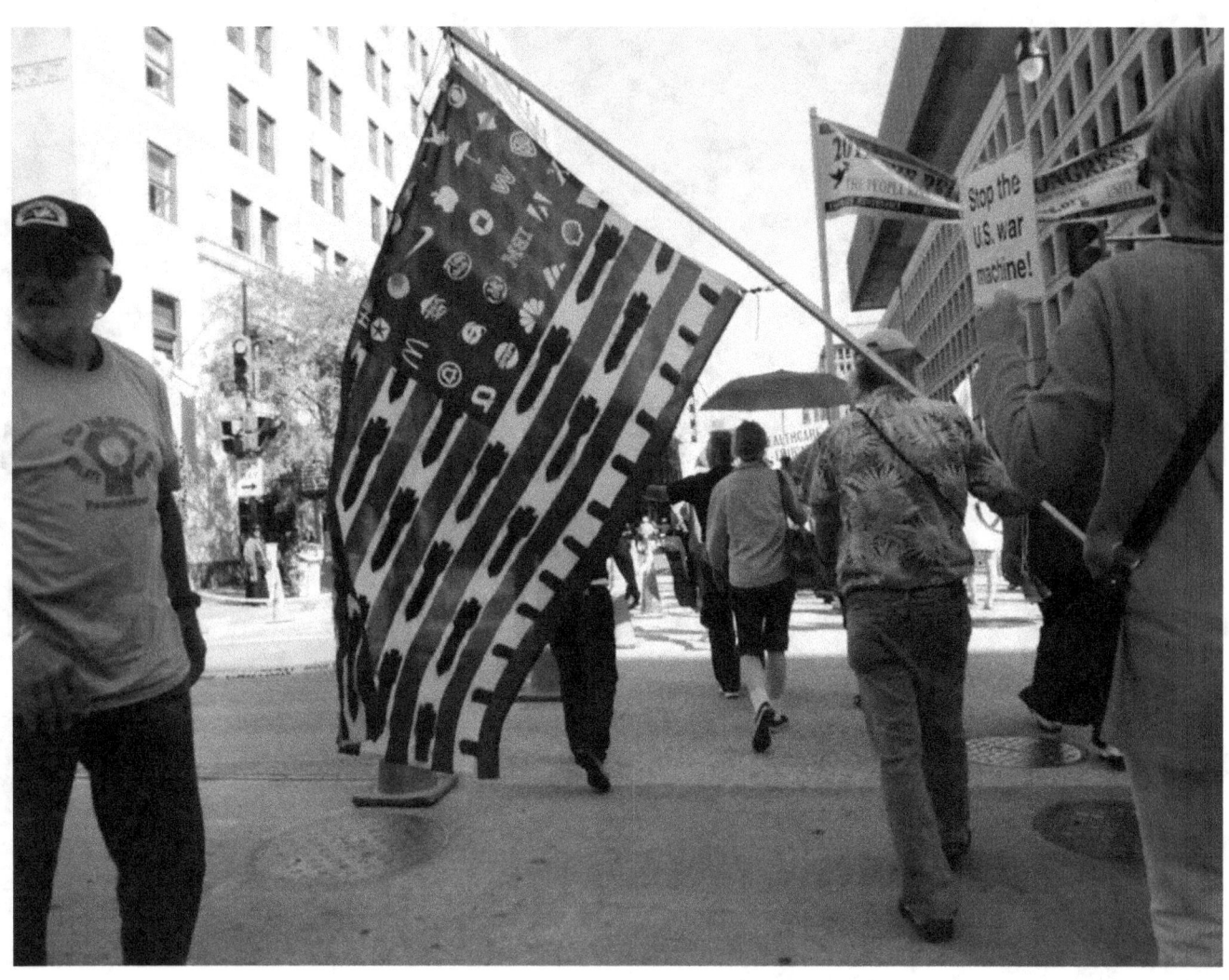

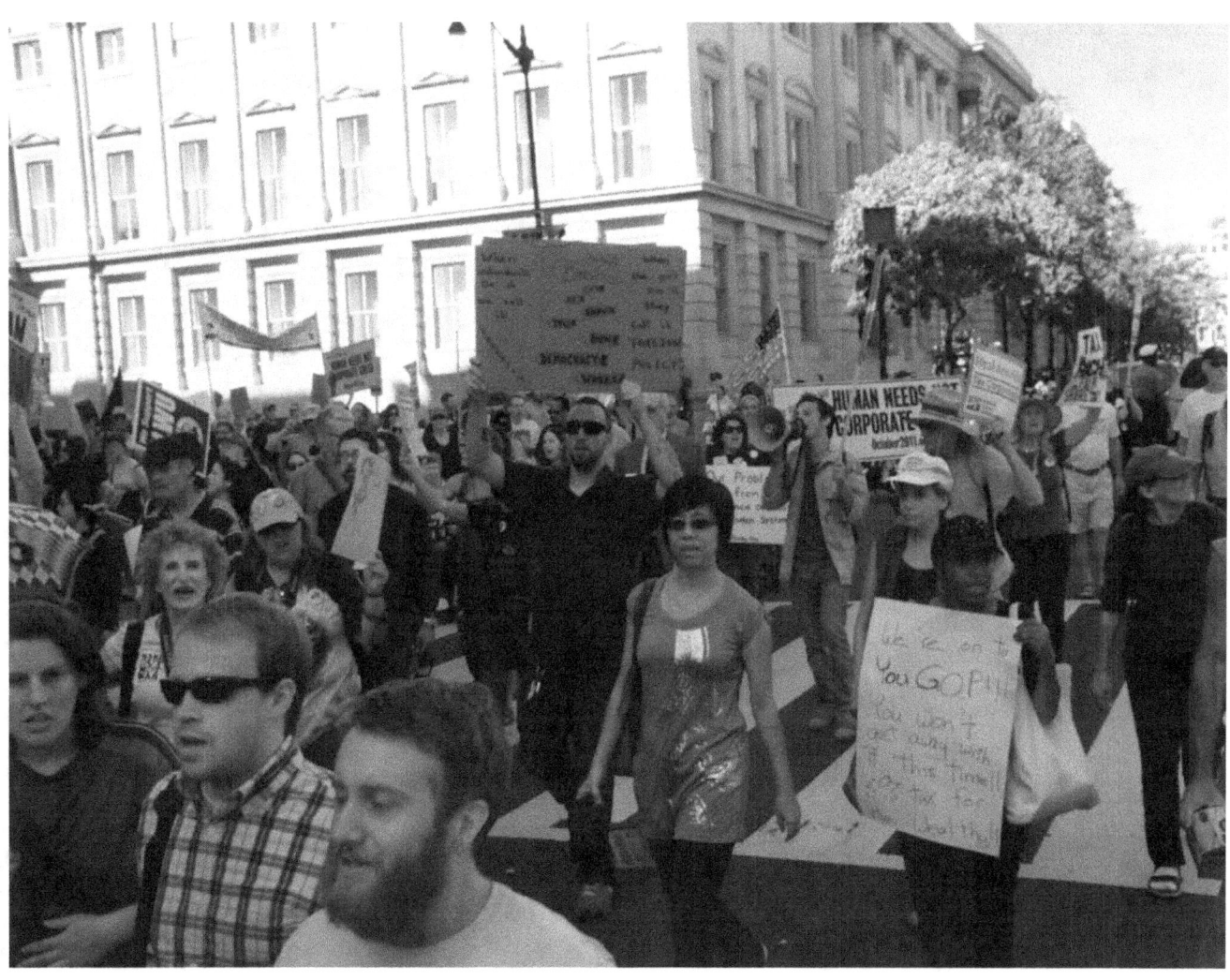

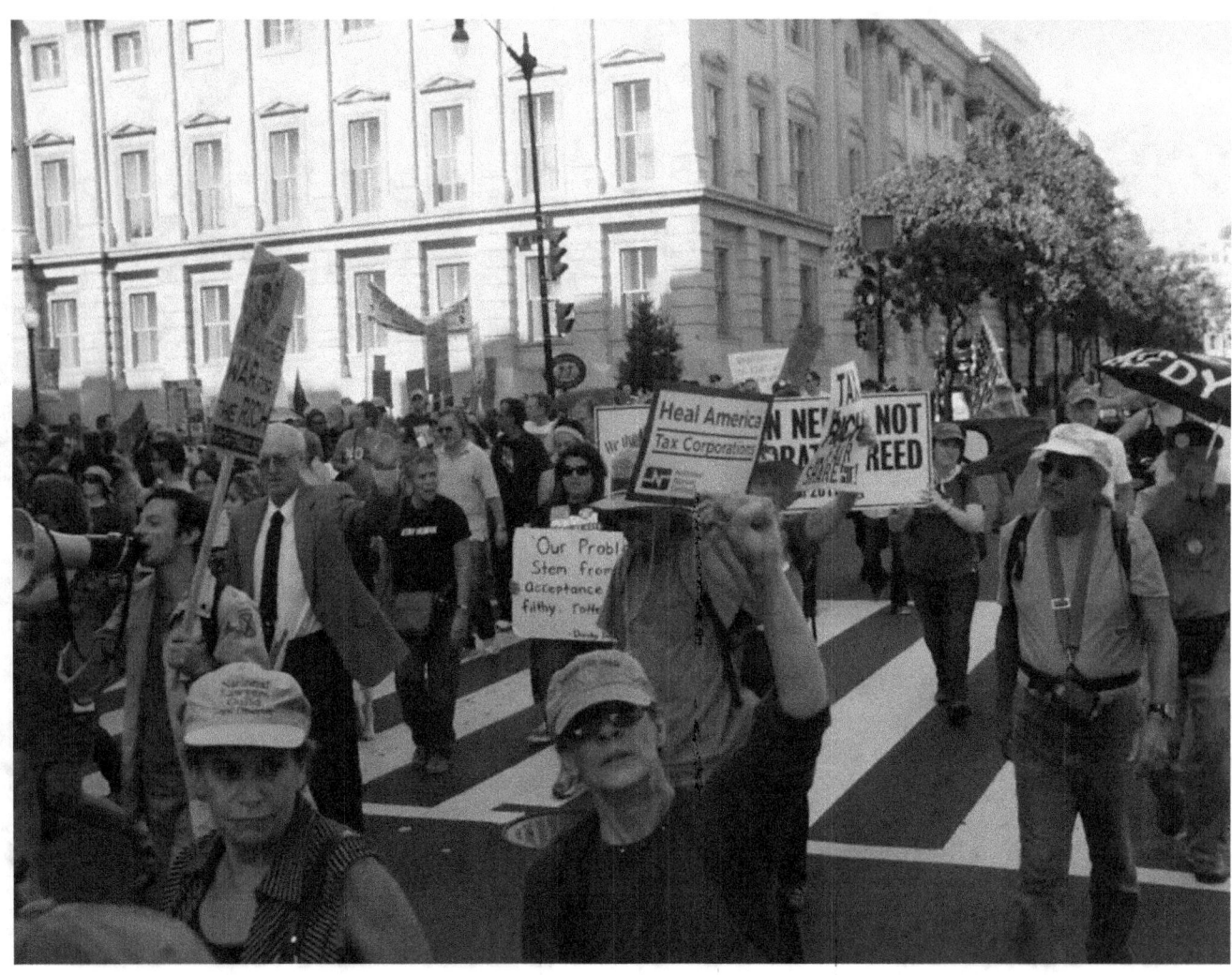

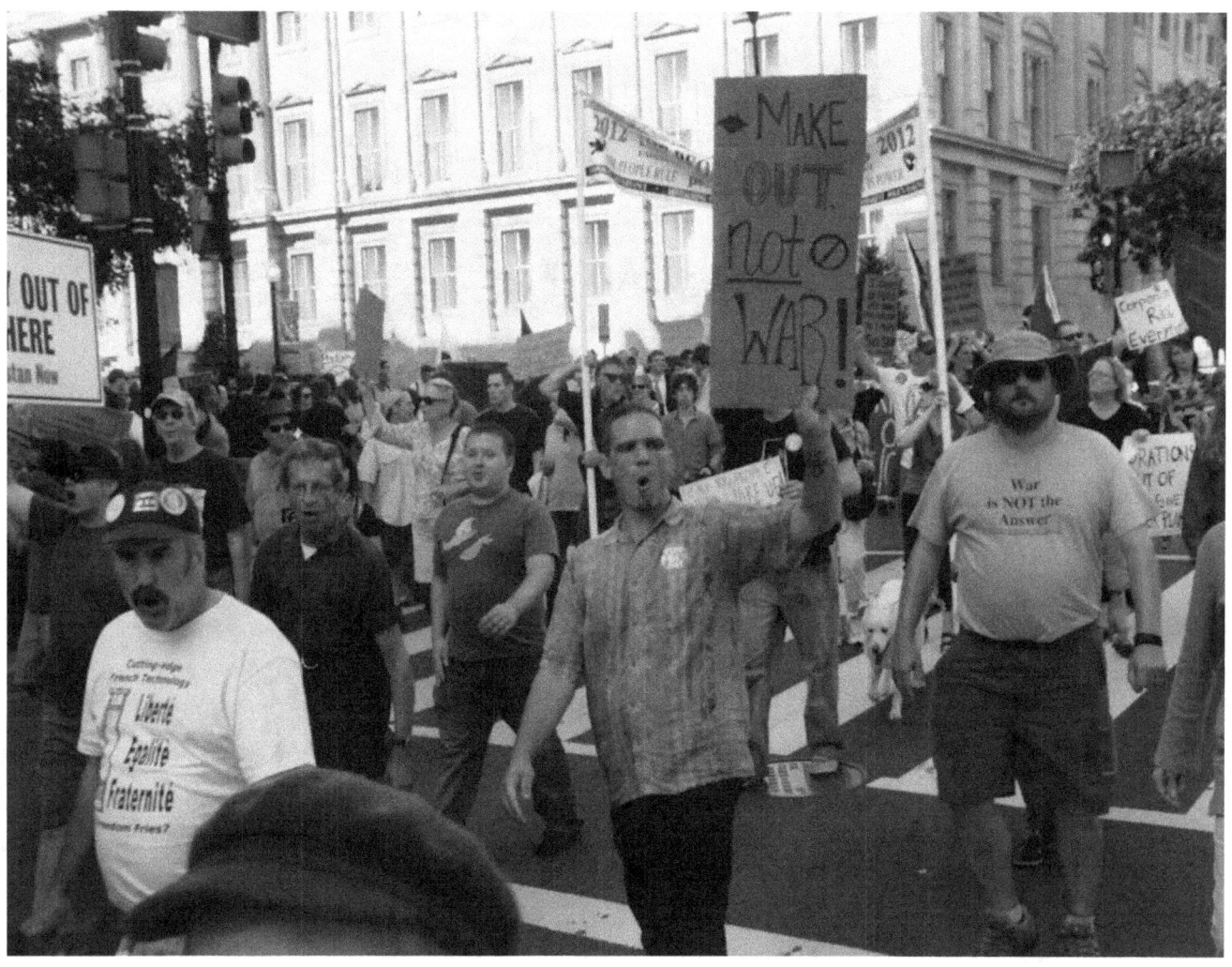

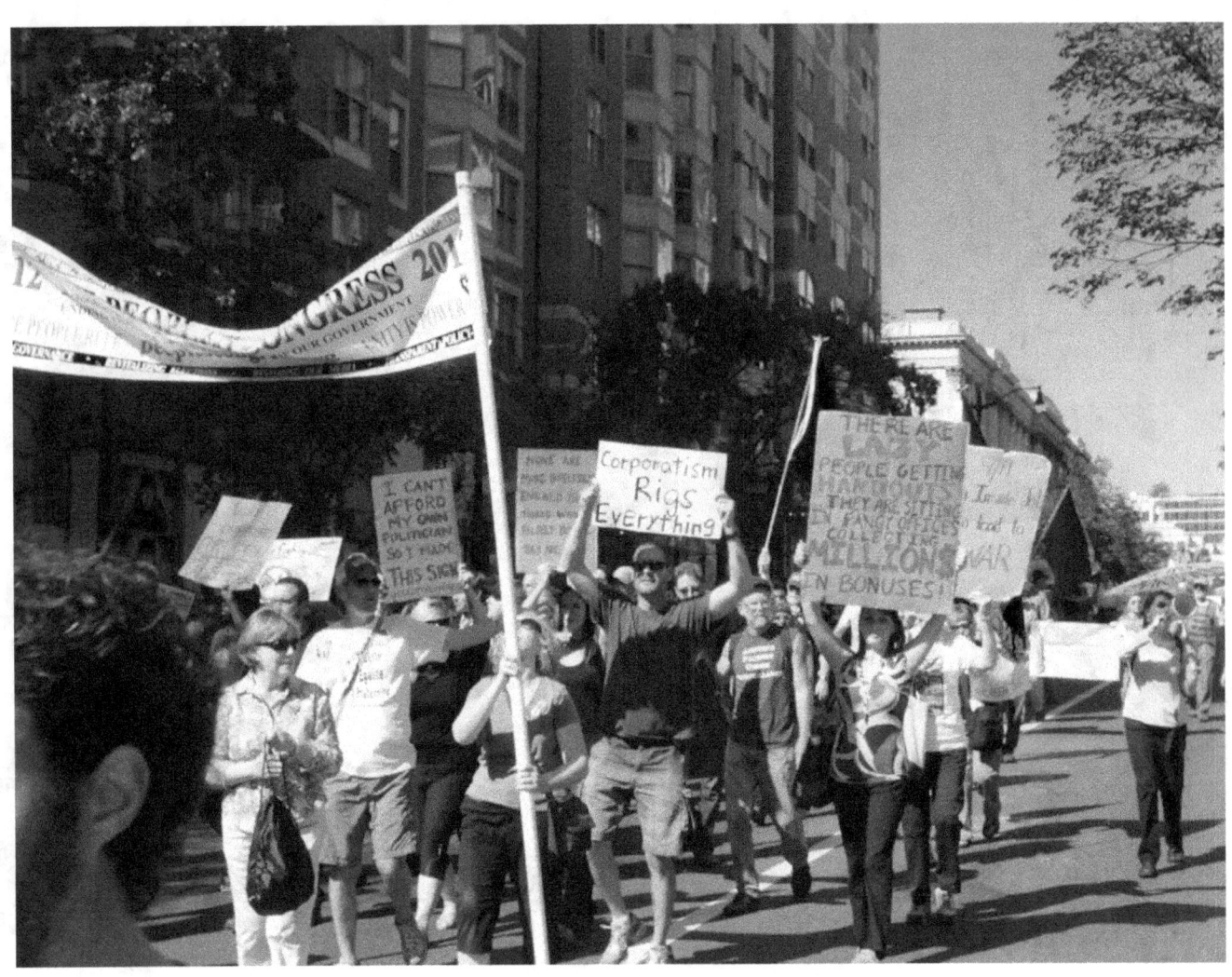

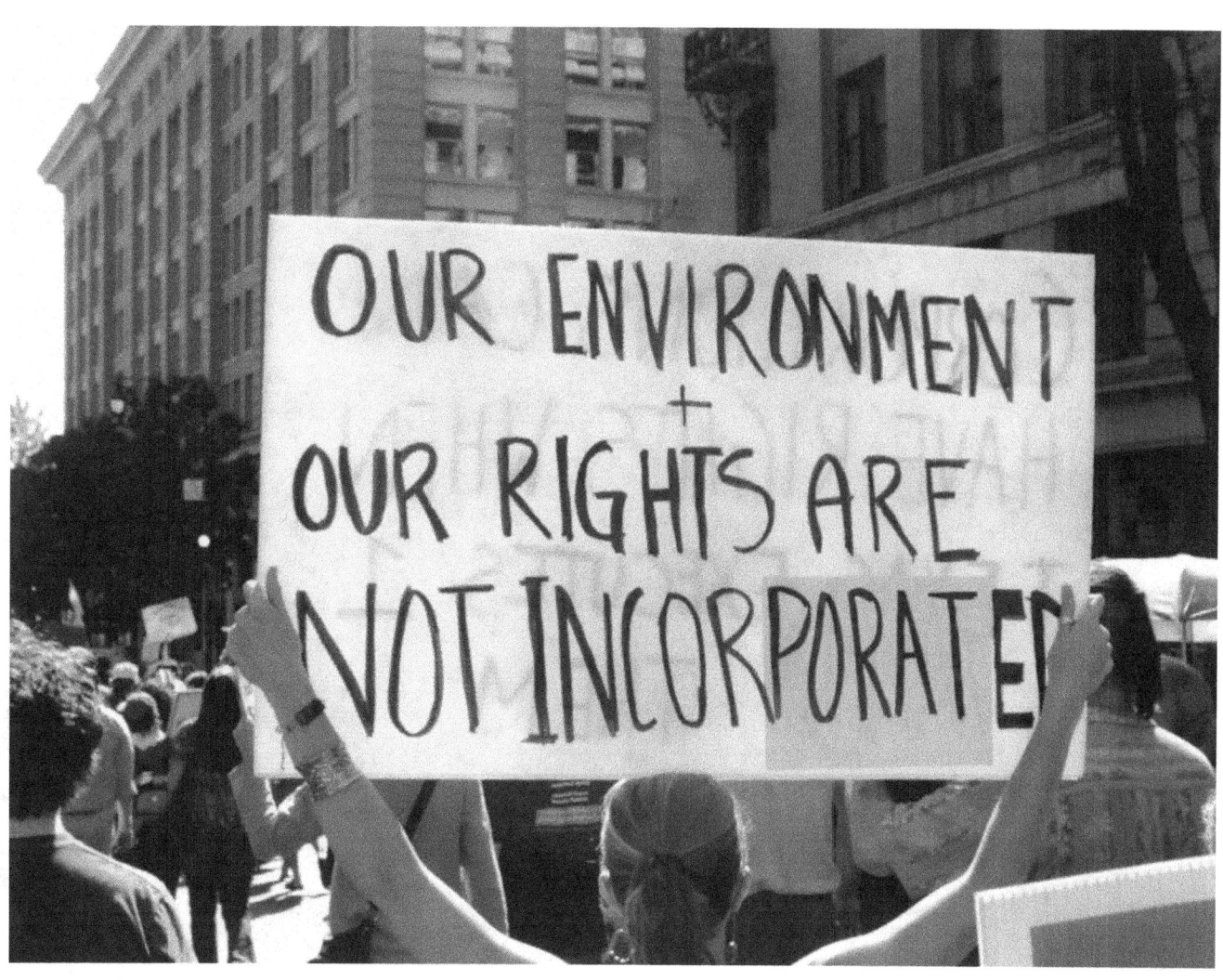

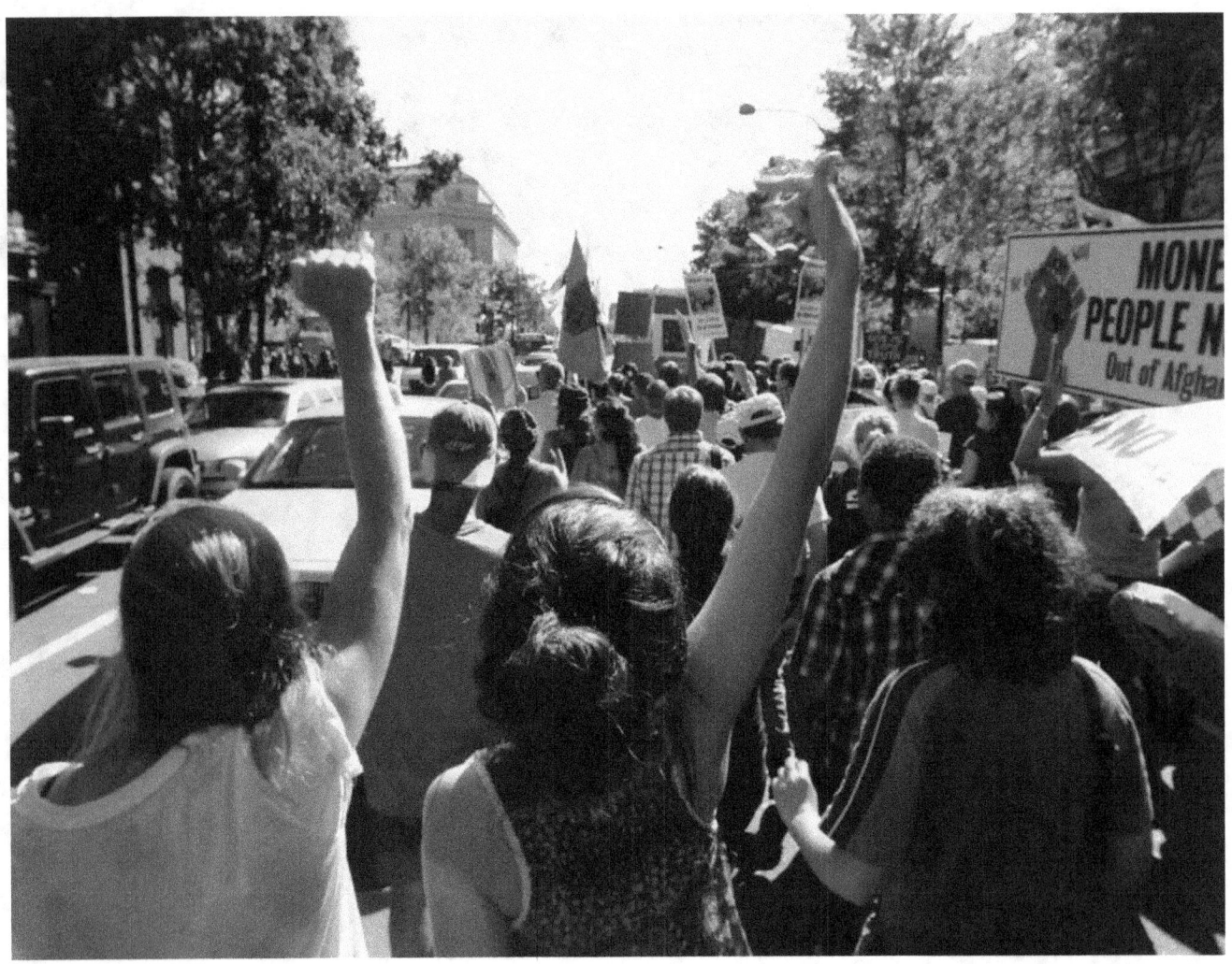

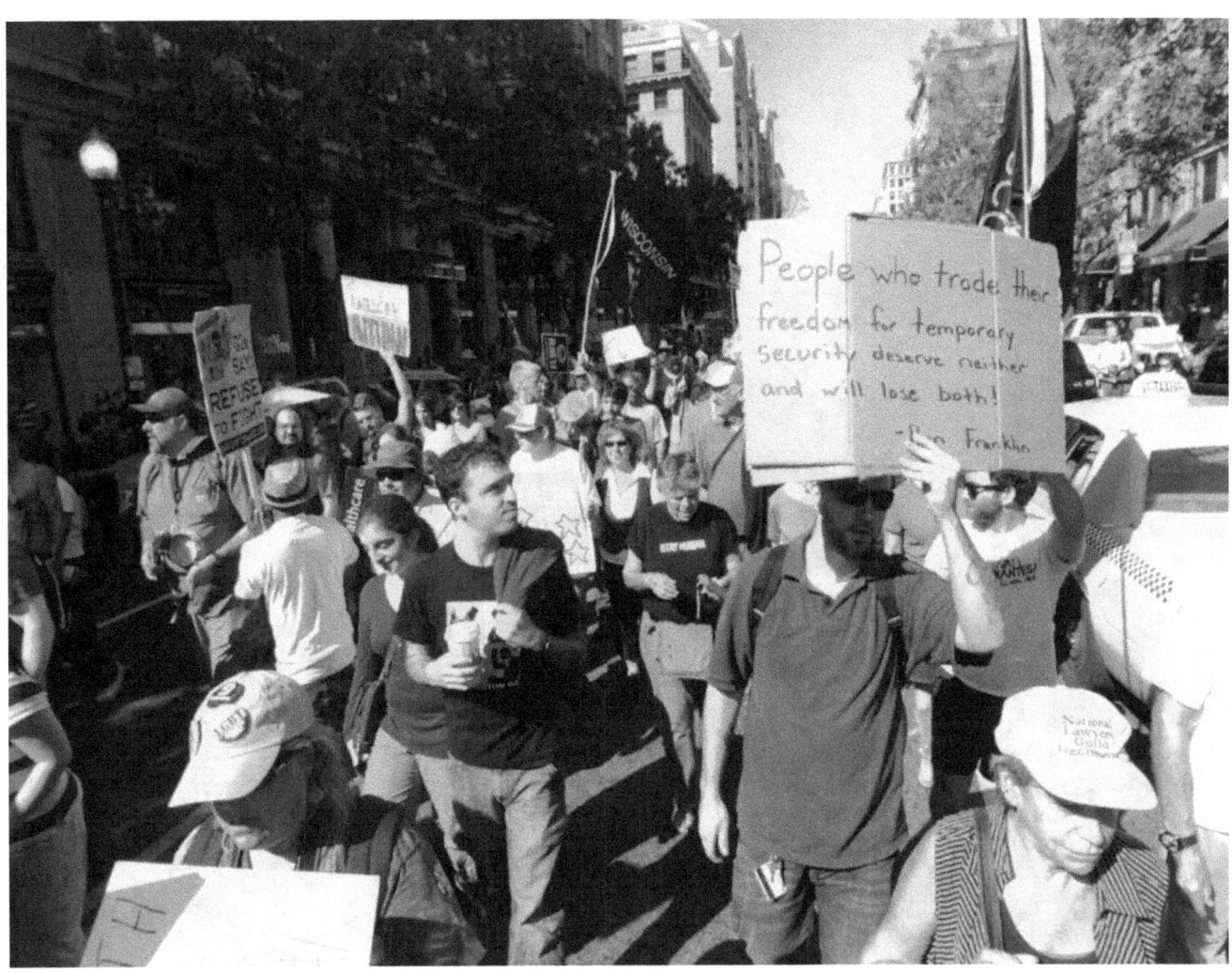

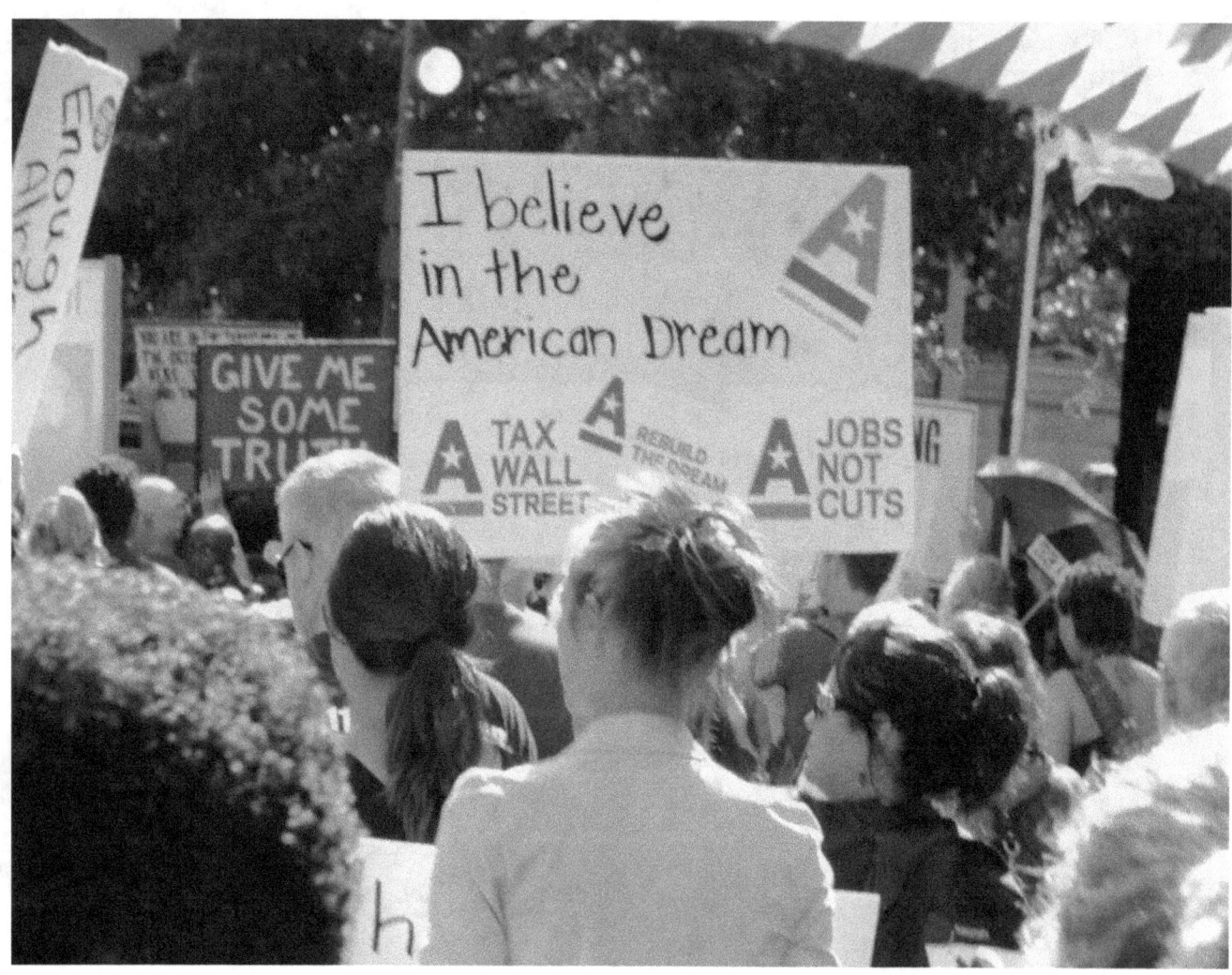

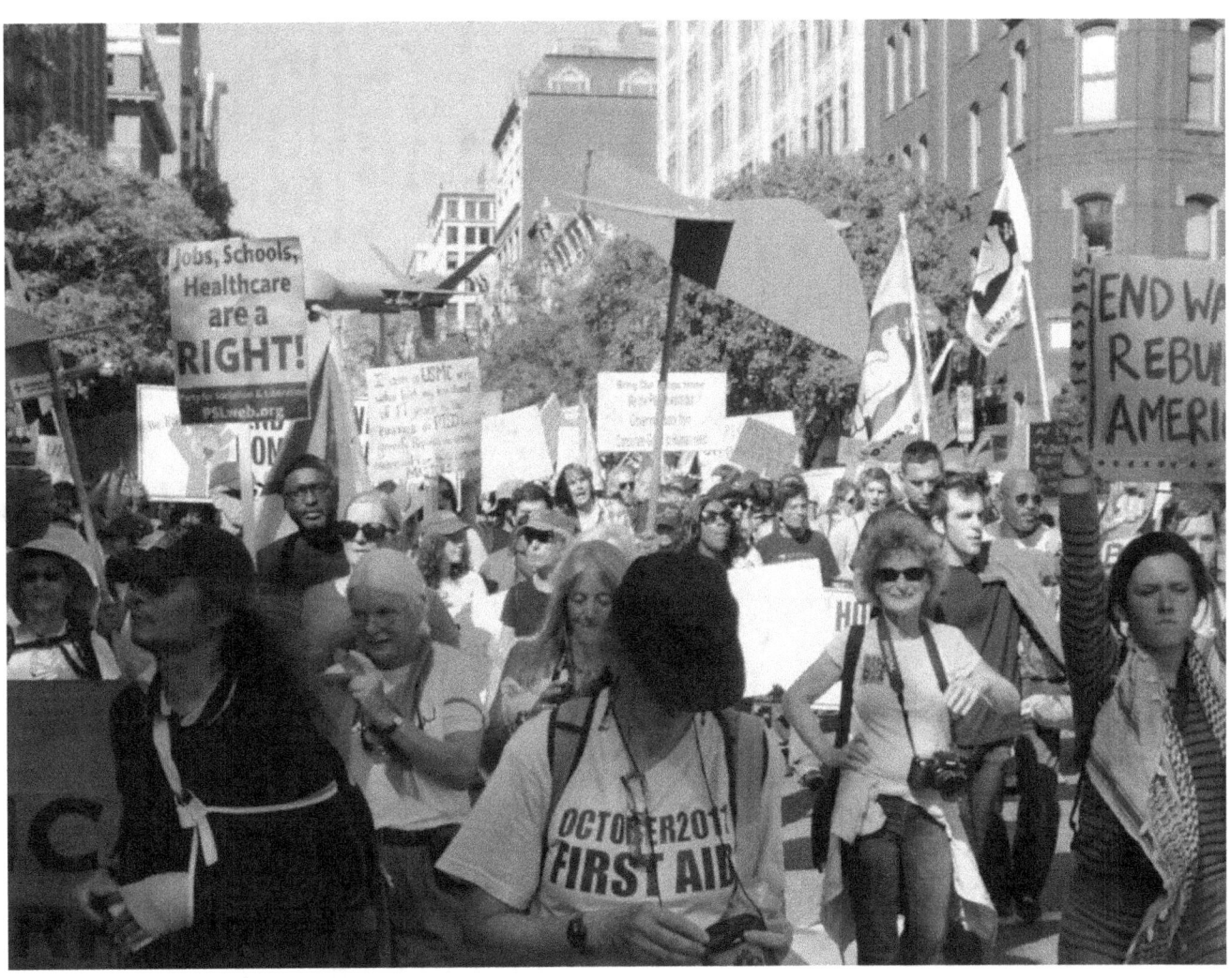

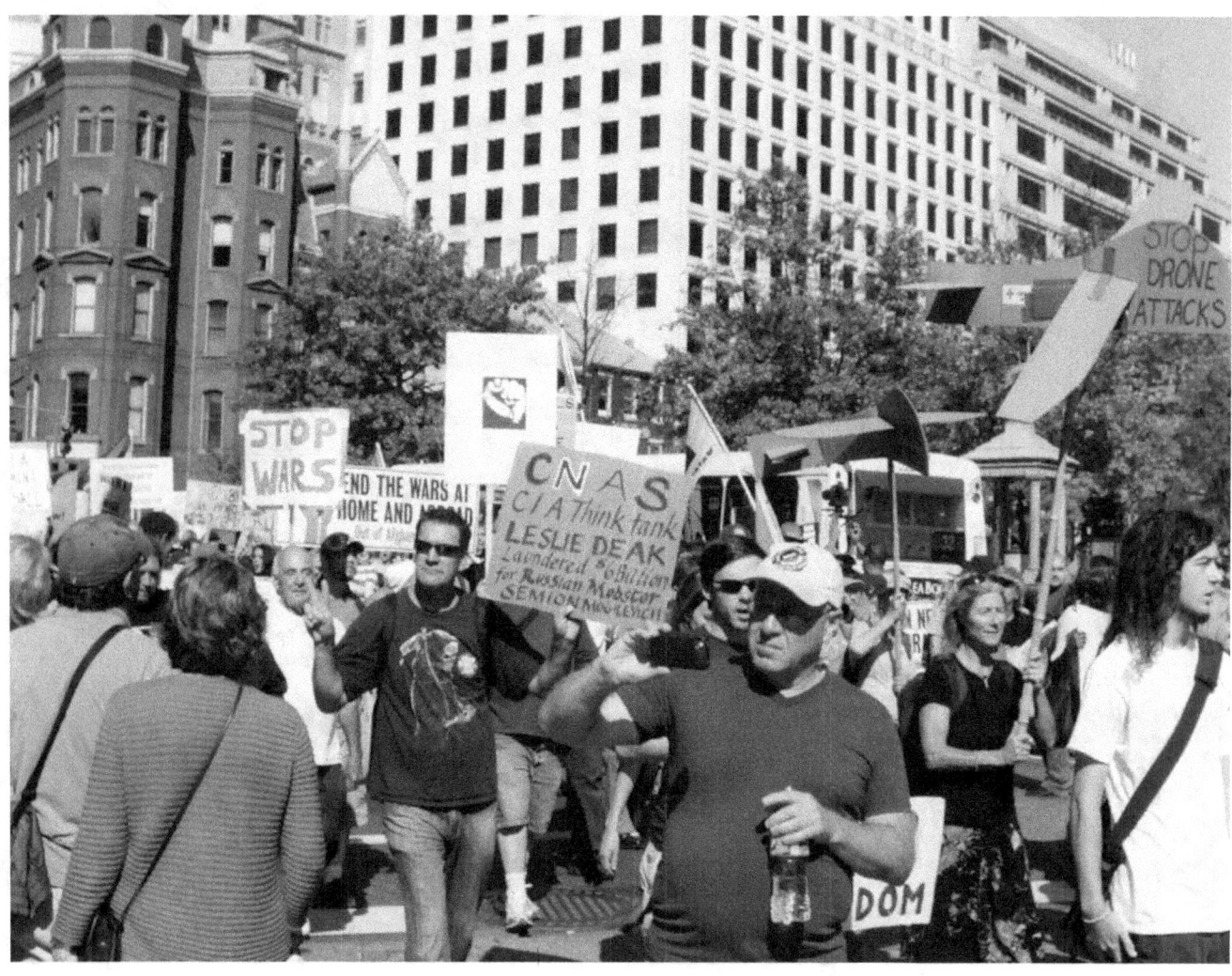

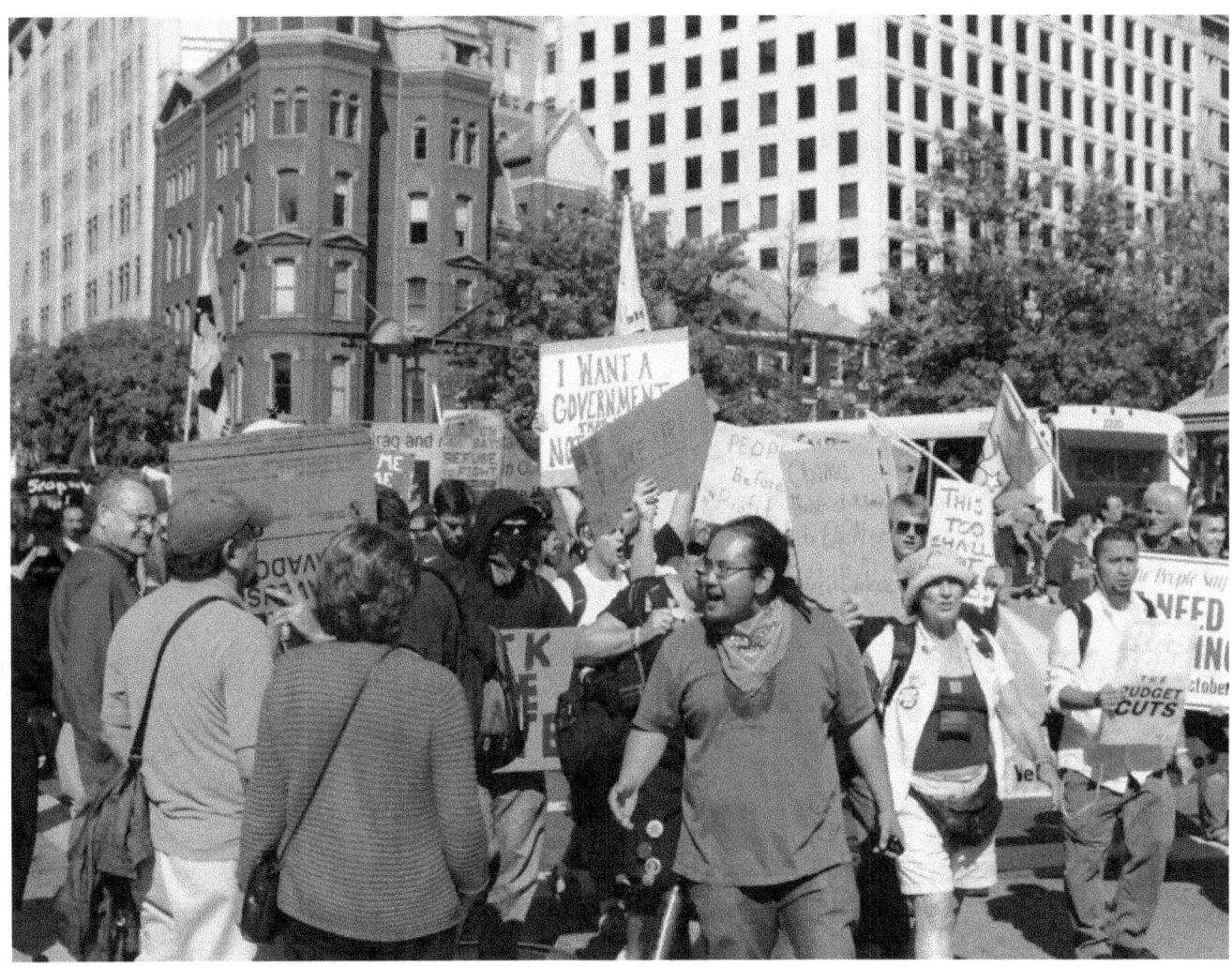

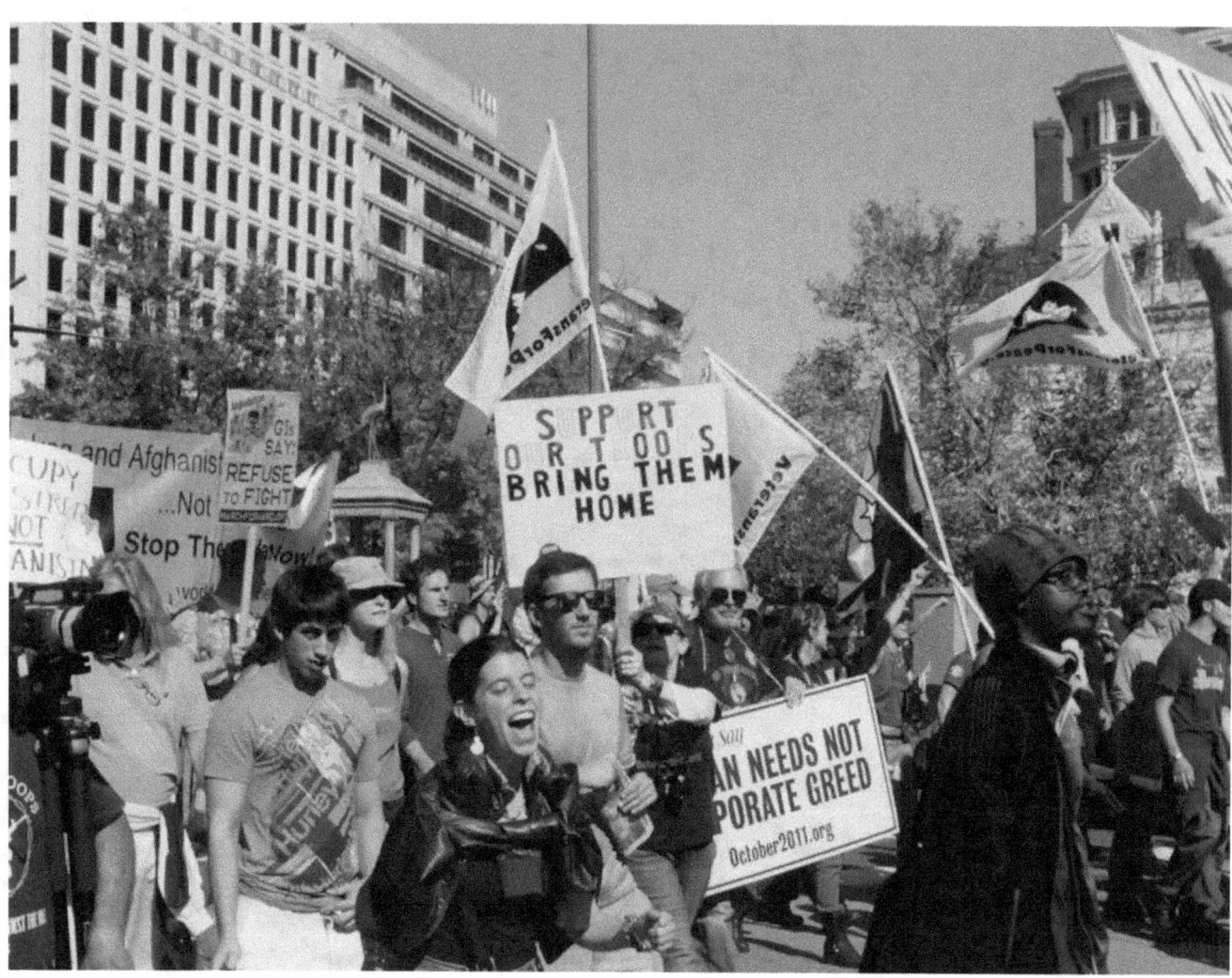

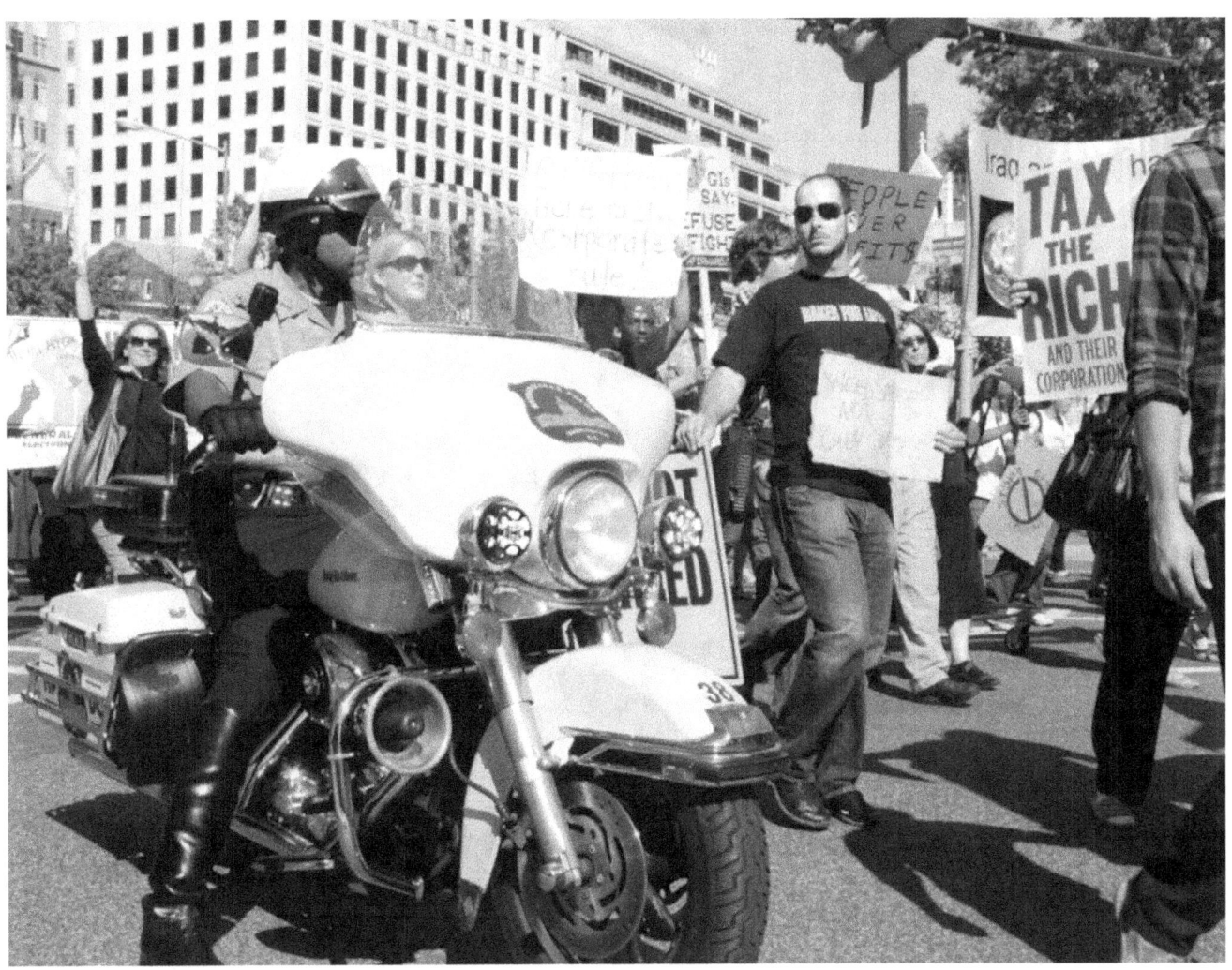

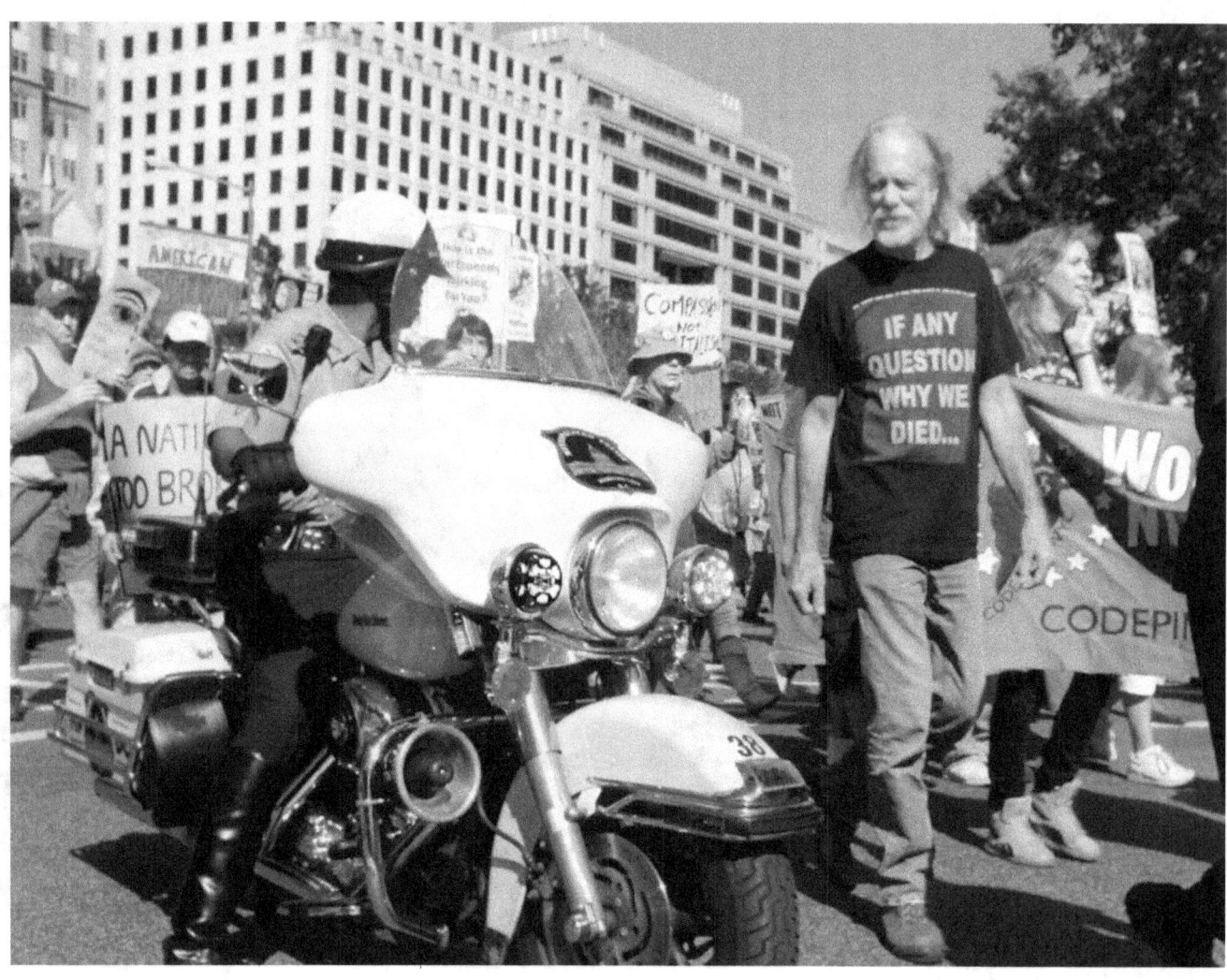

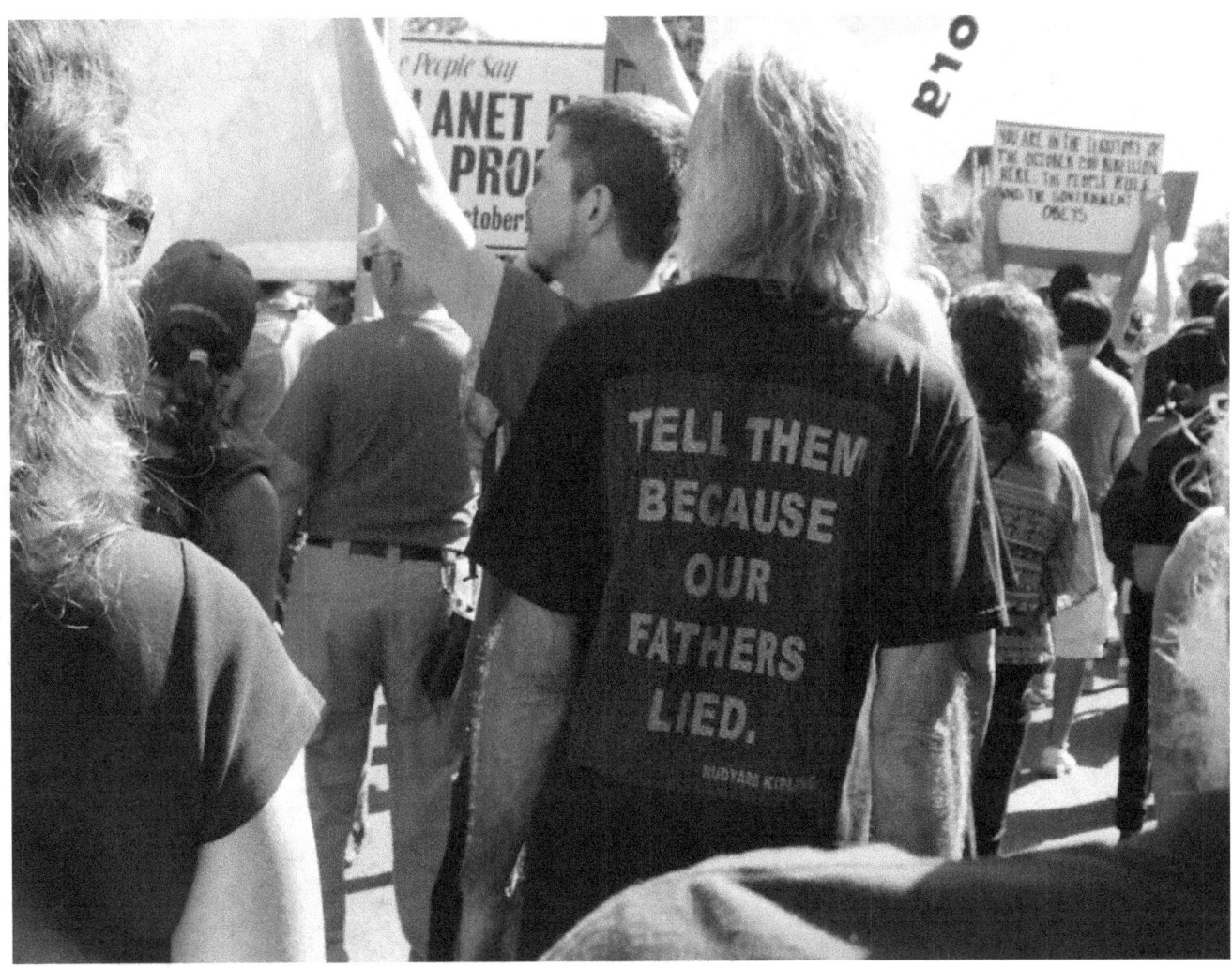

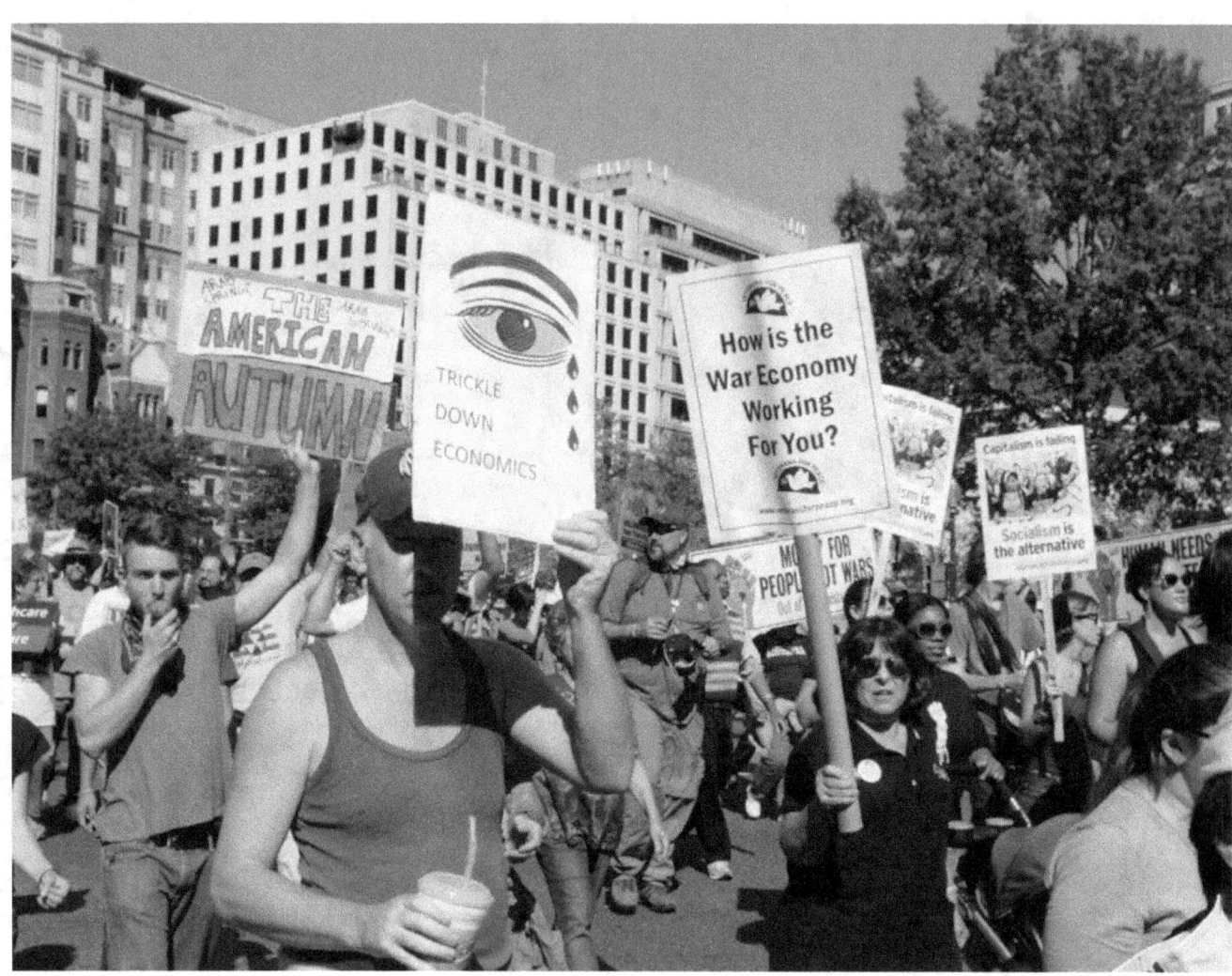

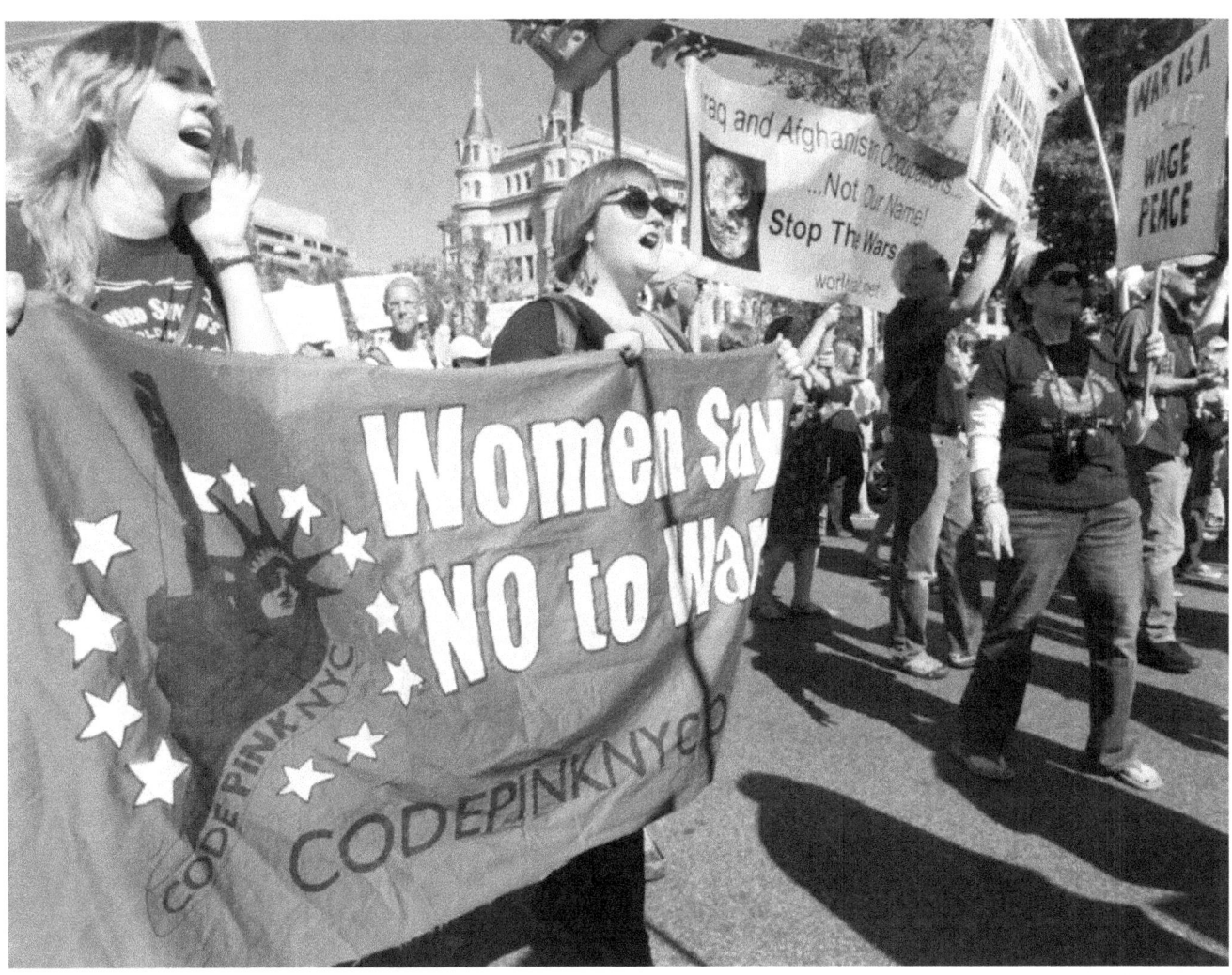

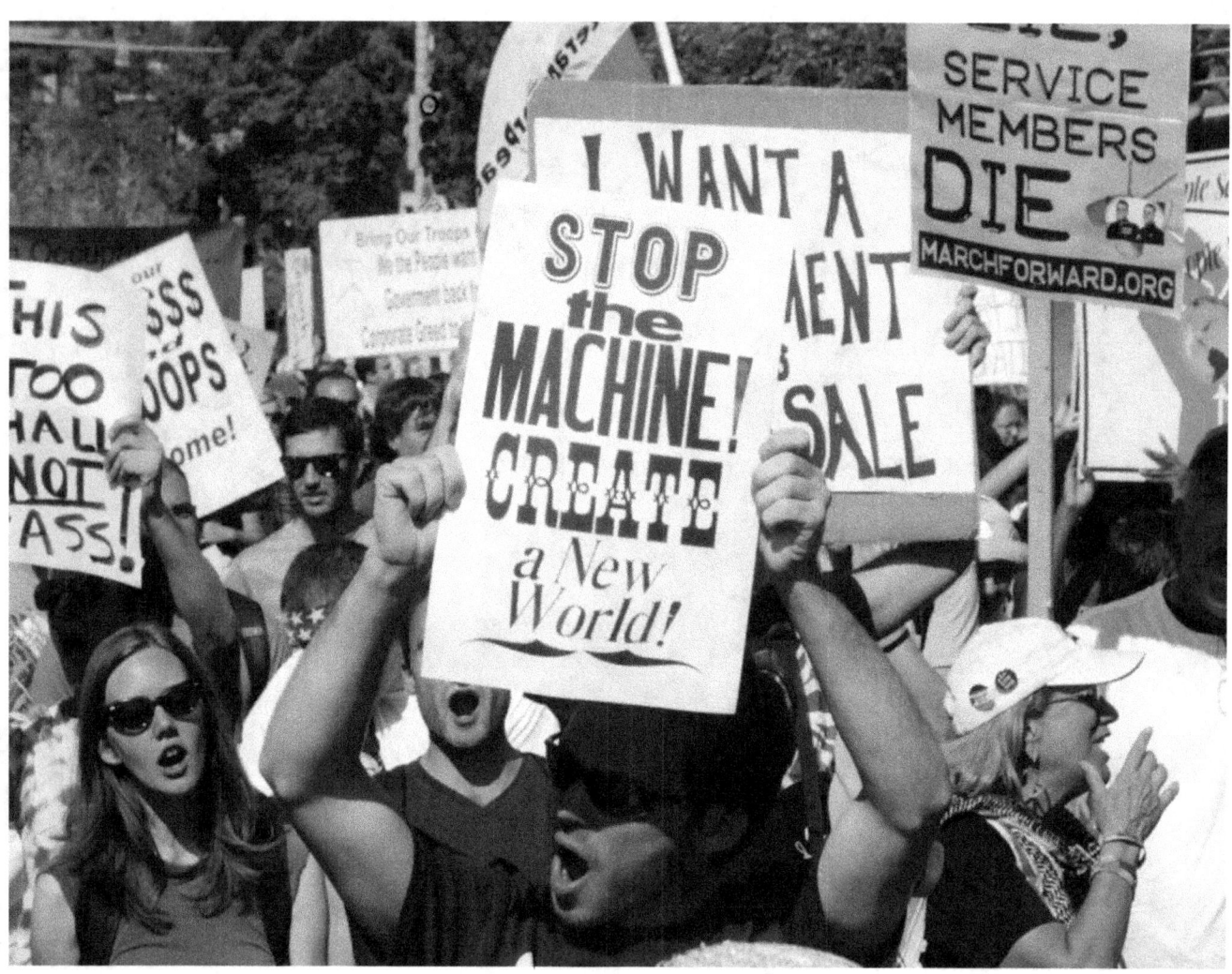

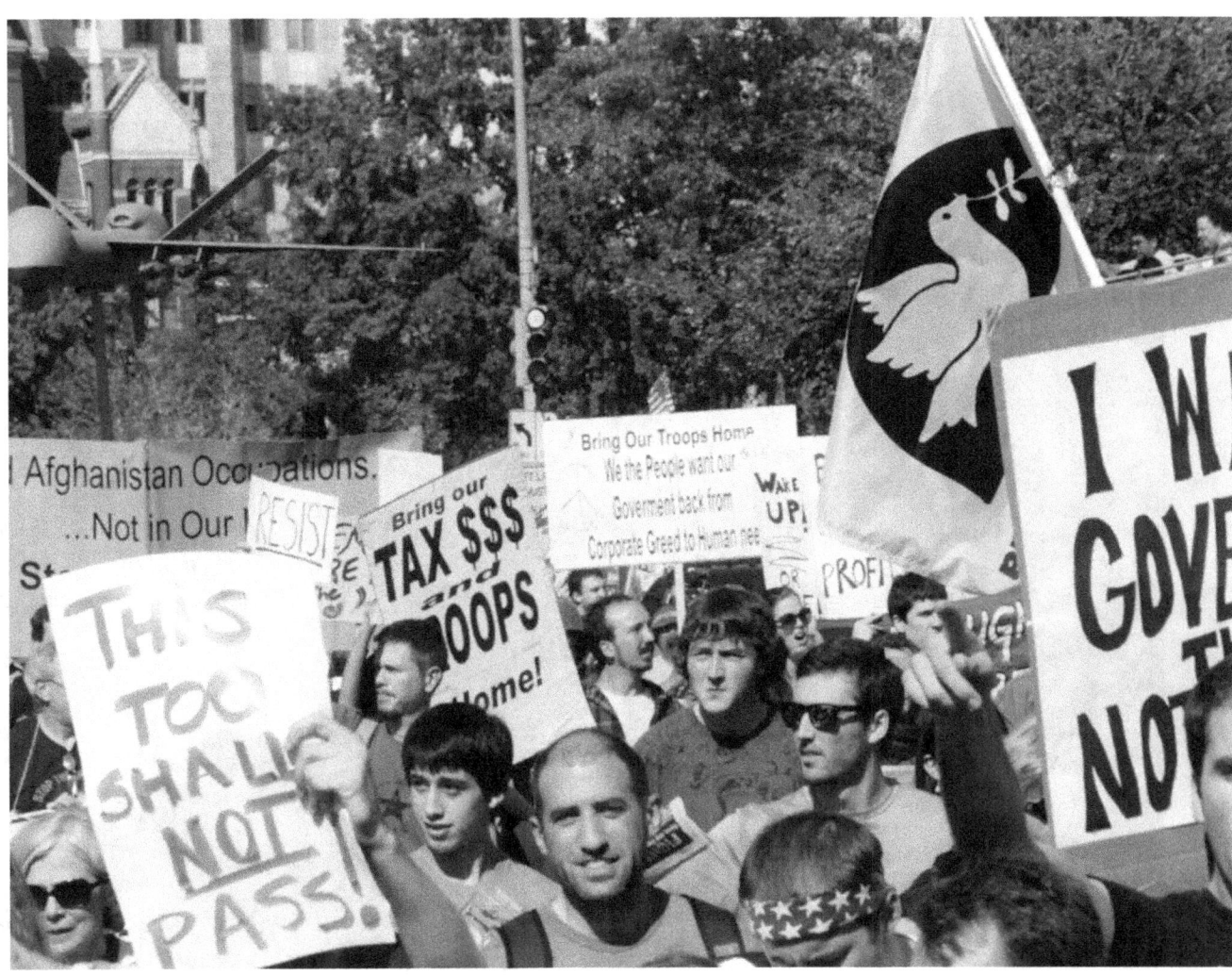

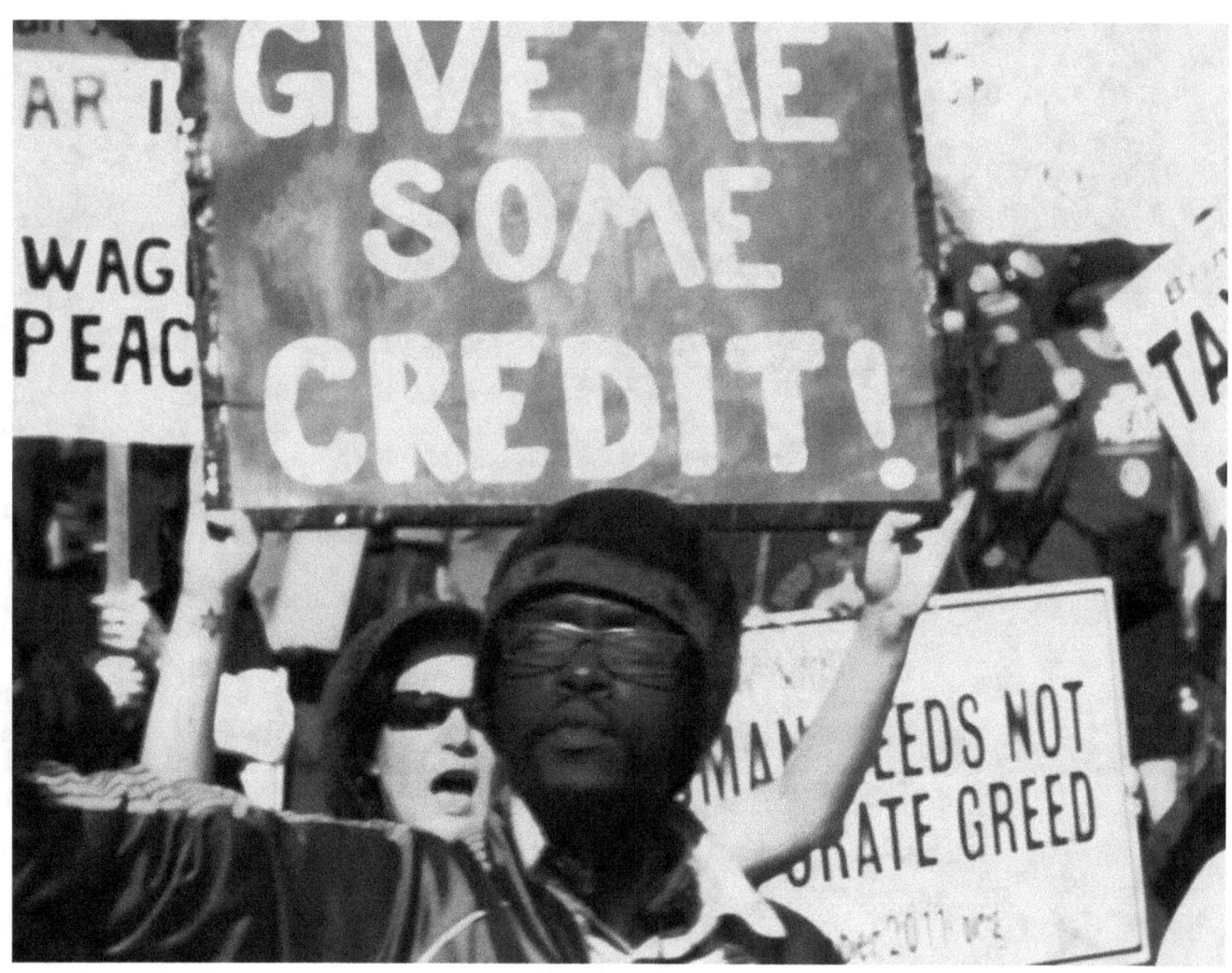

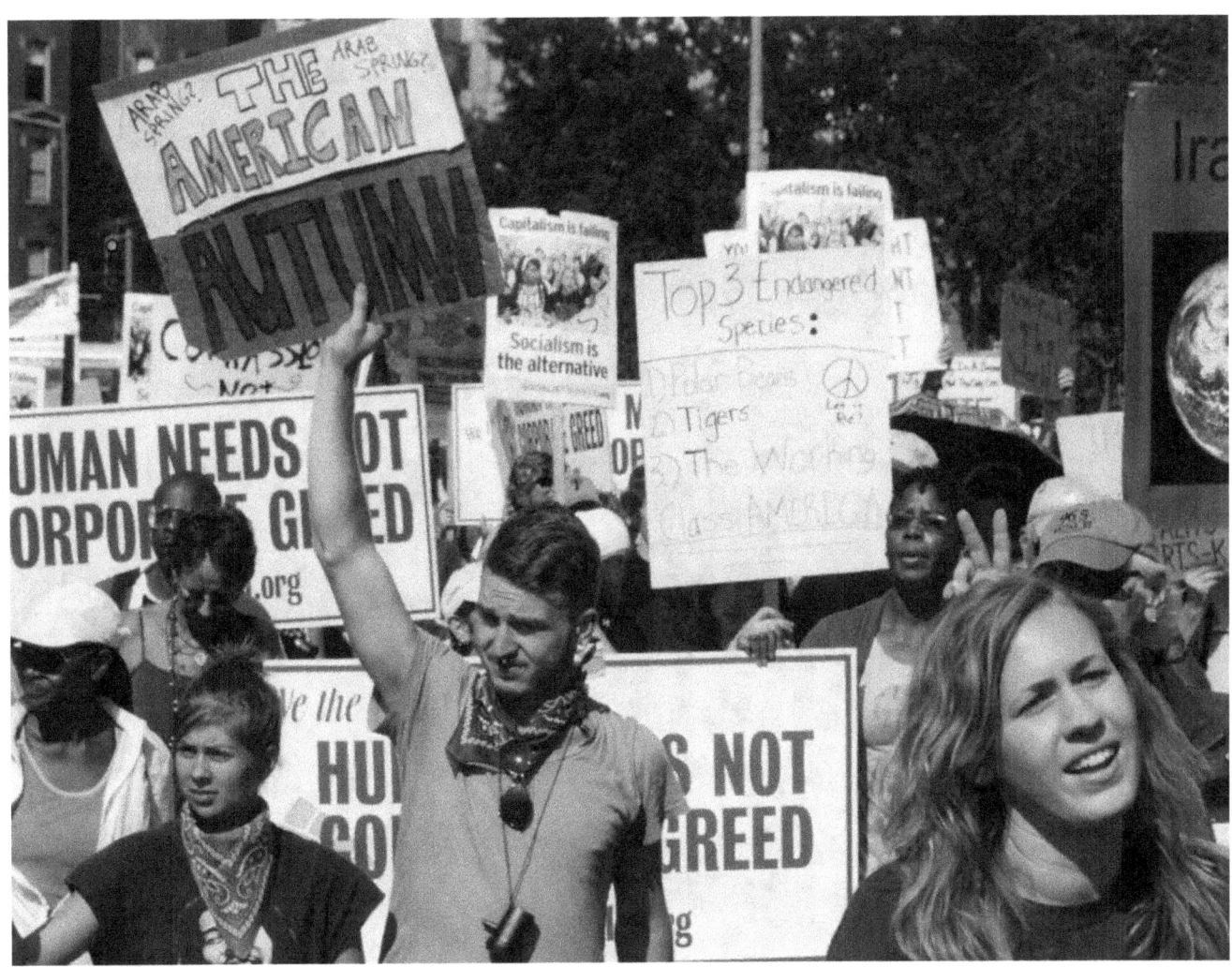

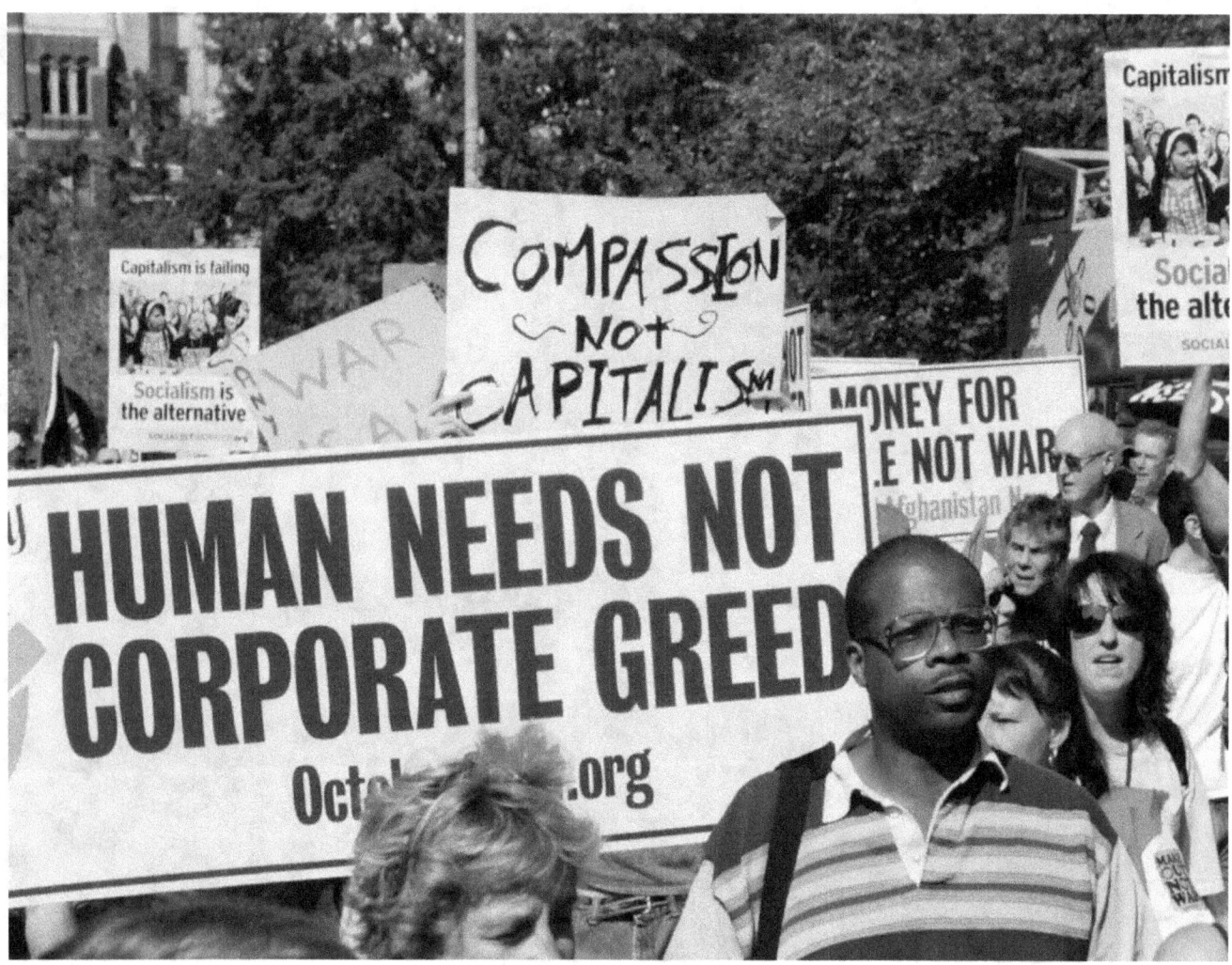

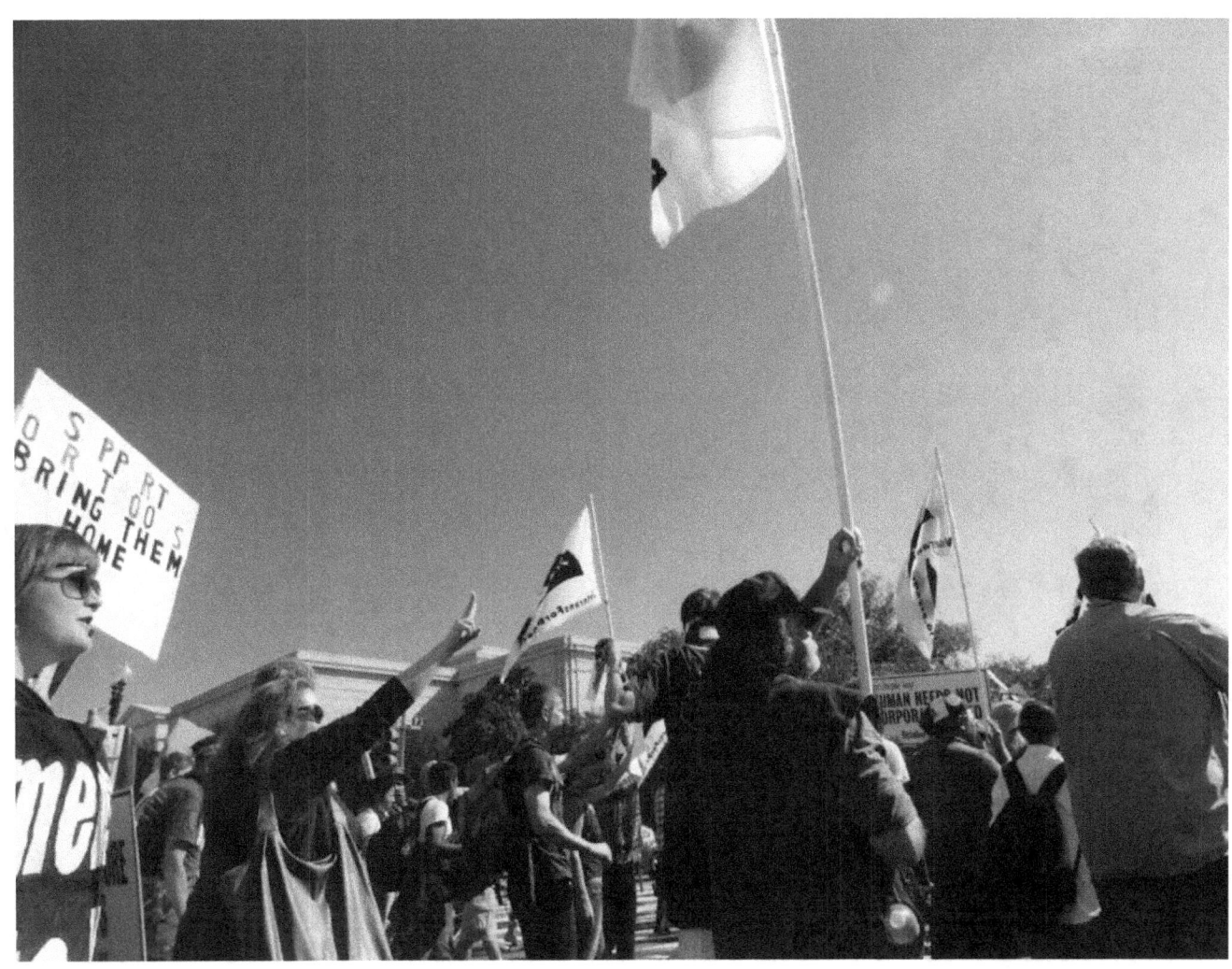

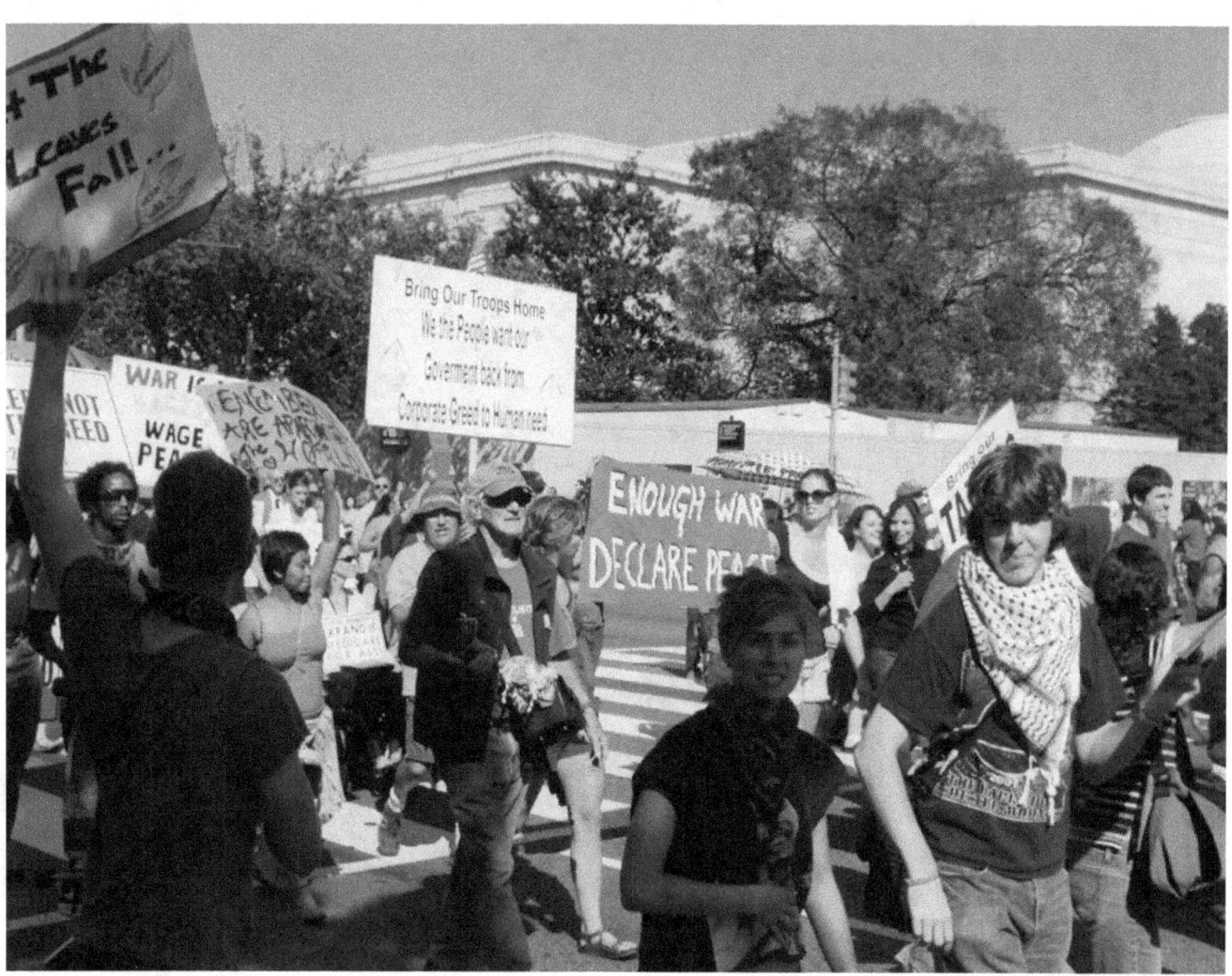

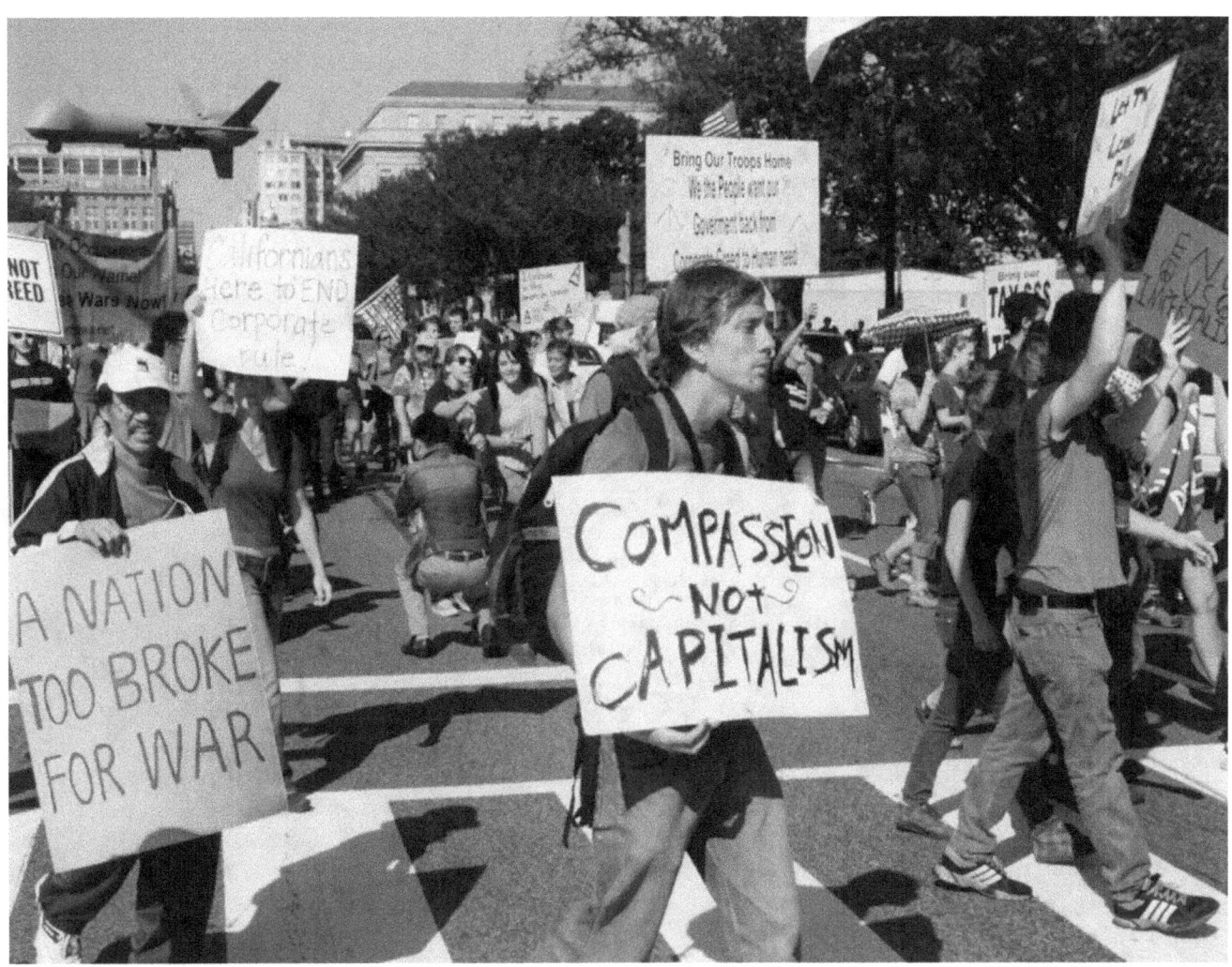

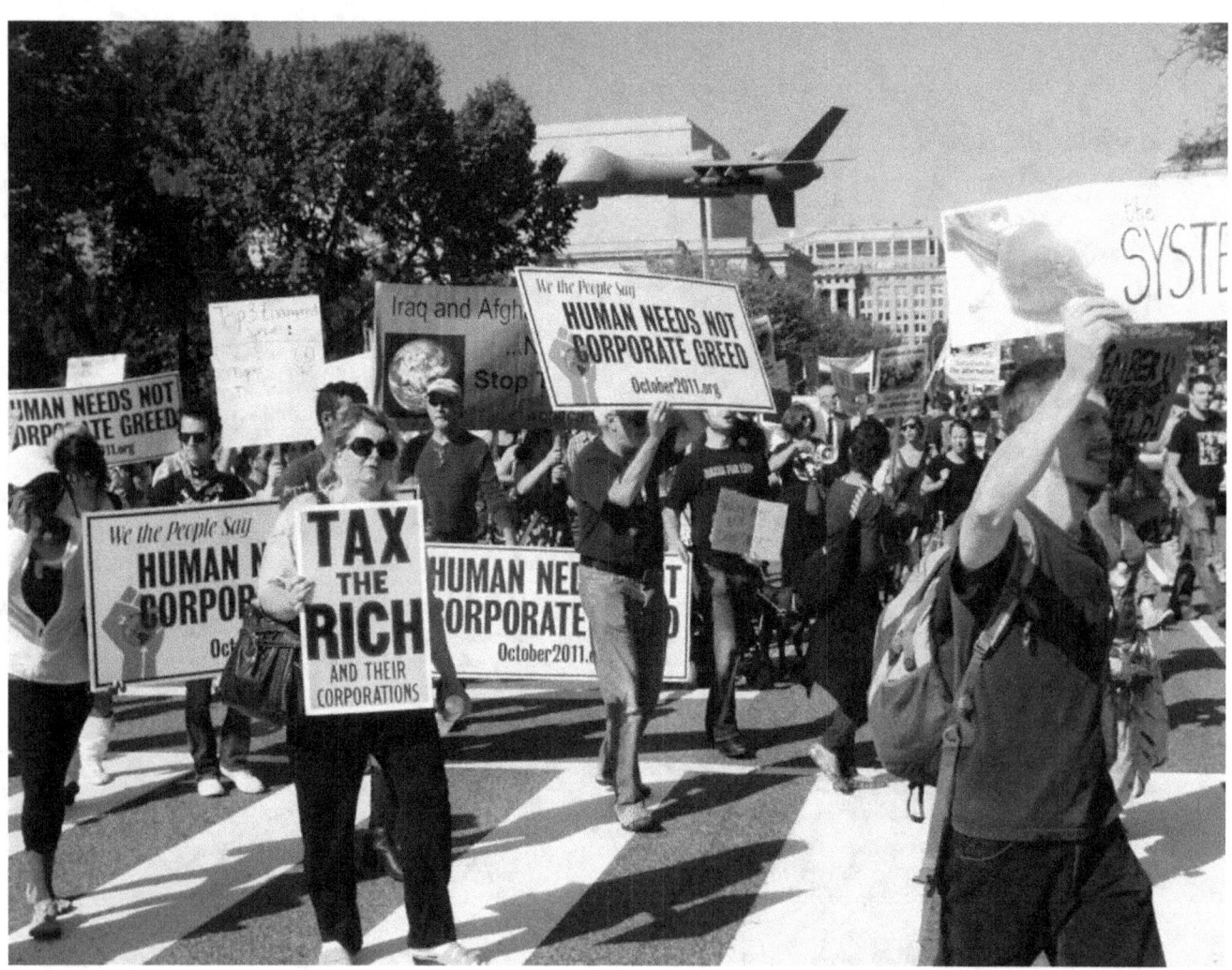

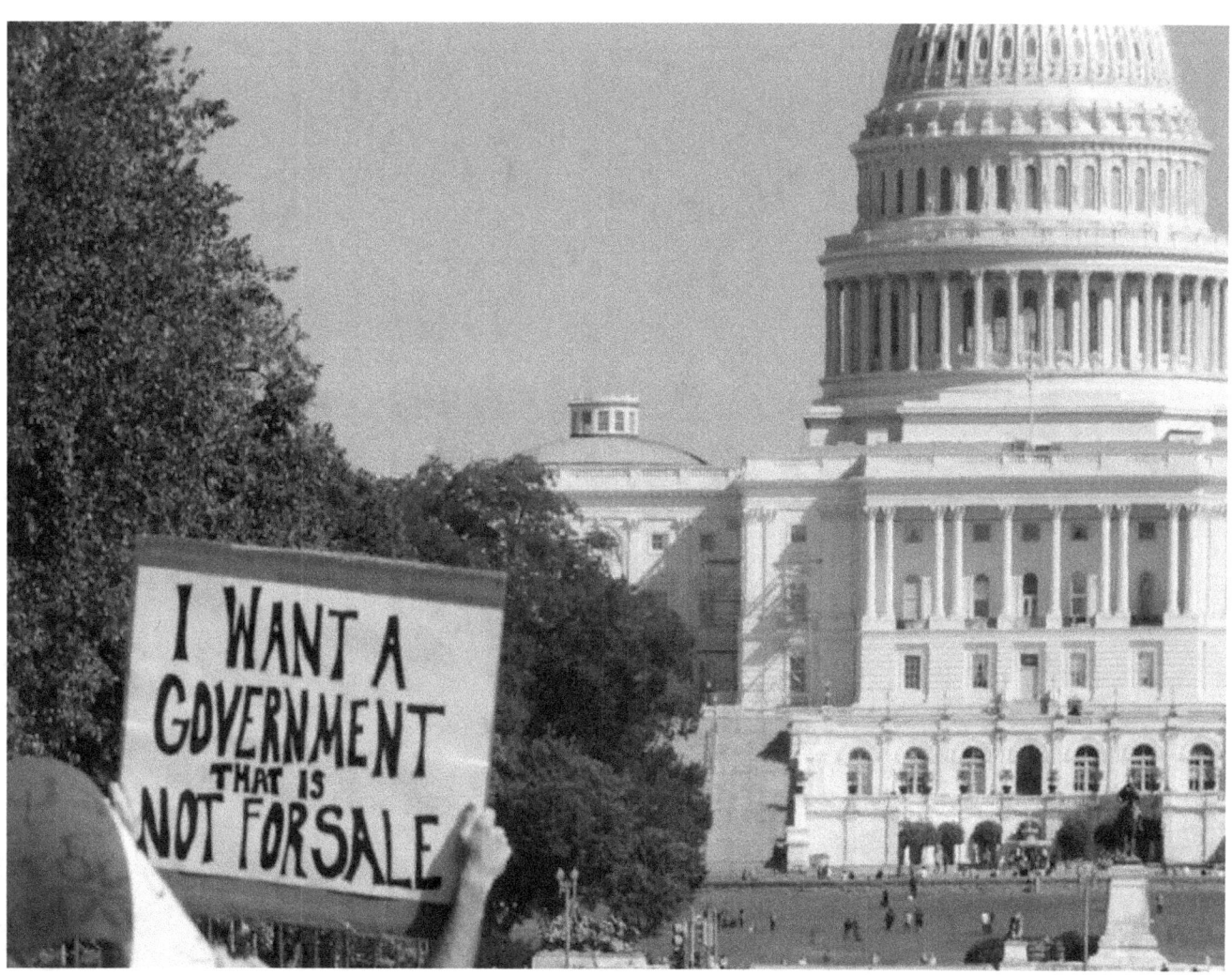

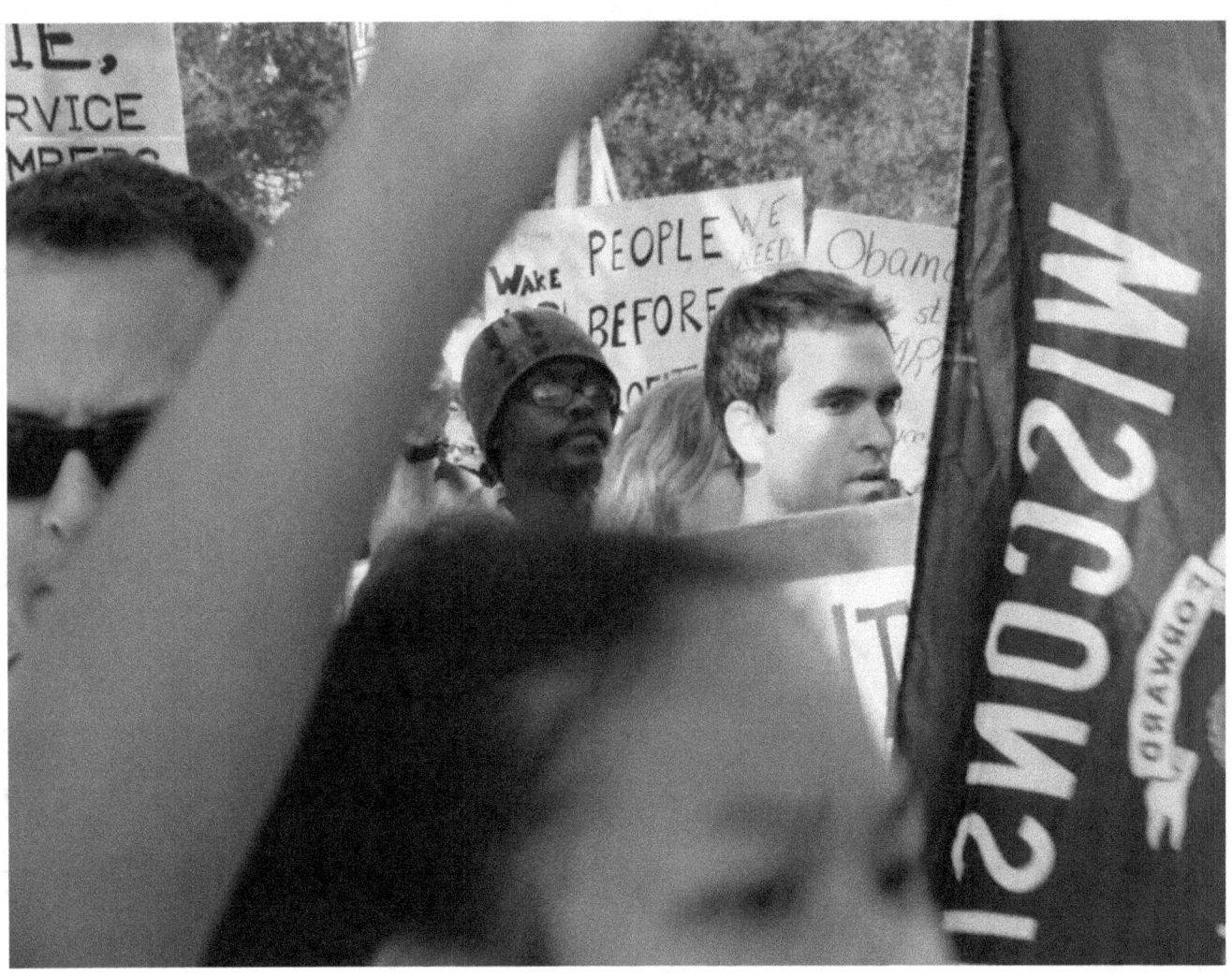

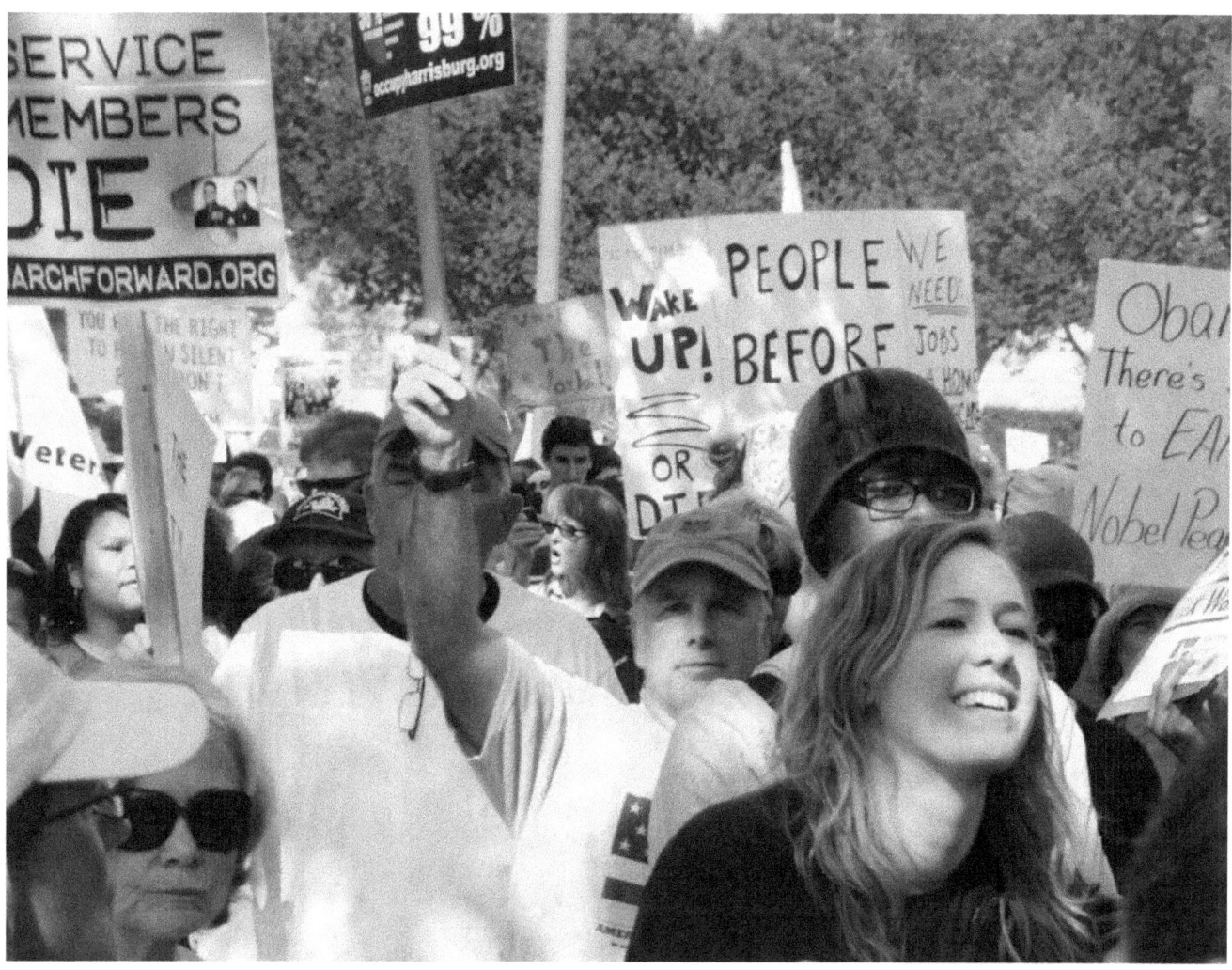

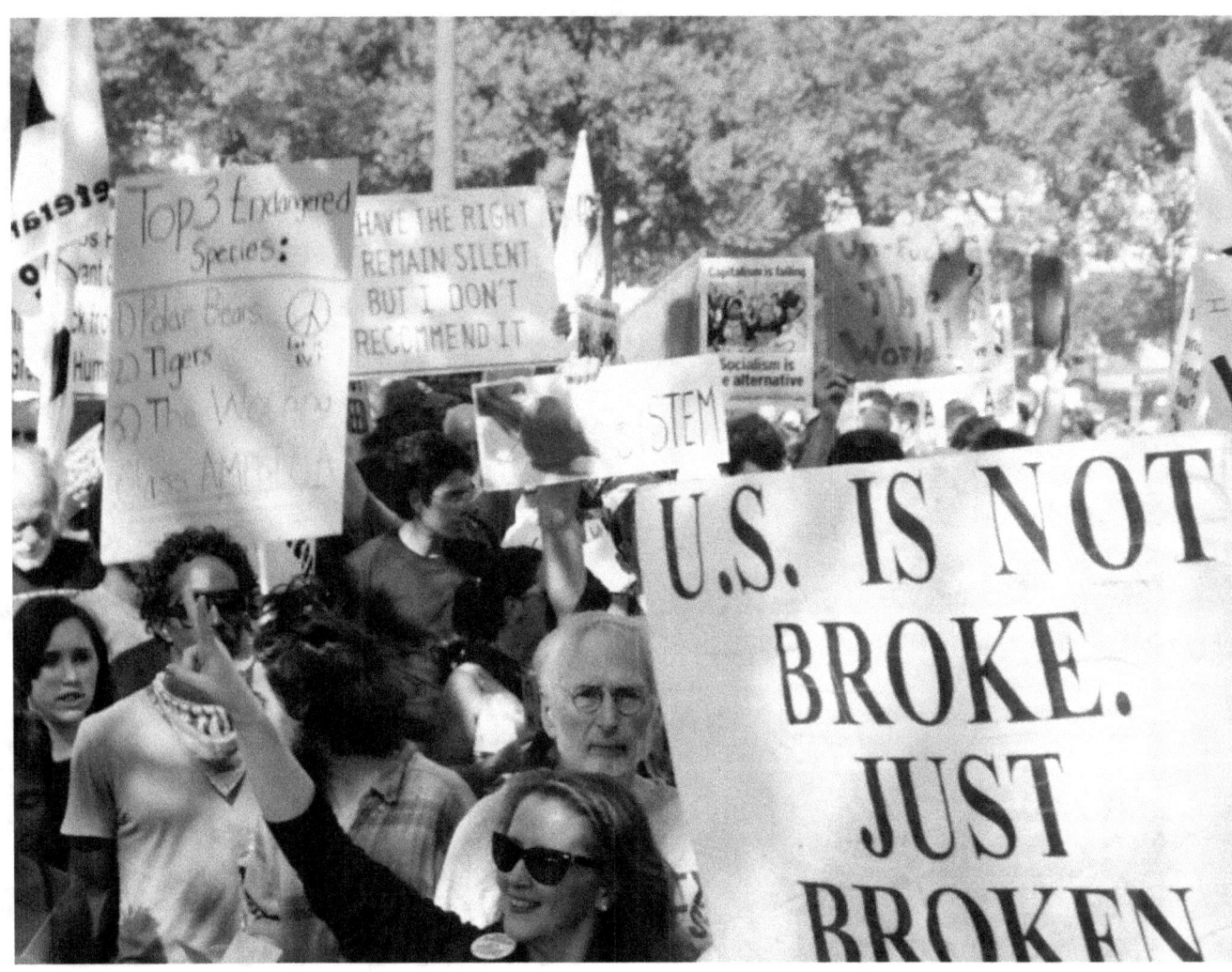

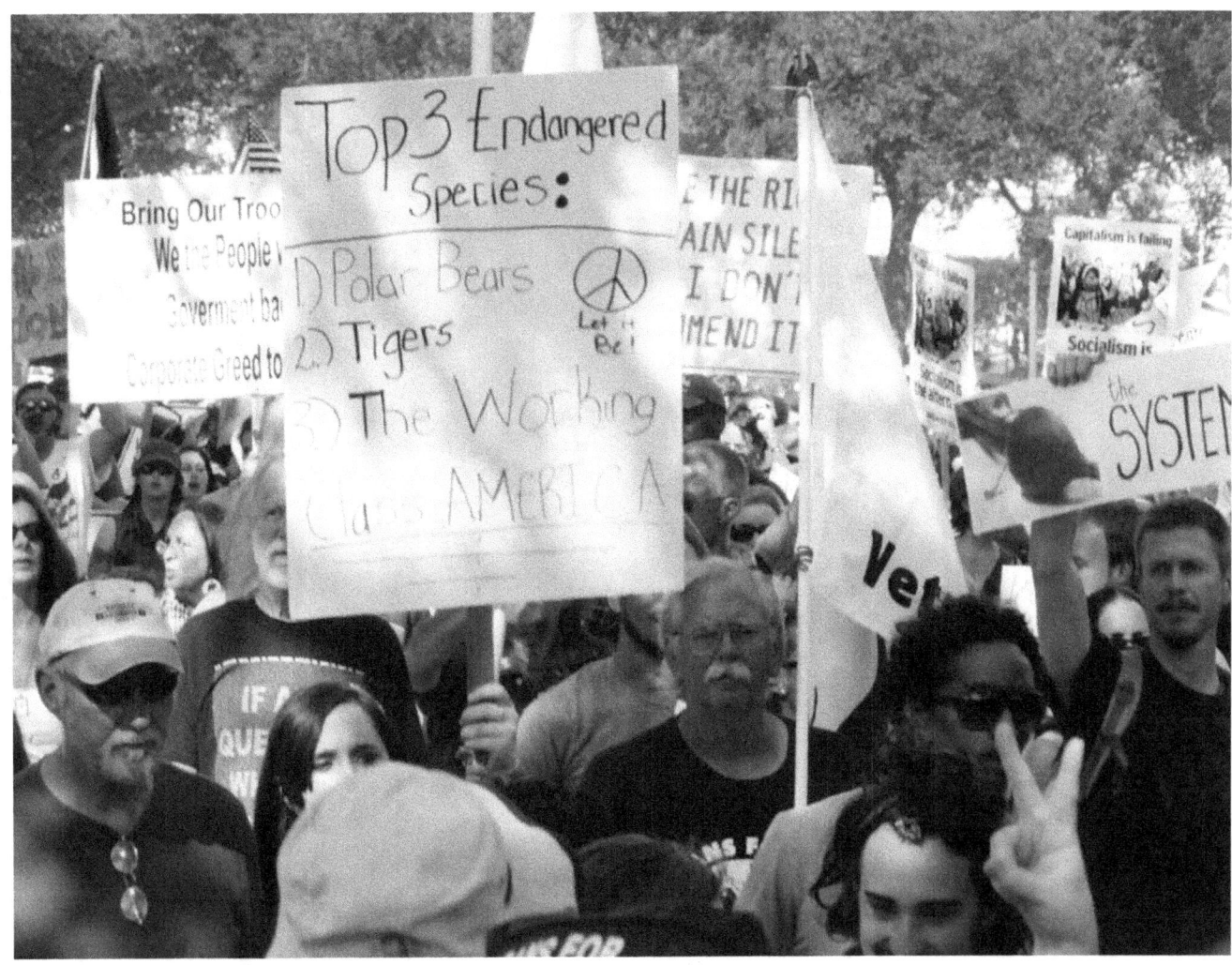

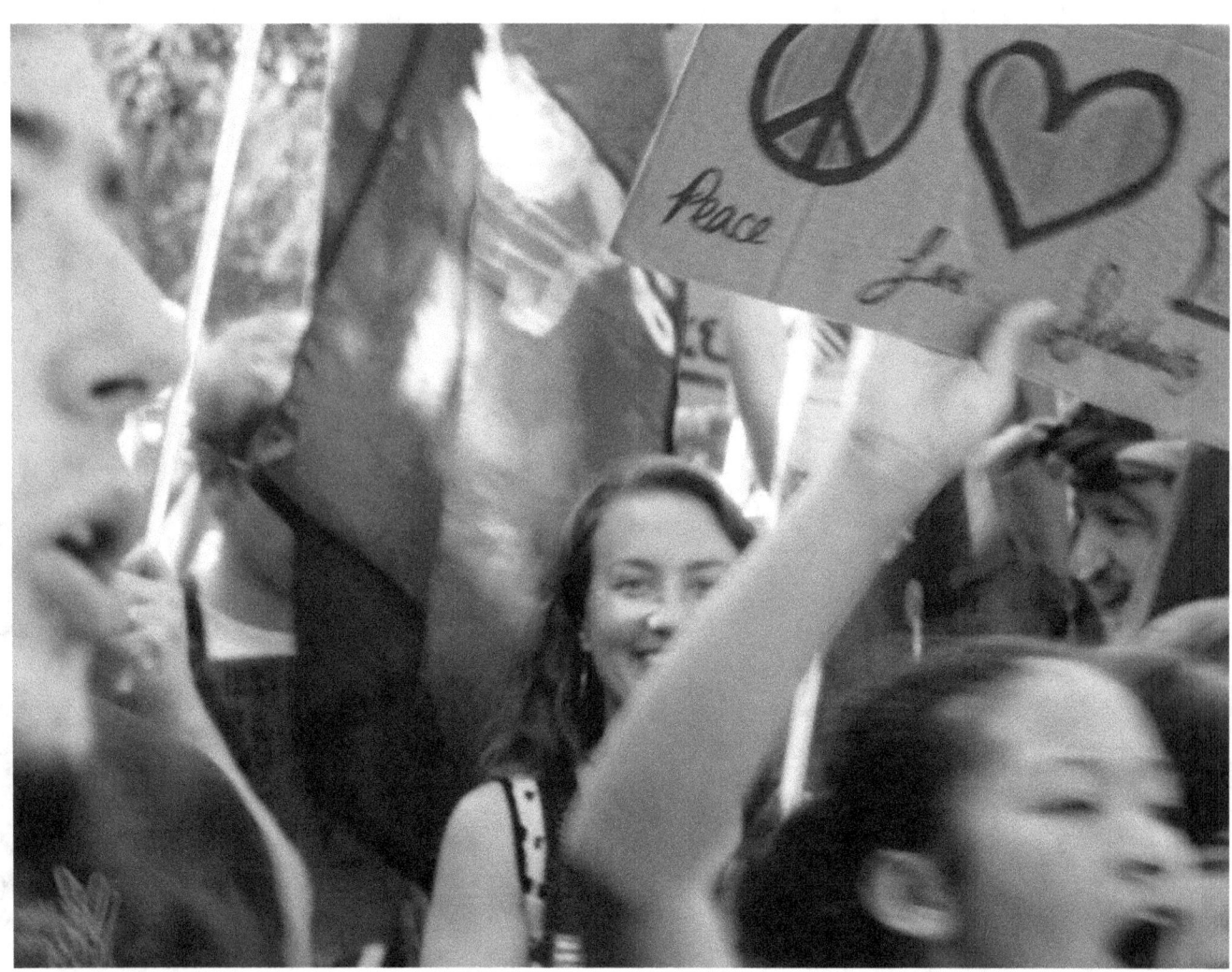

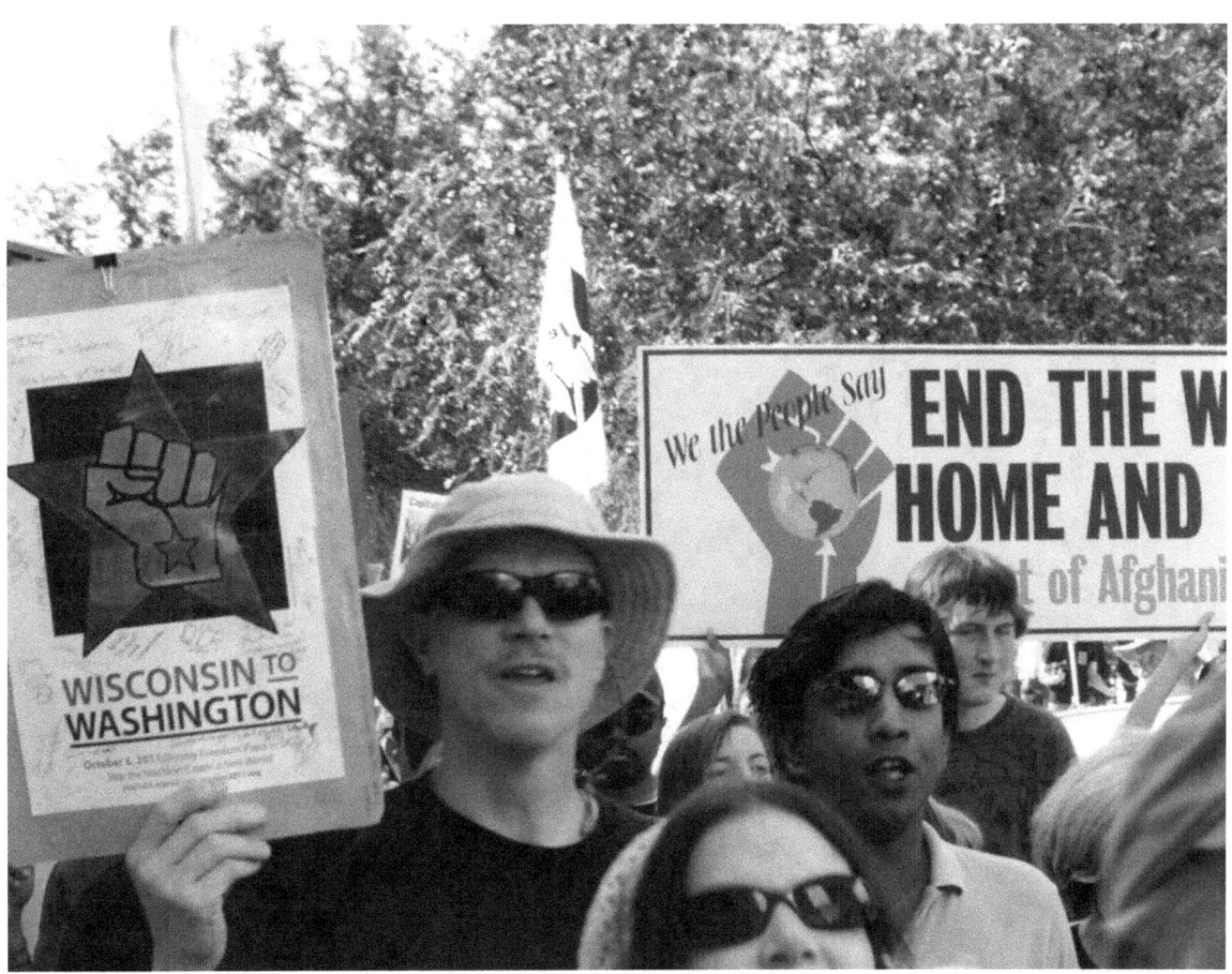

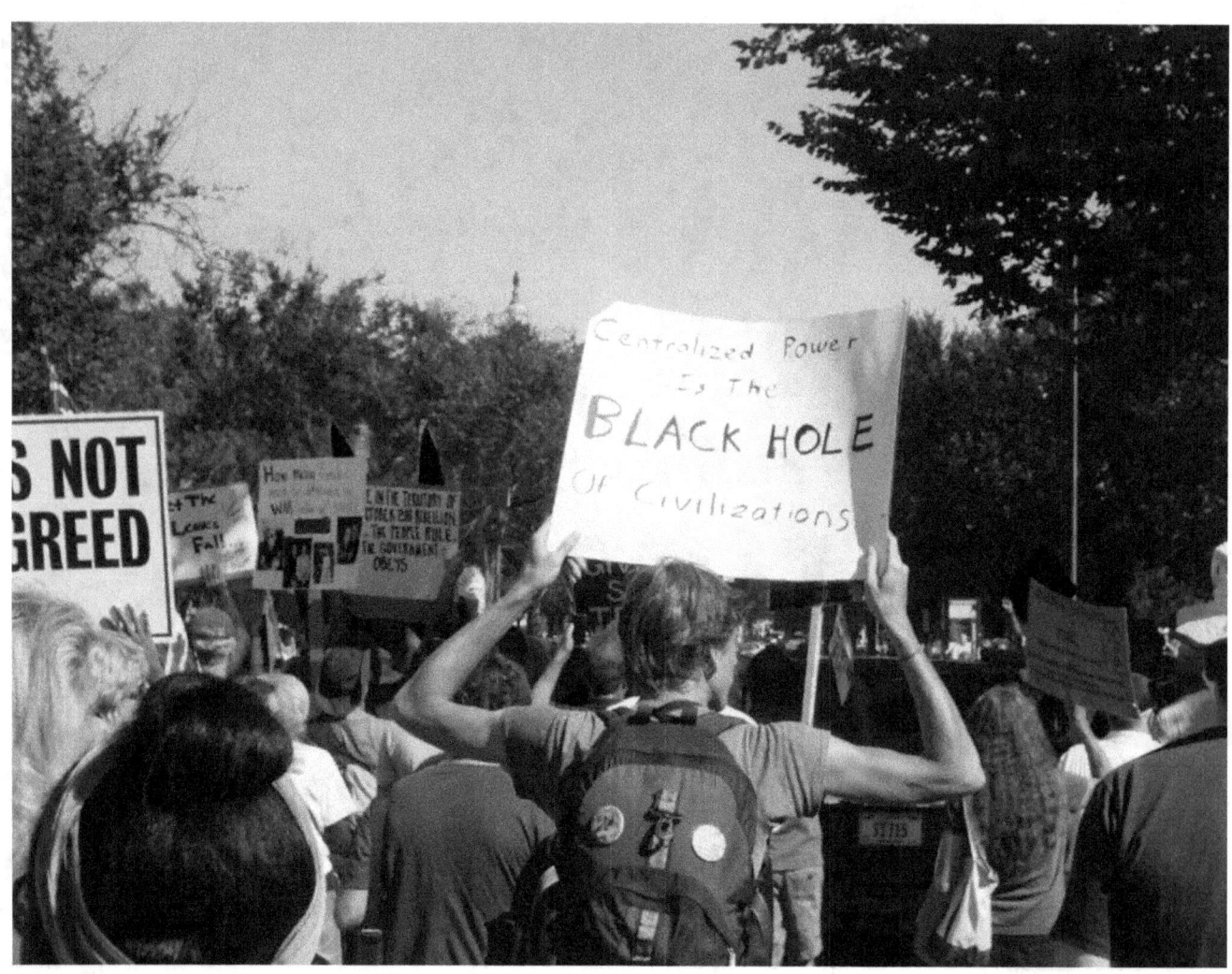

4 AT THE NATIONAL AIR & SPACE MUSEUM

Assembling on the steps of the National Air & Space Museum.

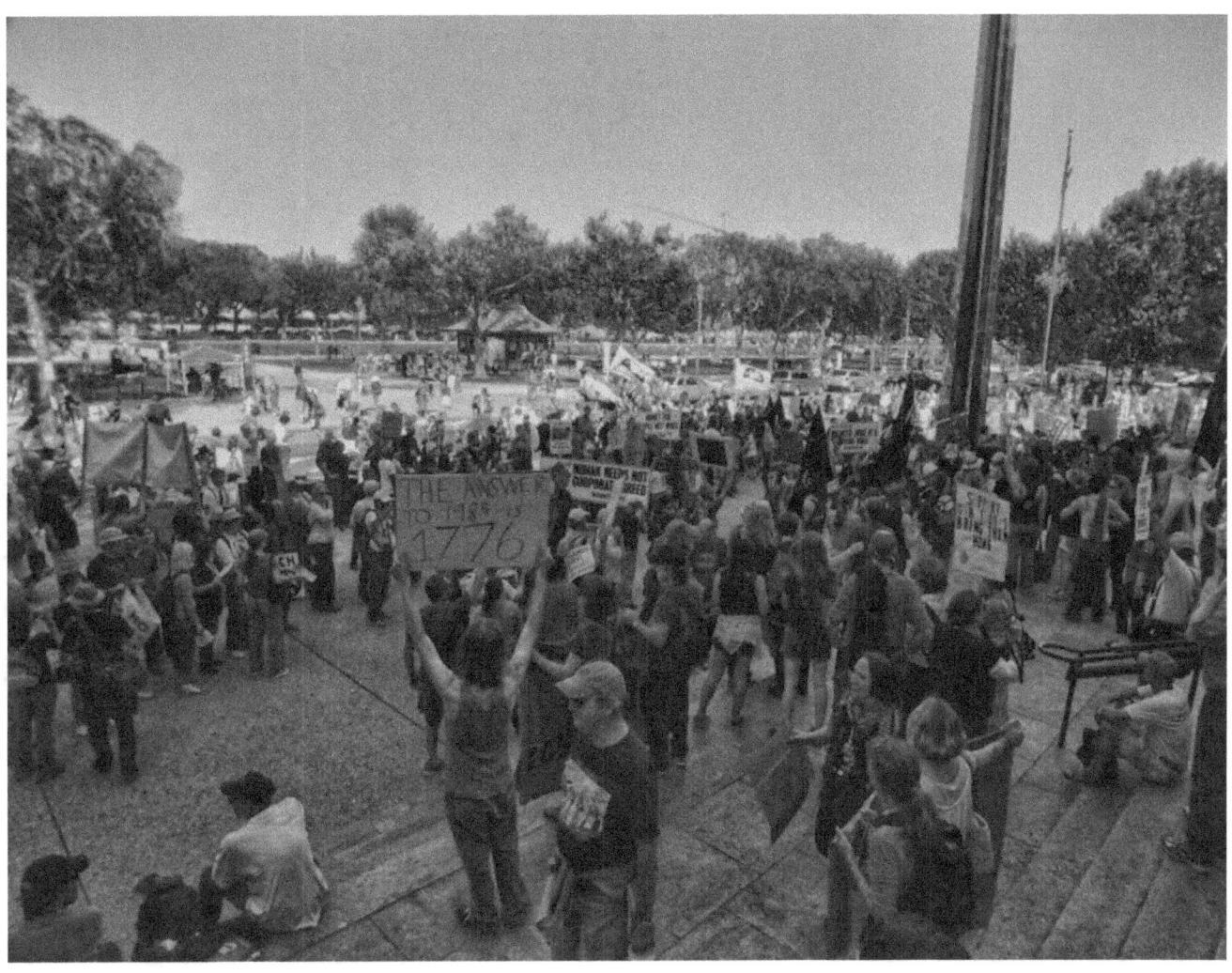

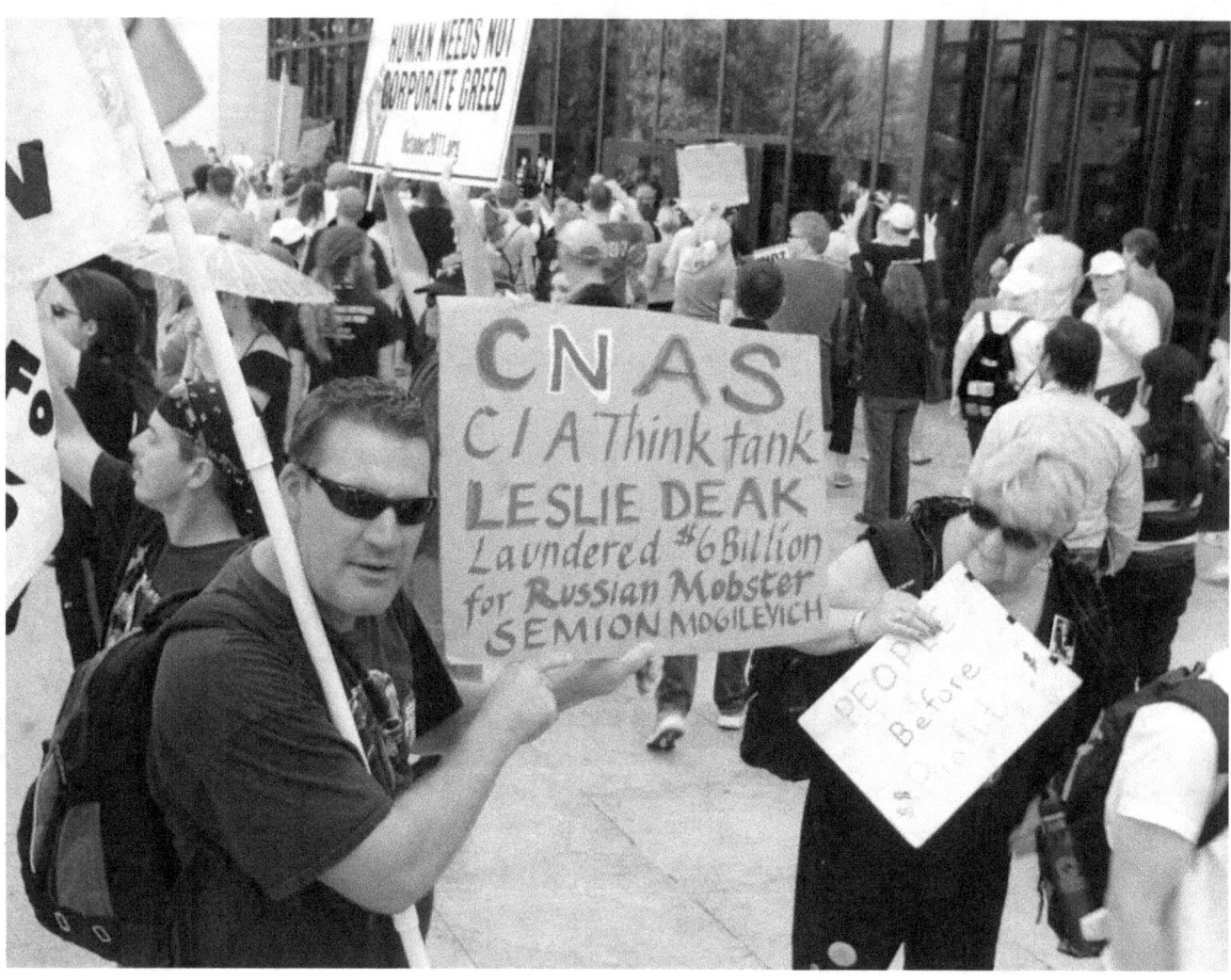

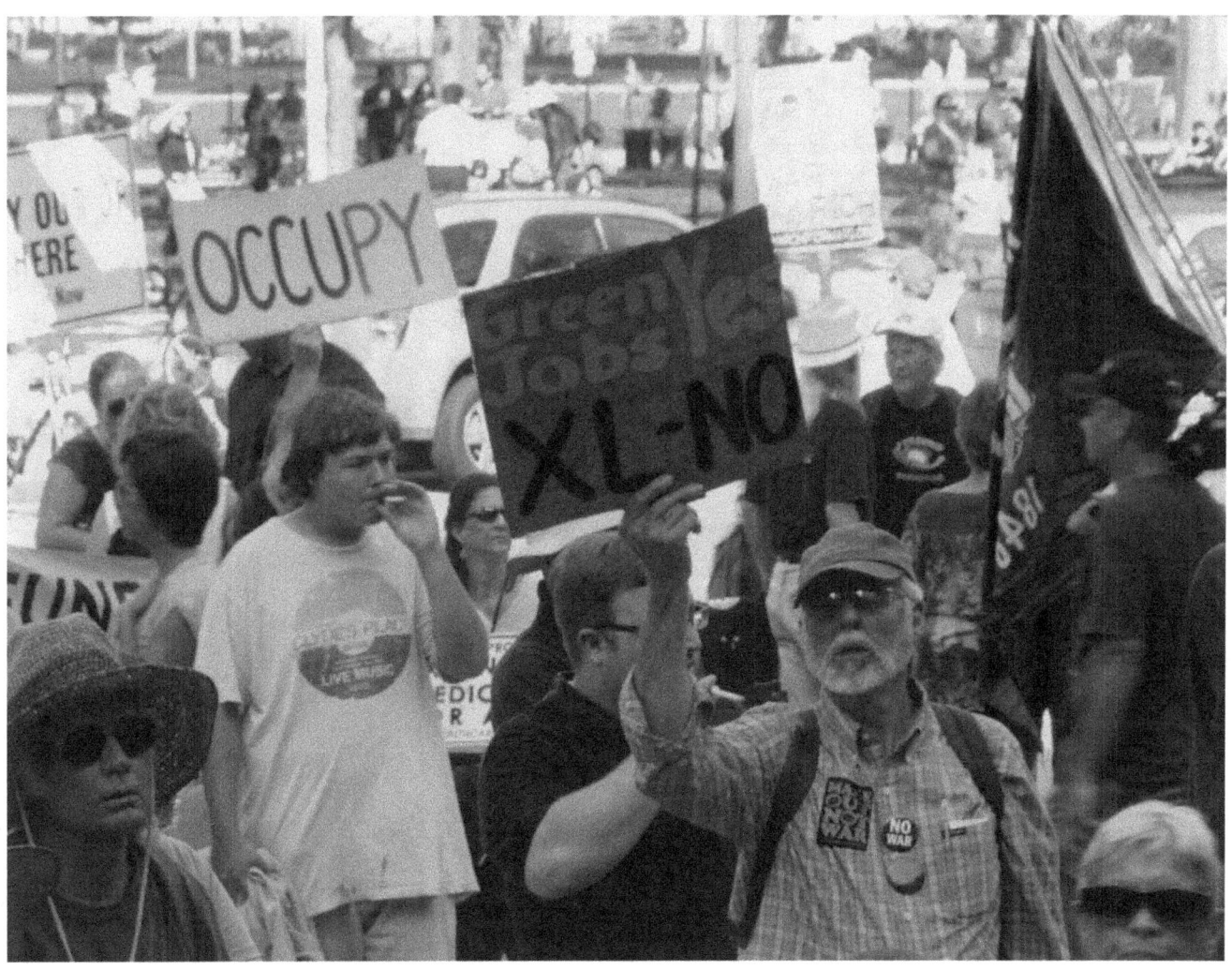

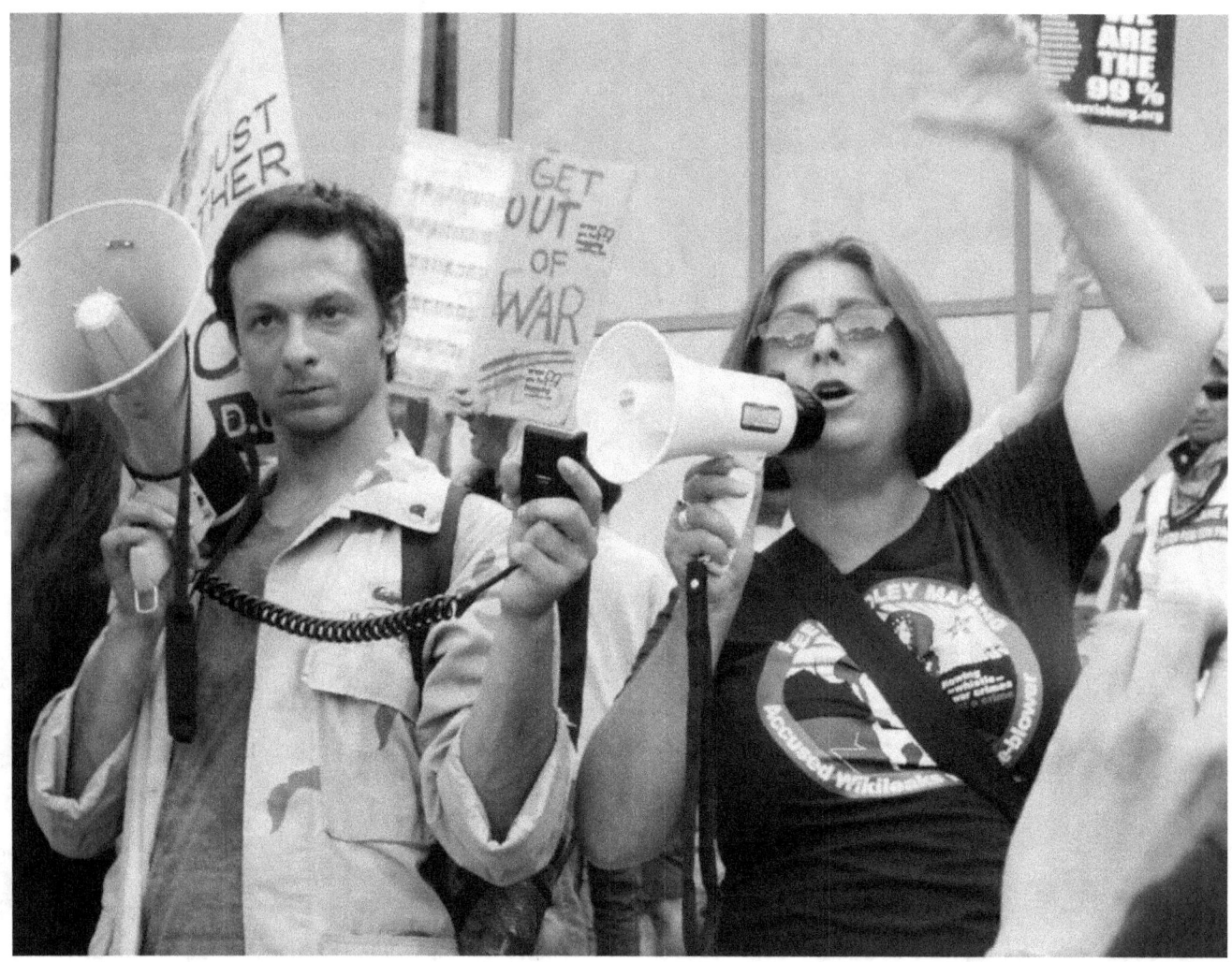

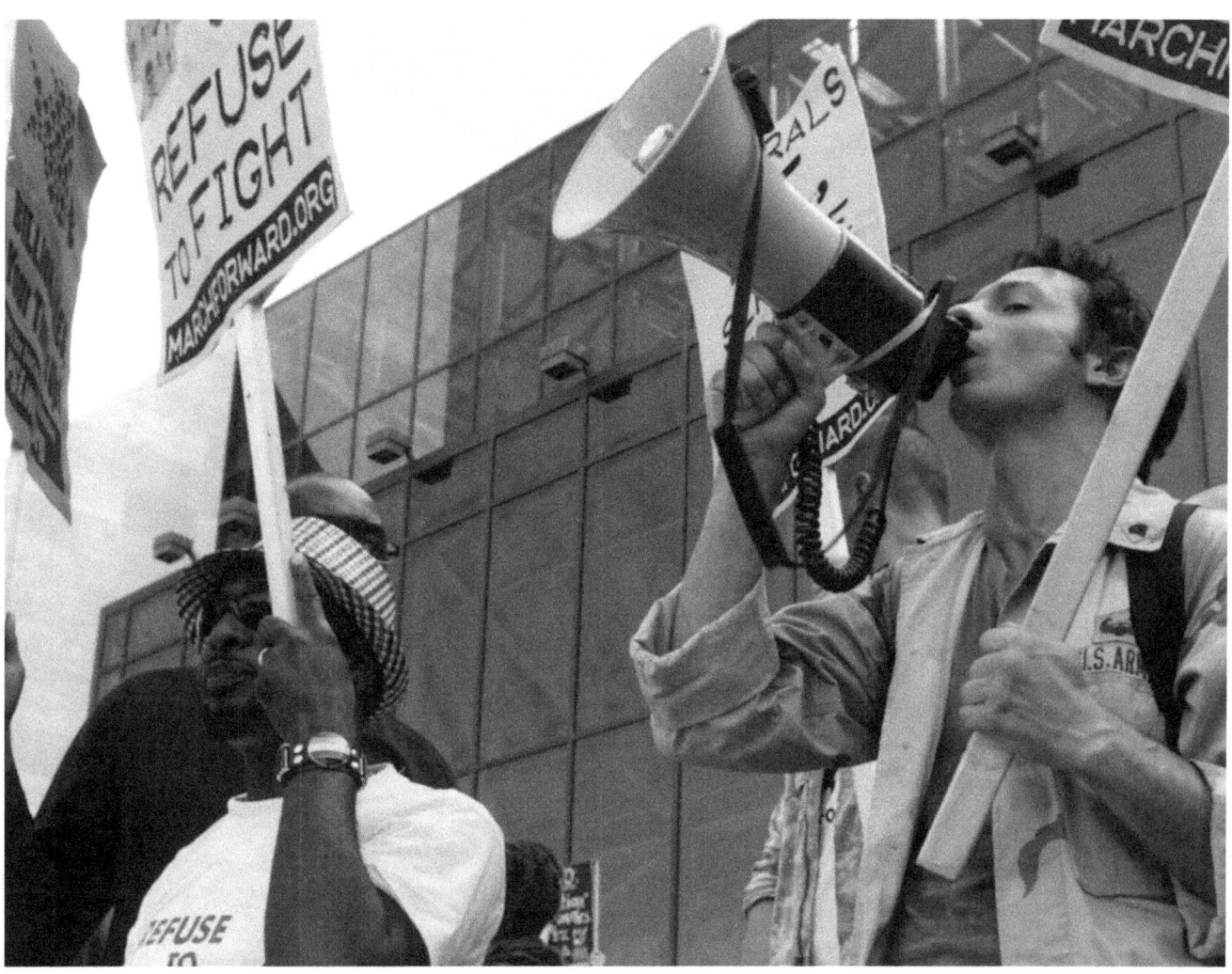

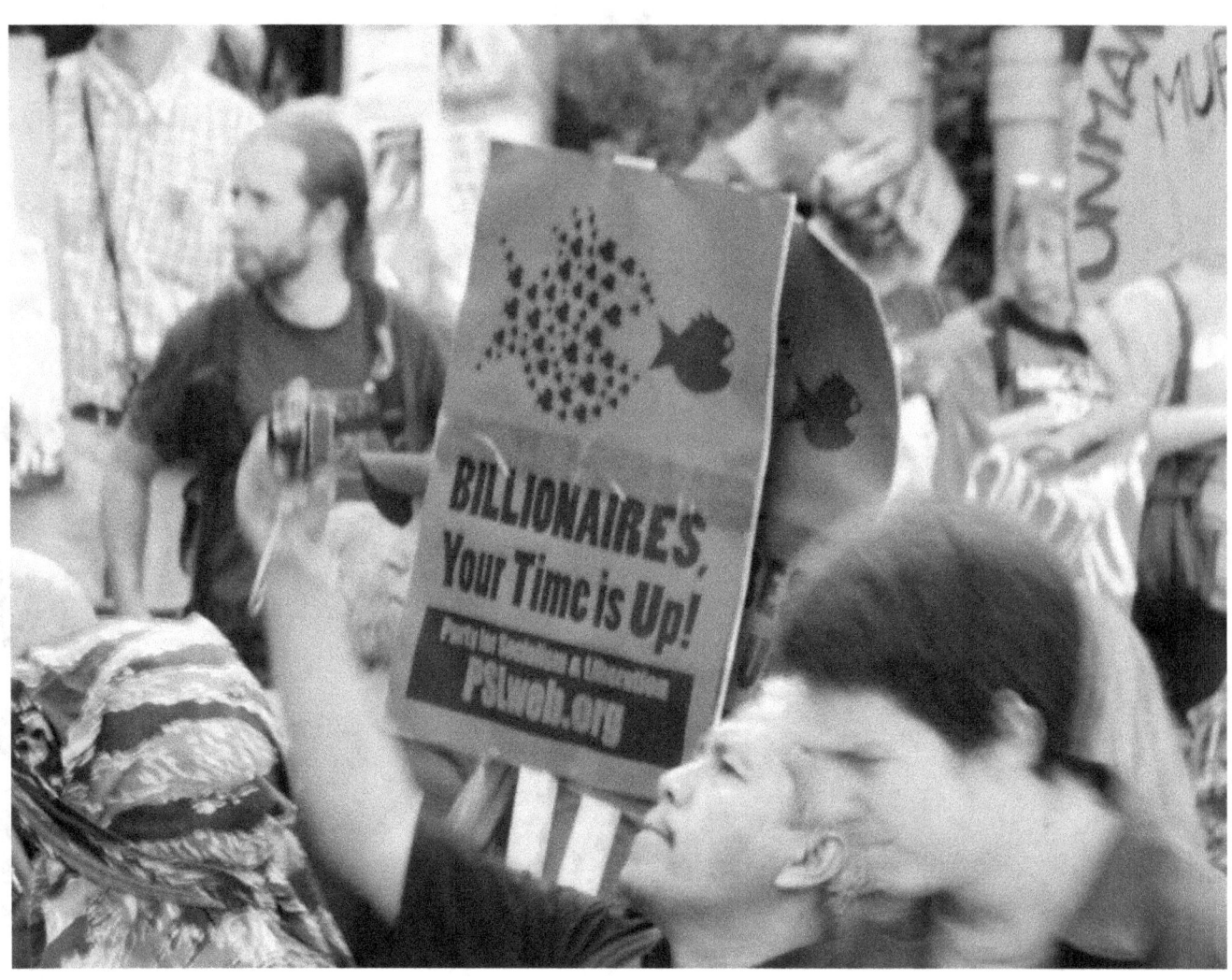

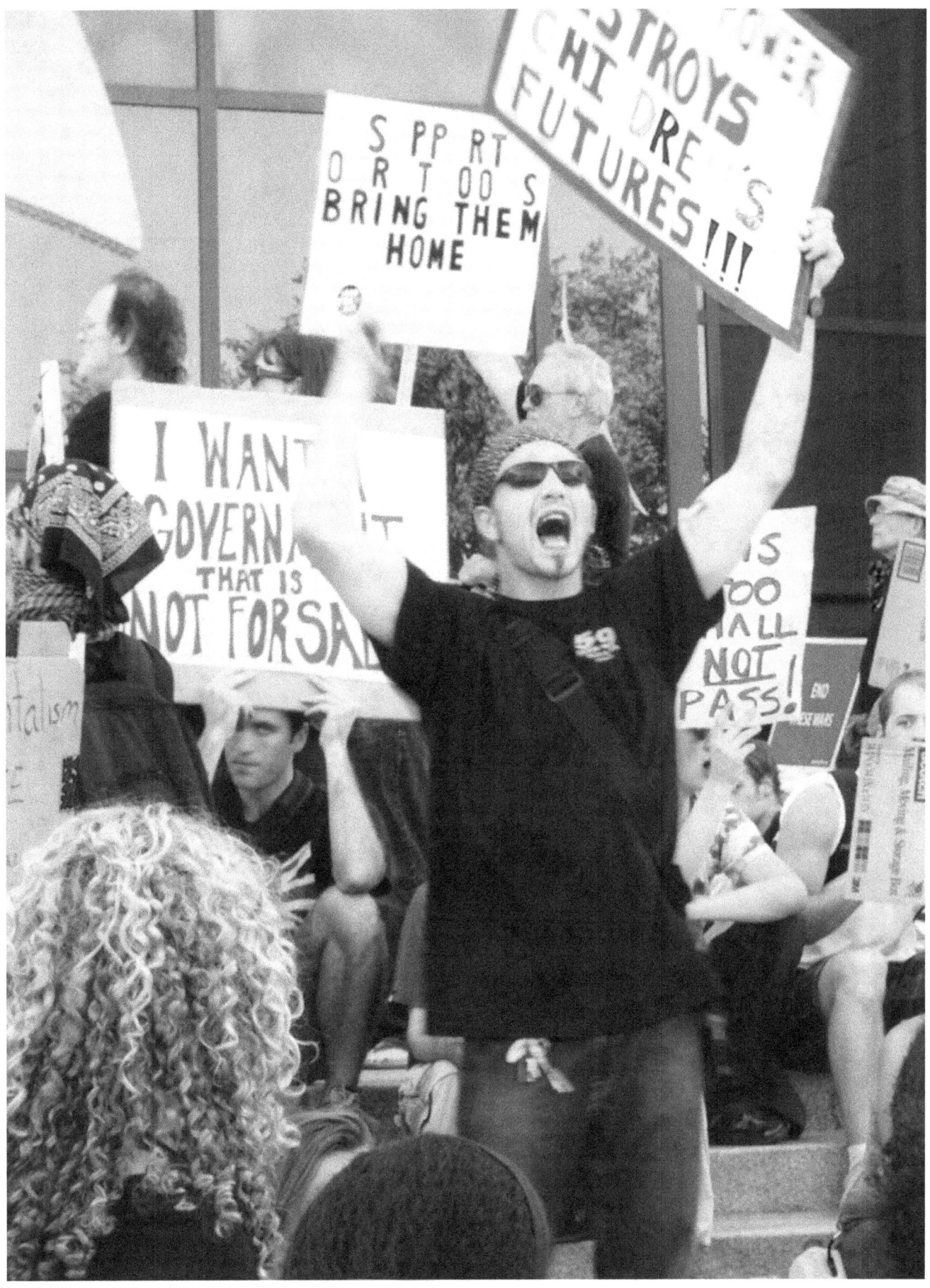

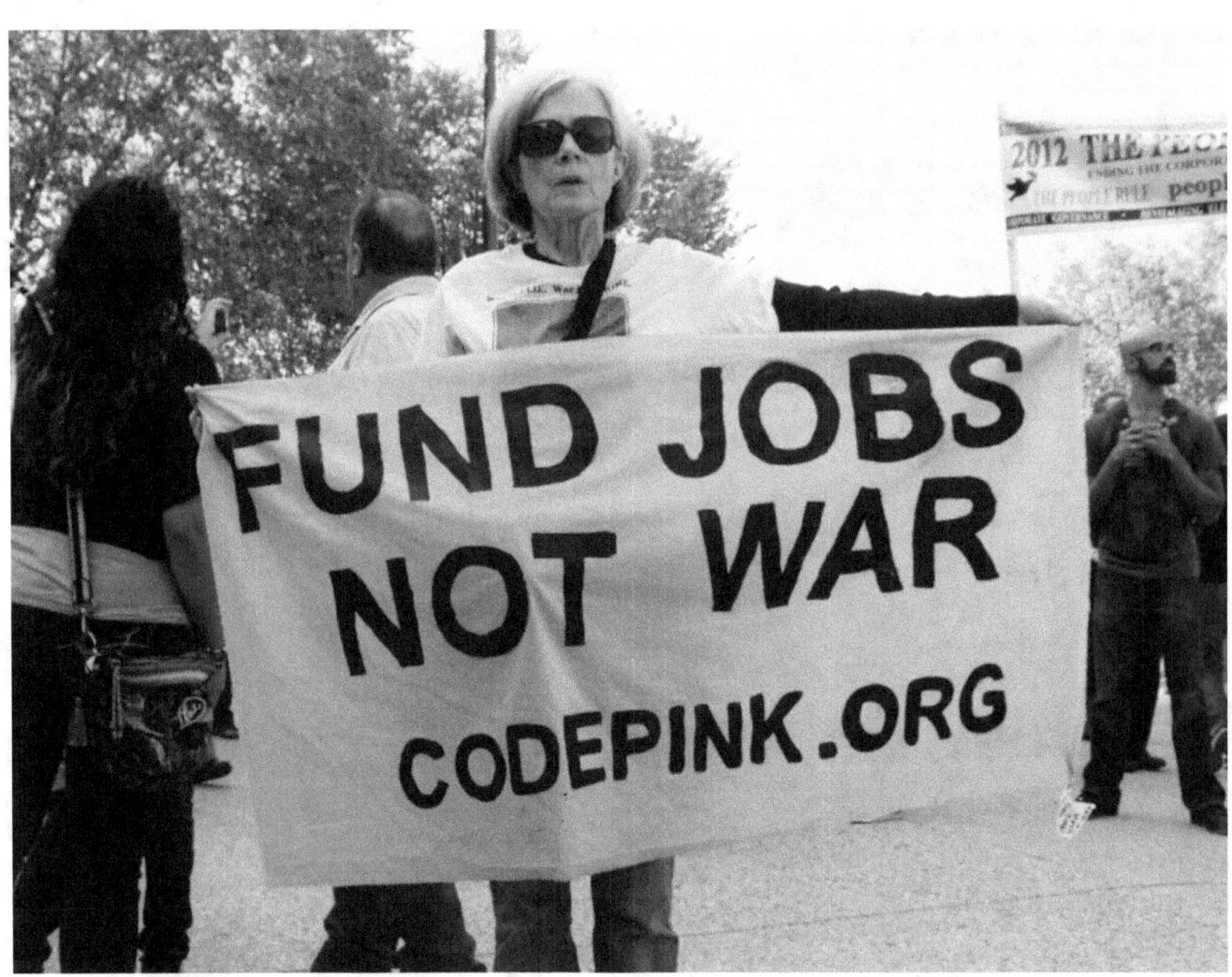

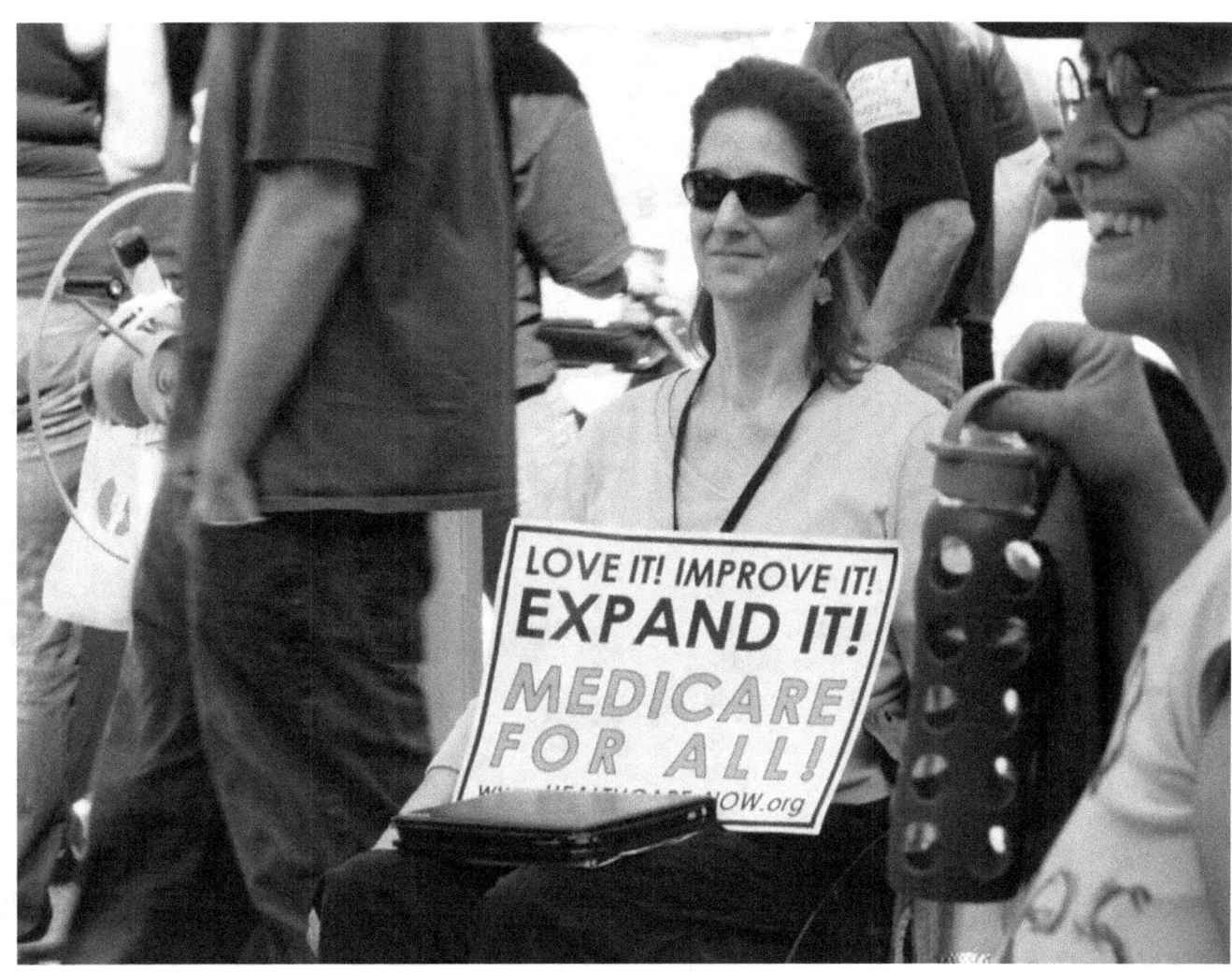

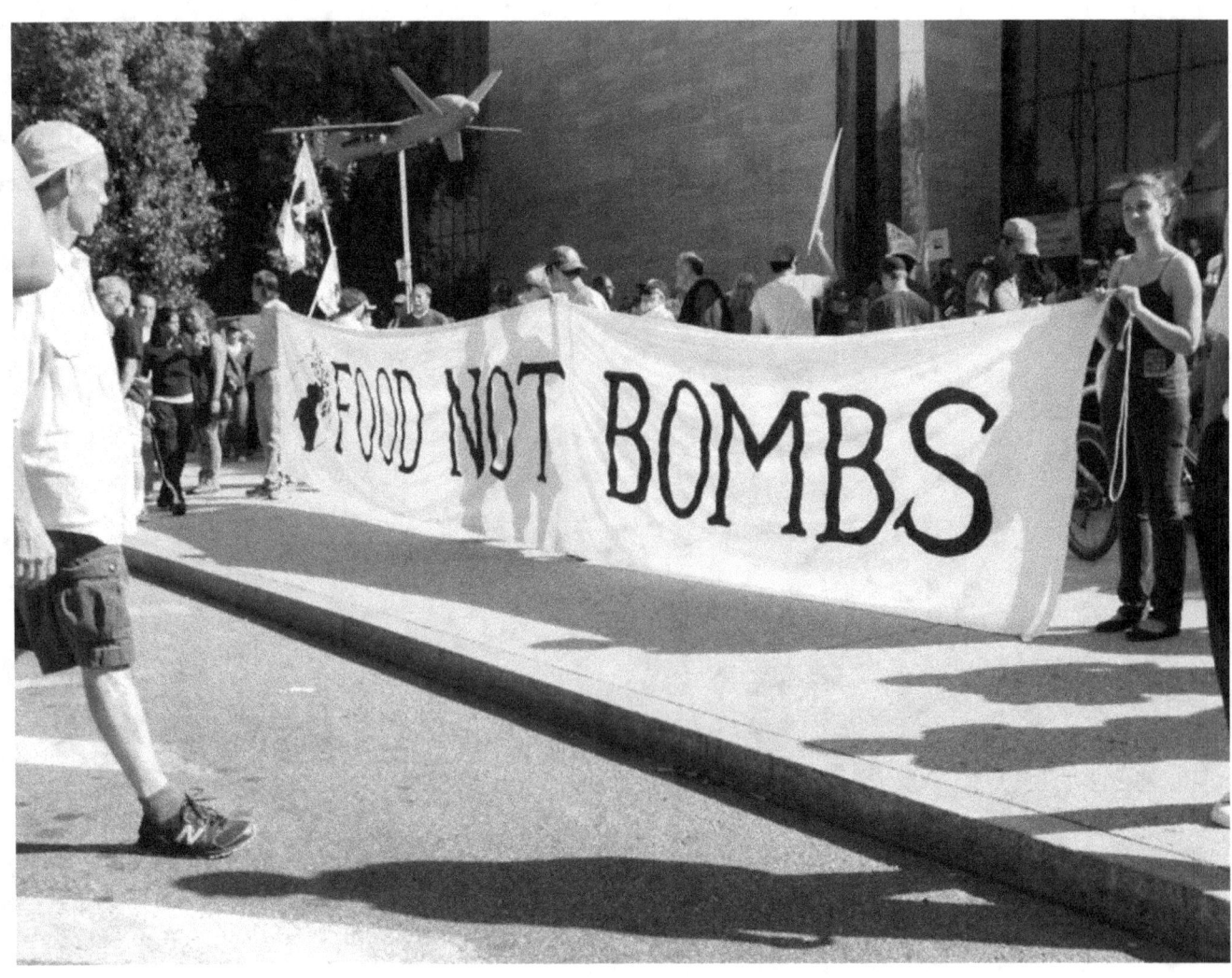

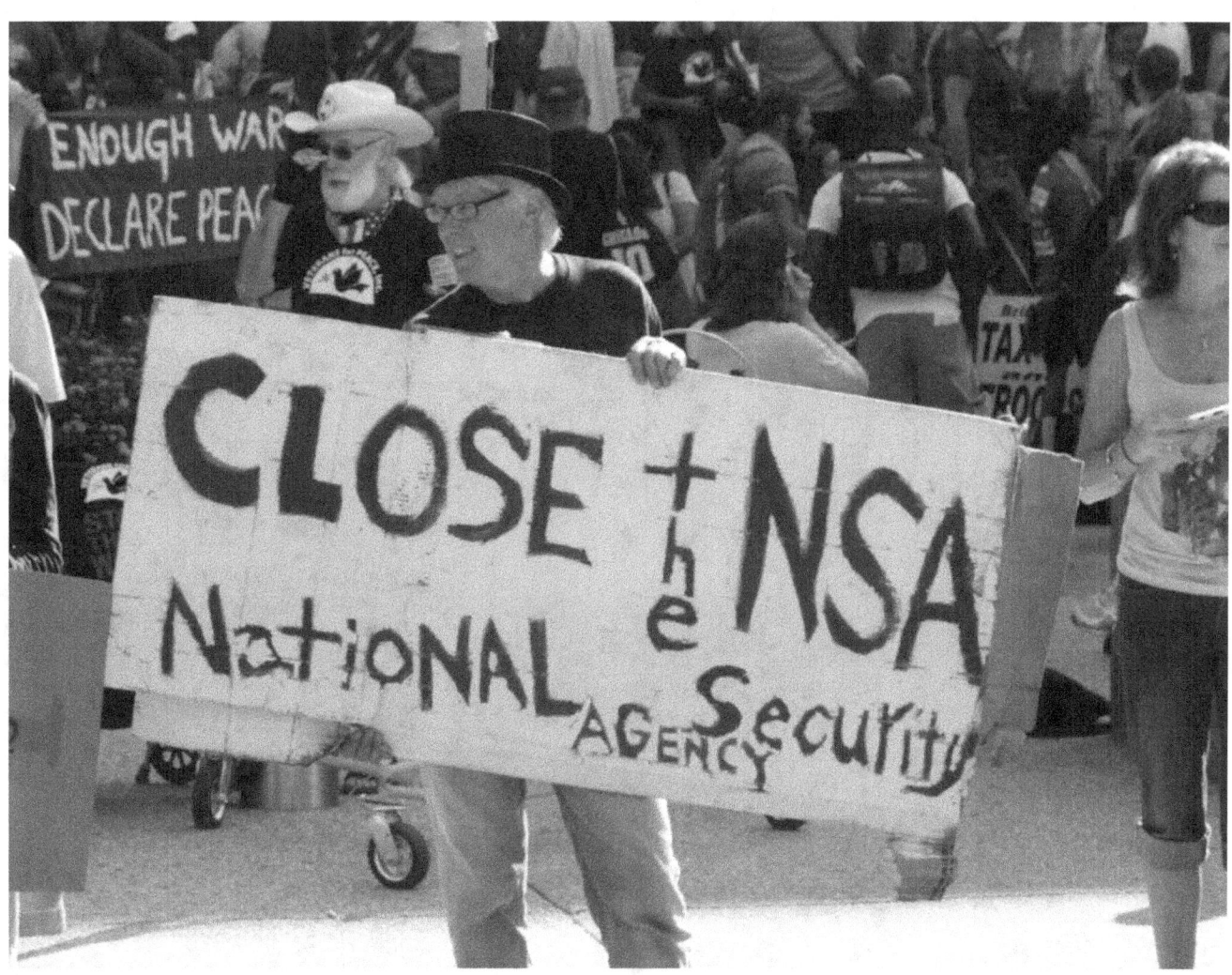

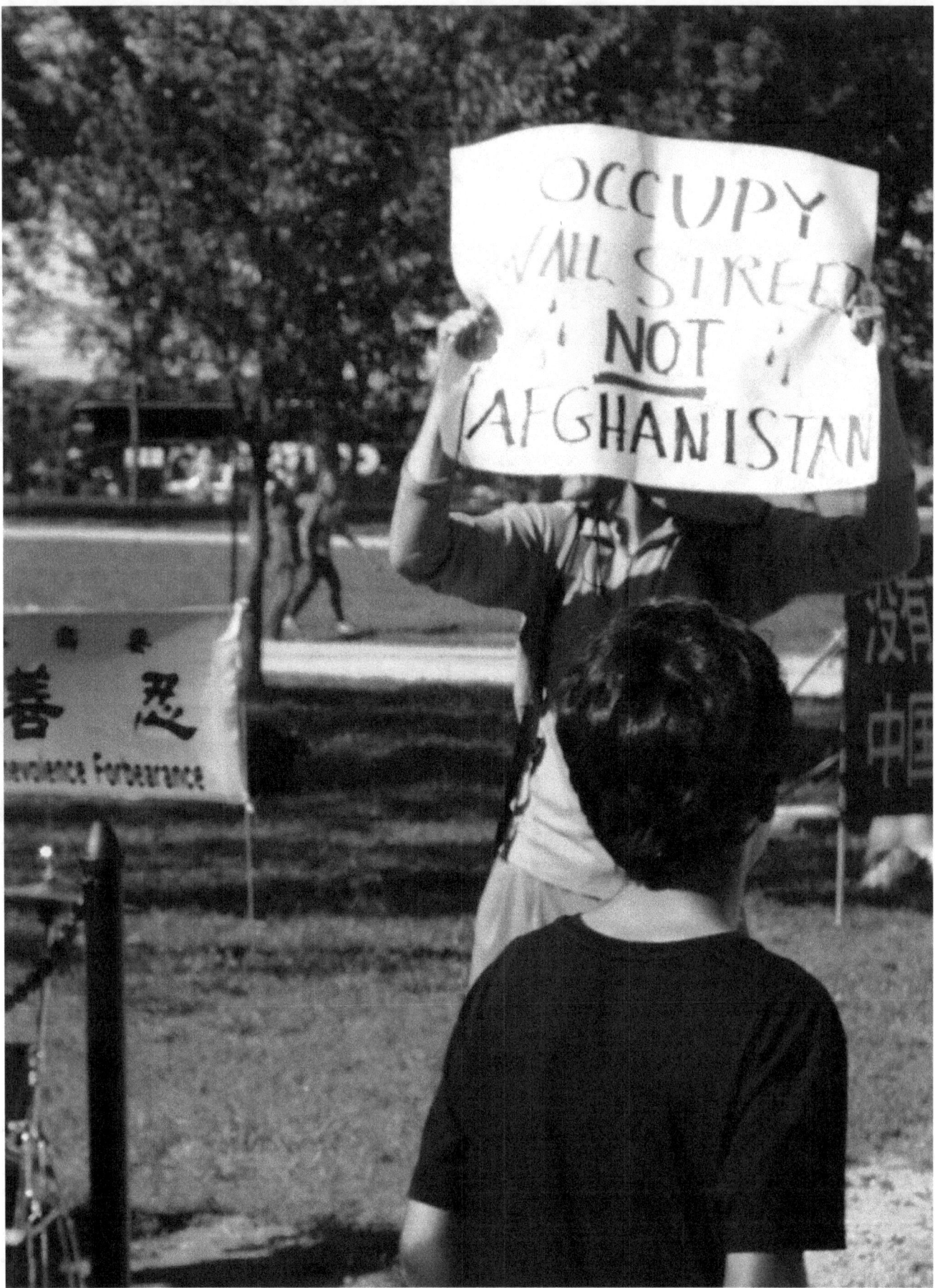

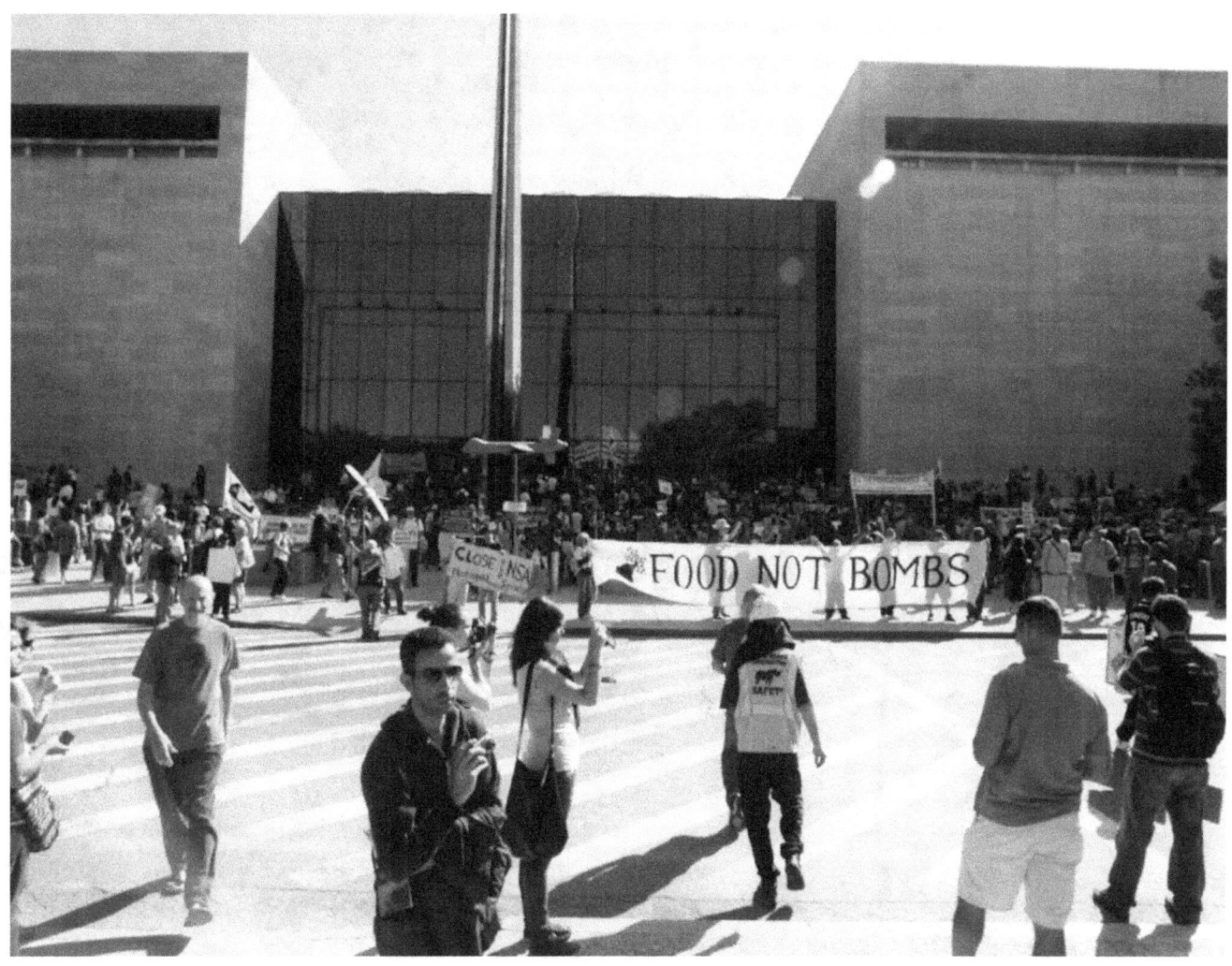

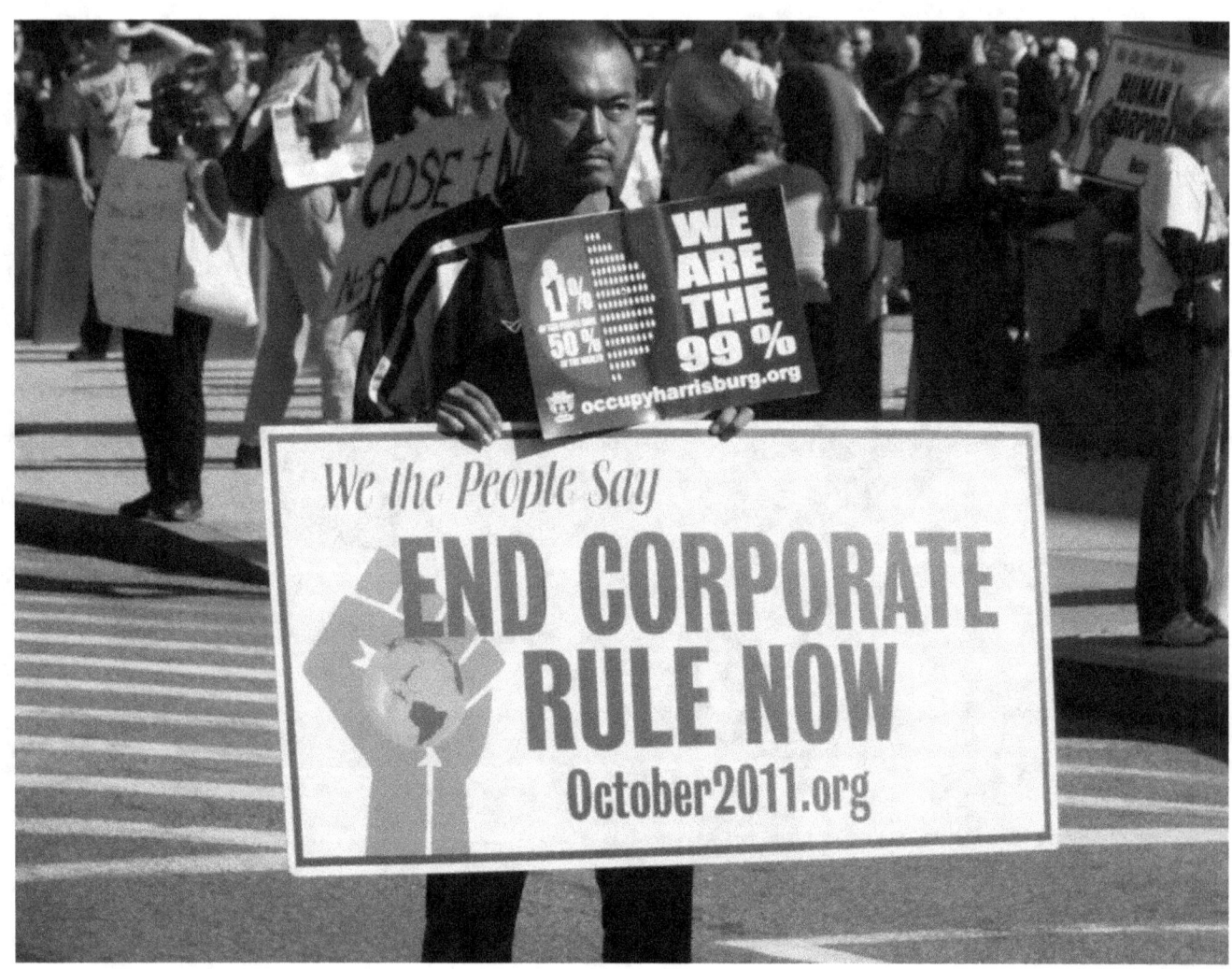

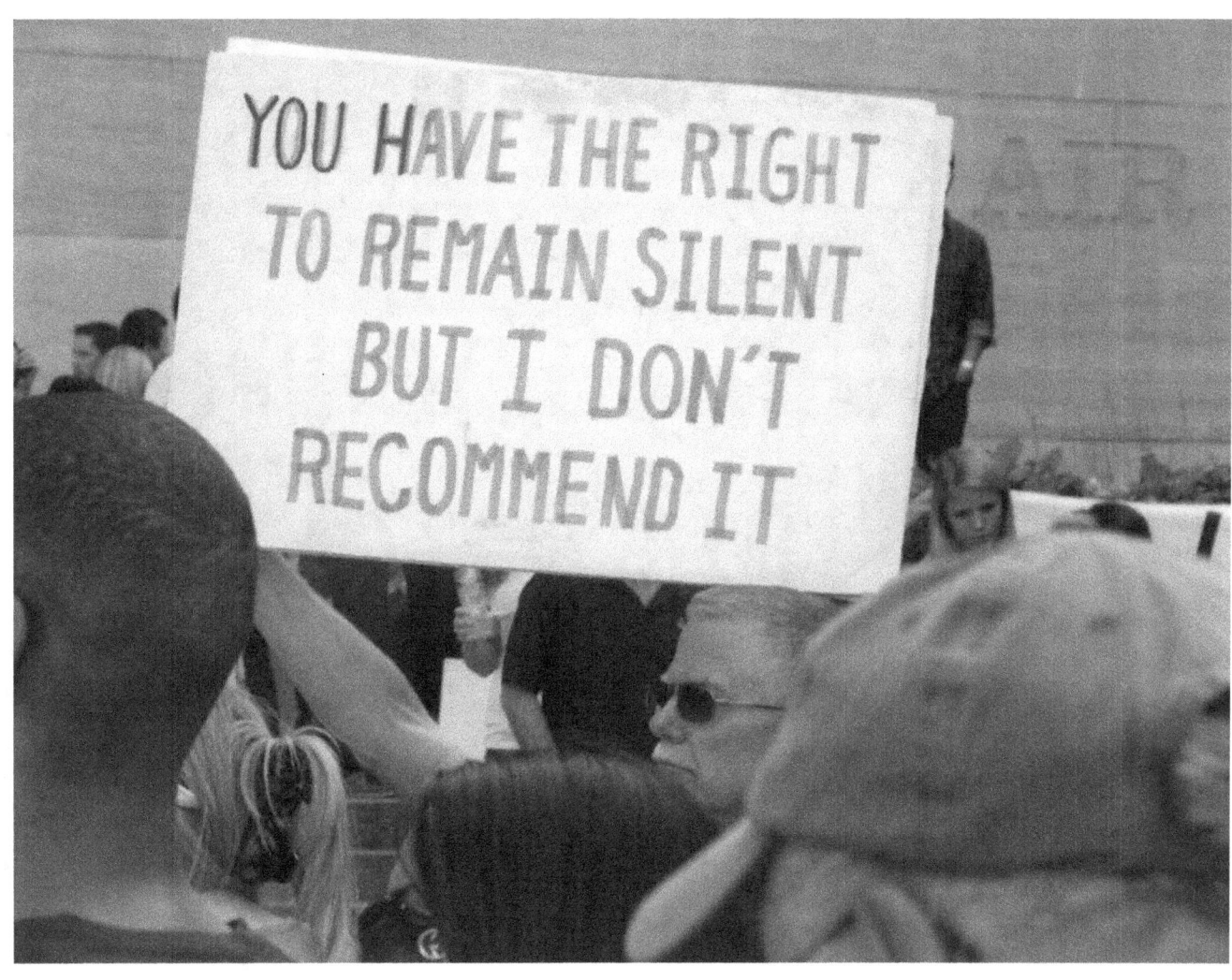

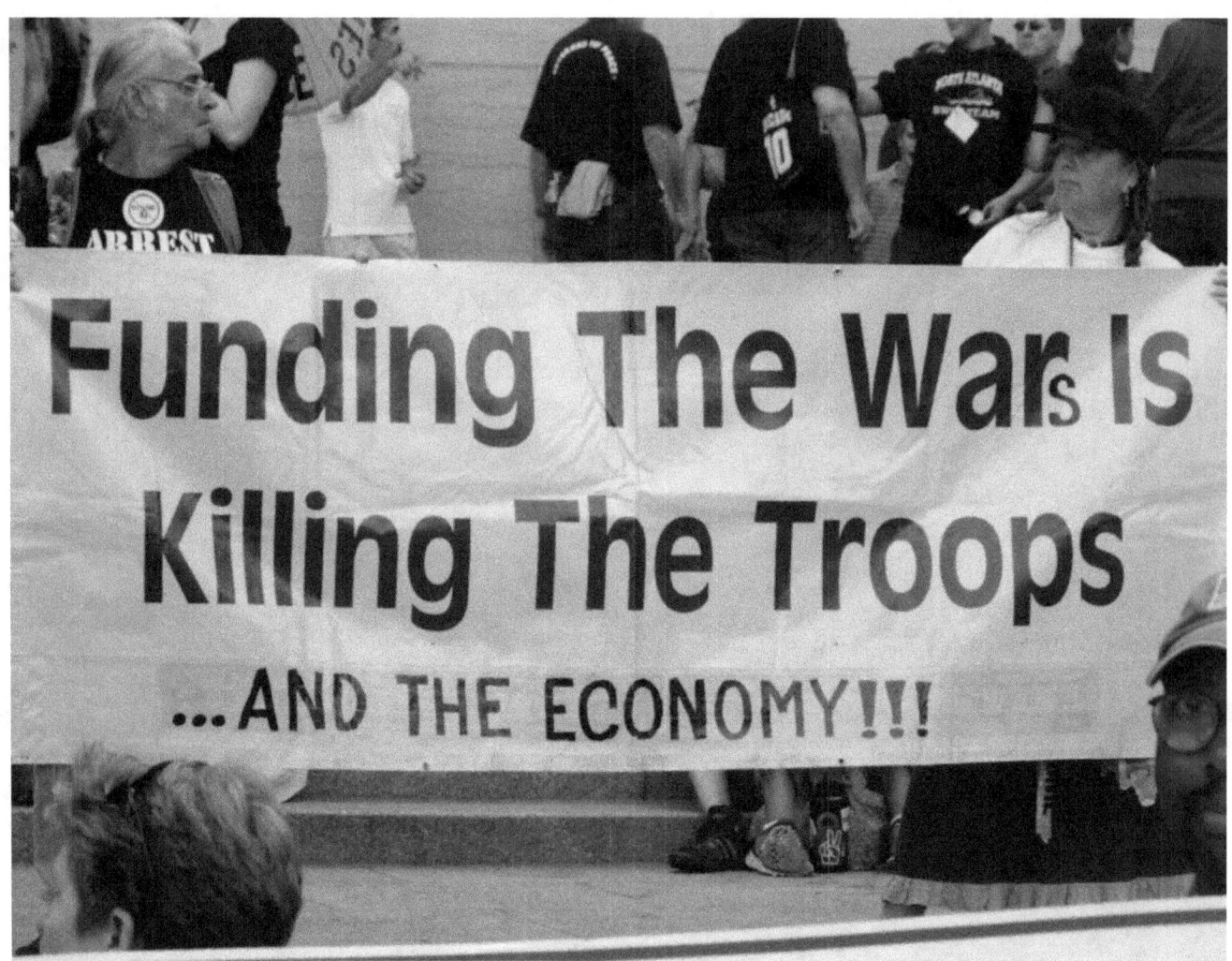

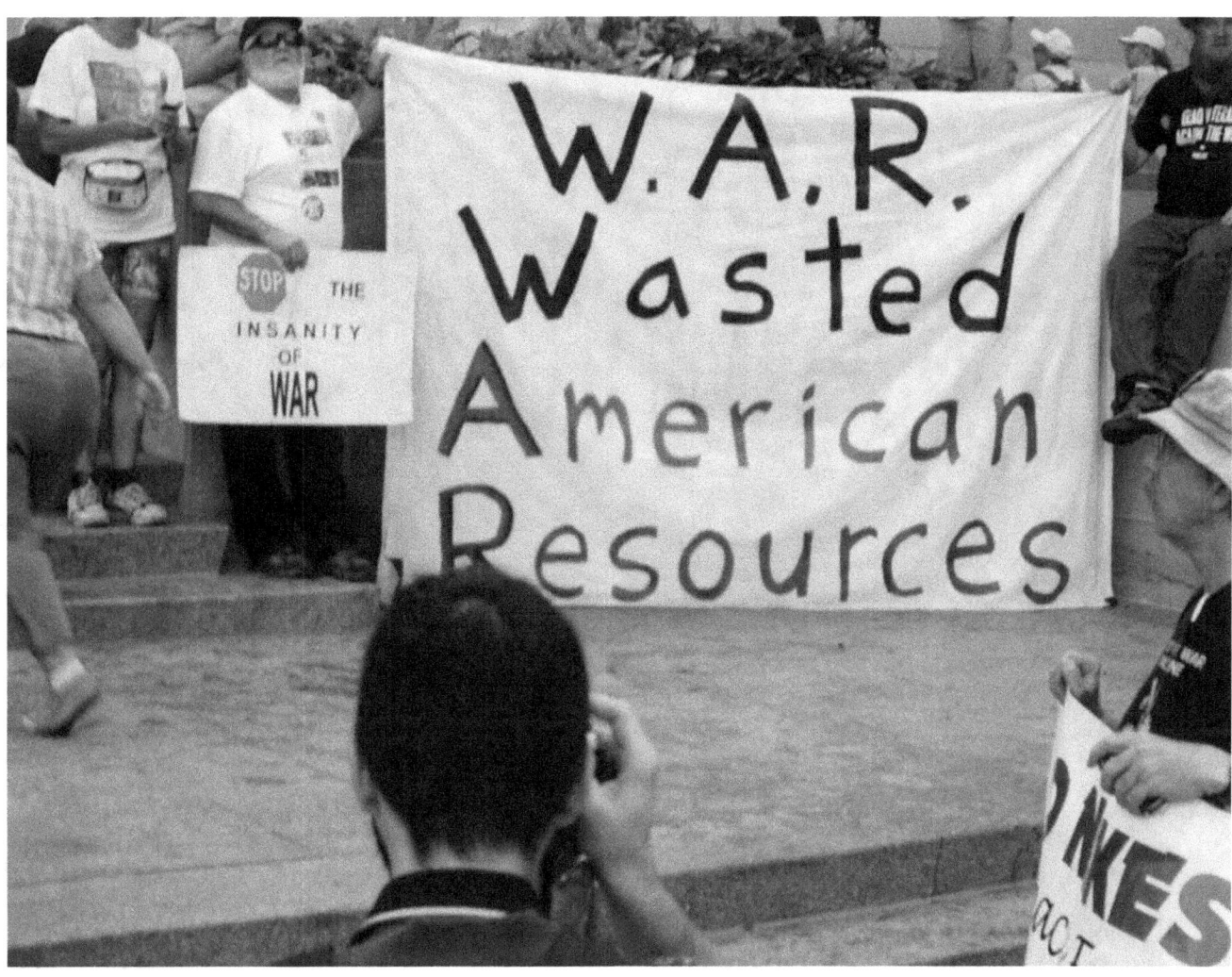

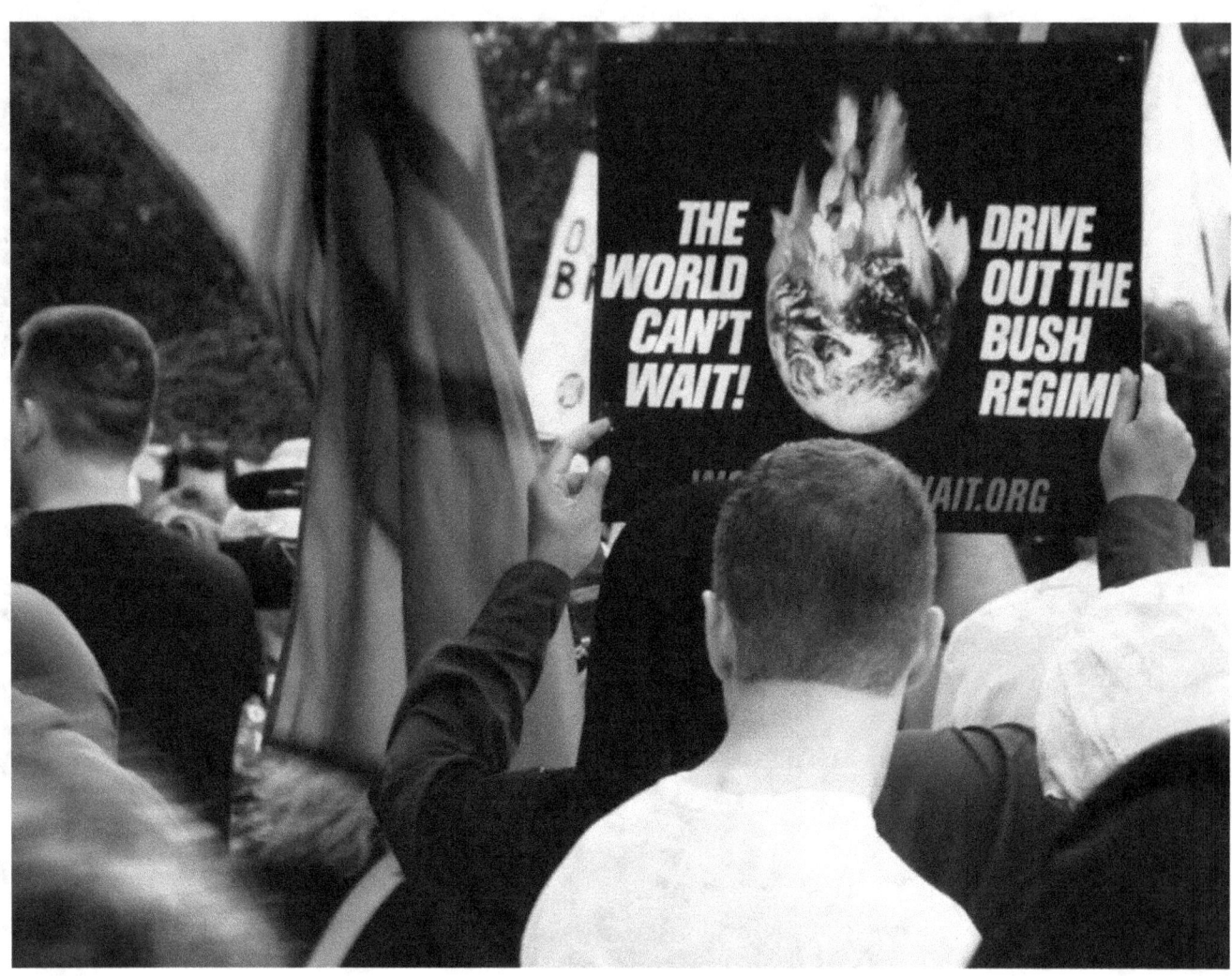

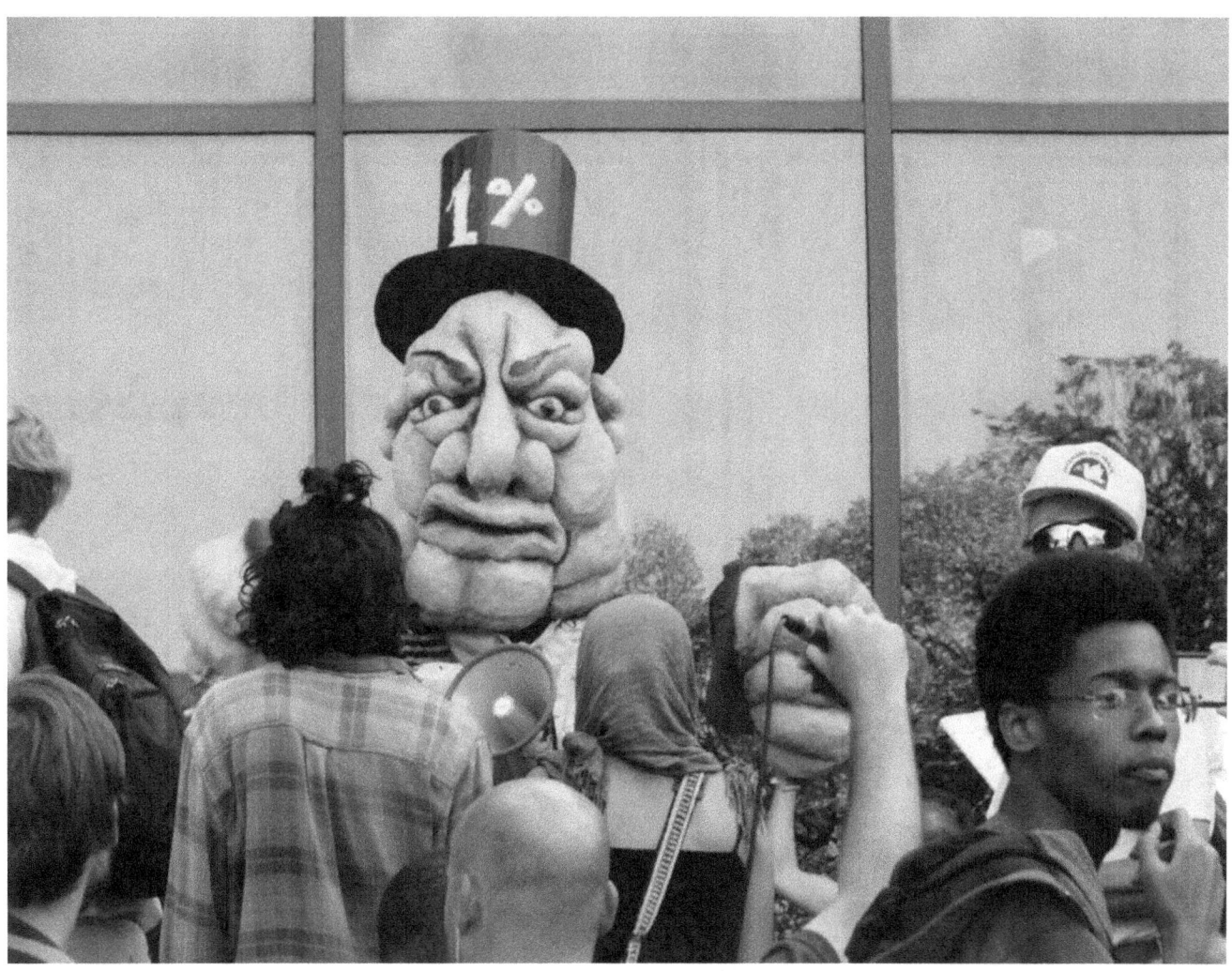

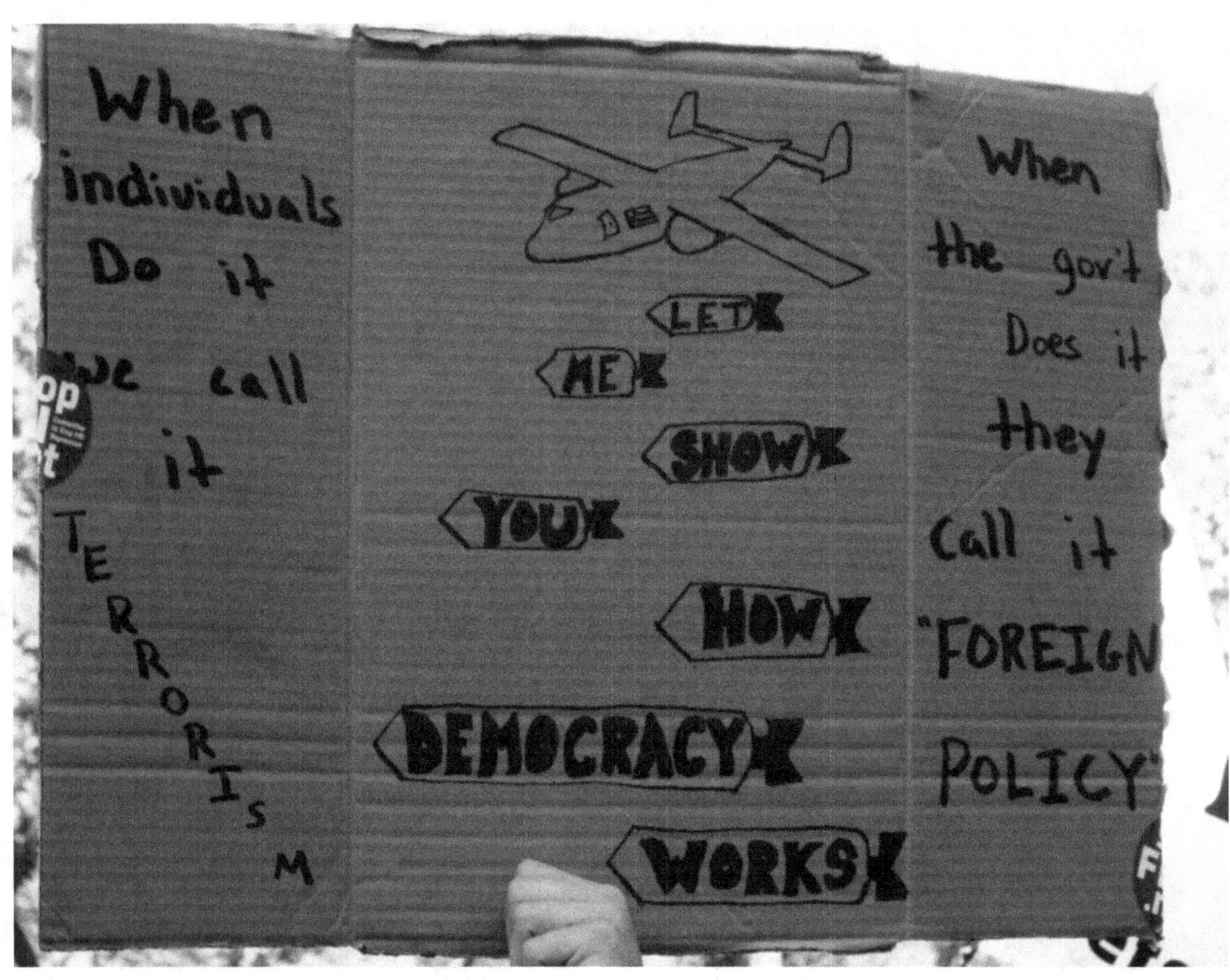

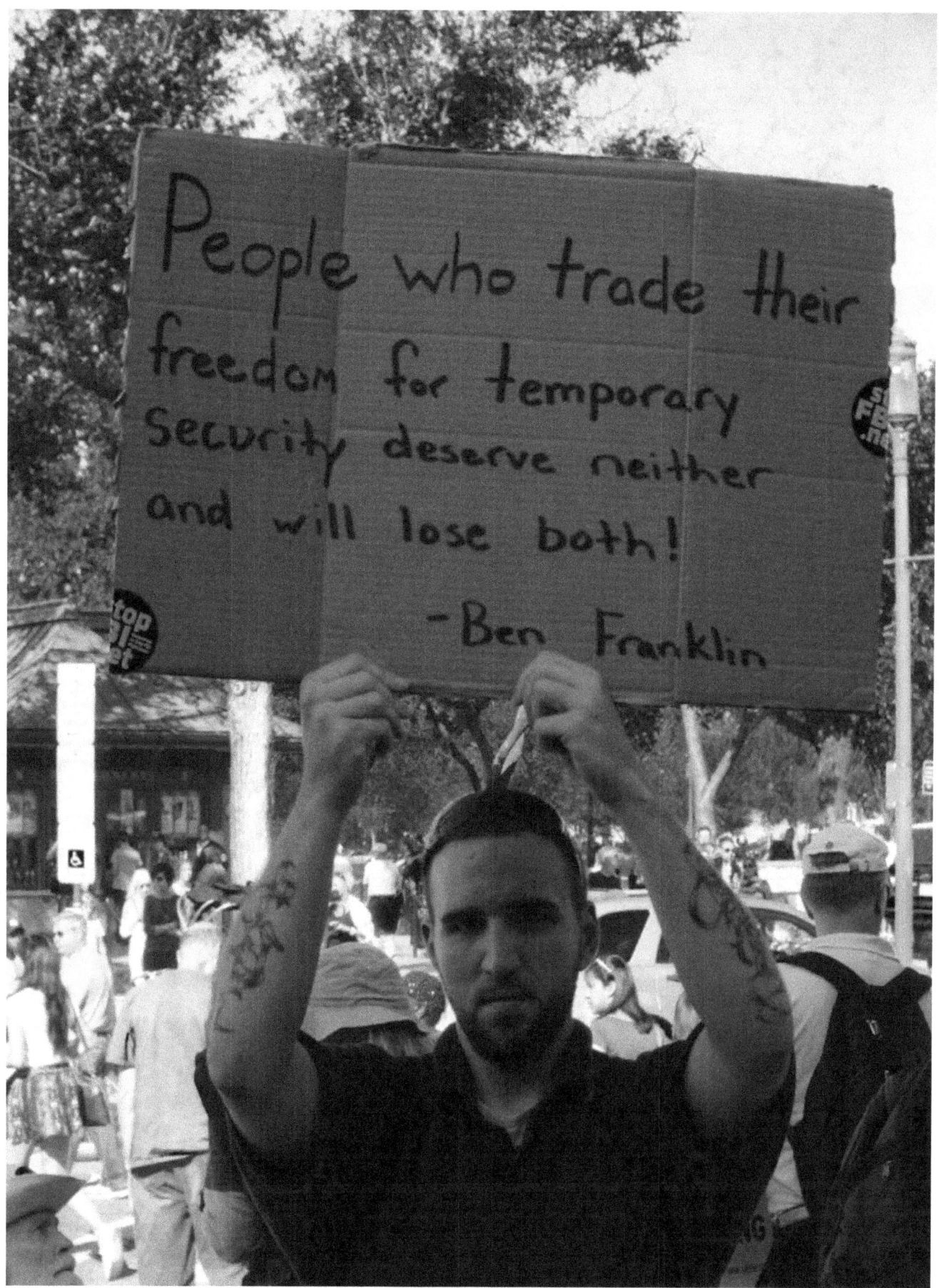

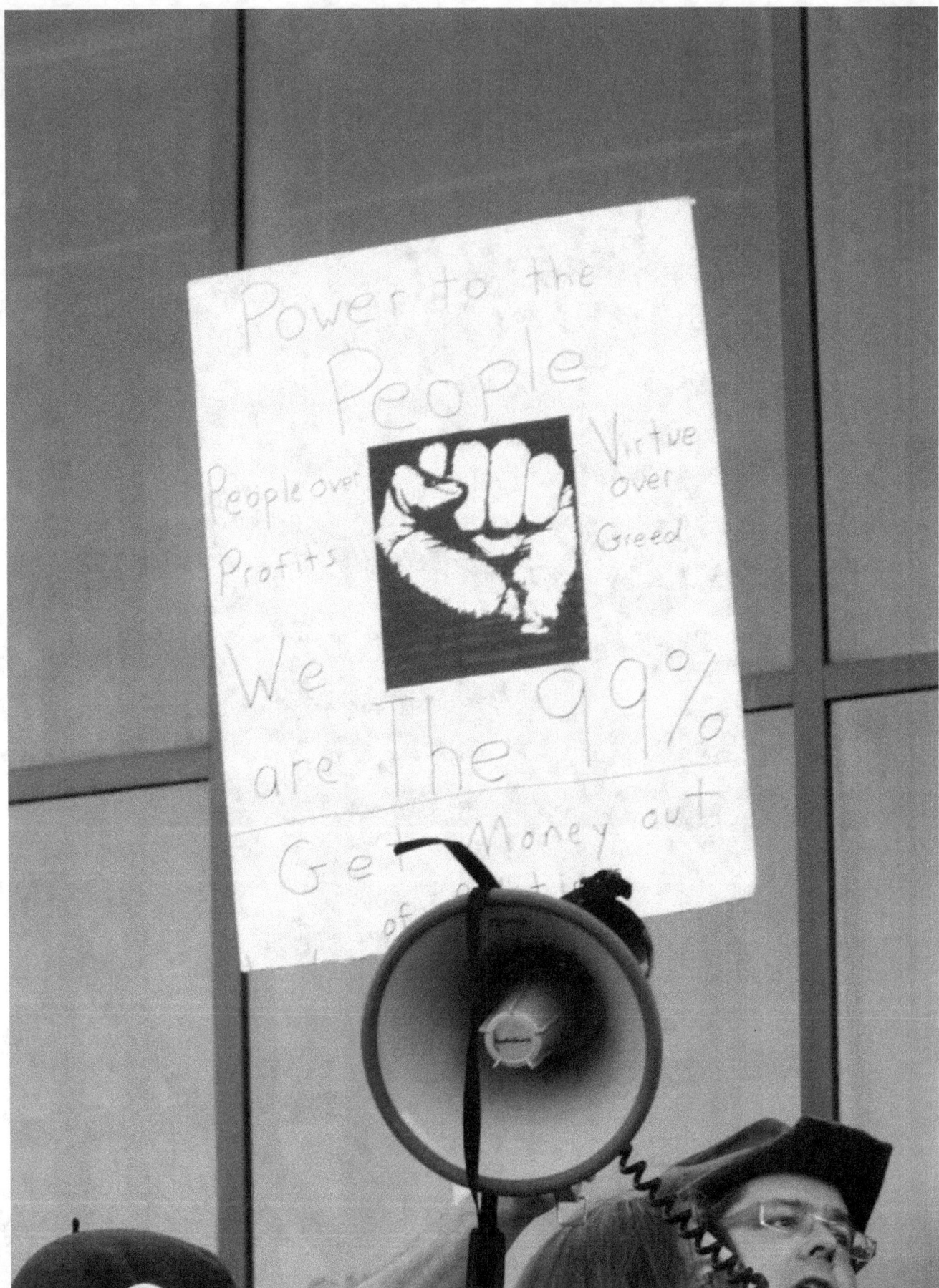

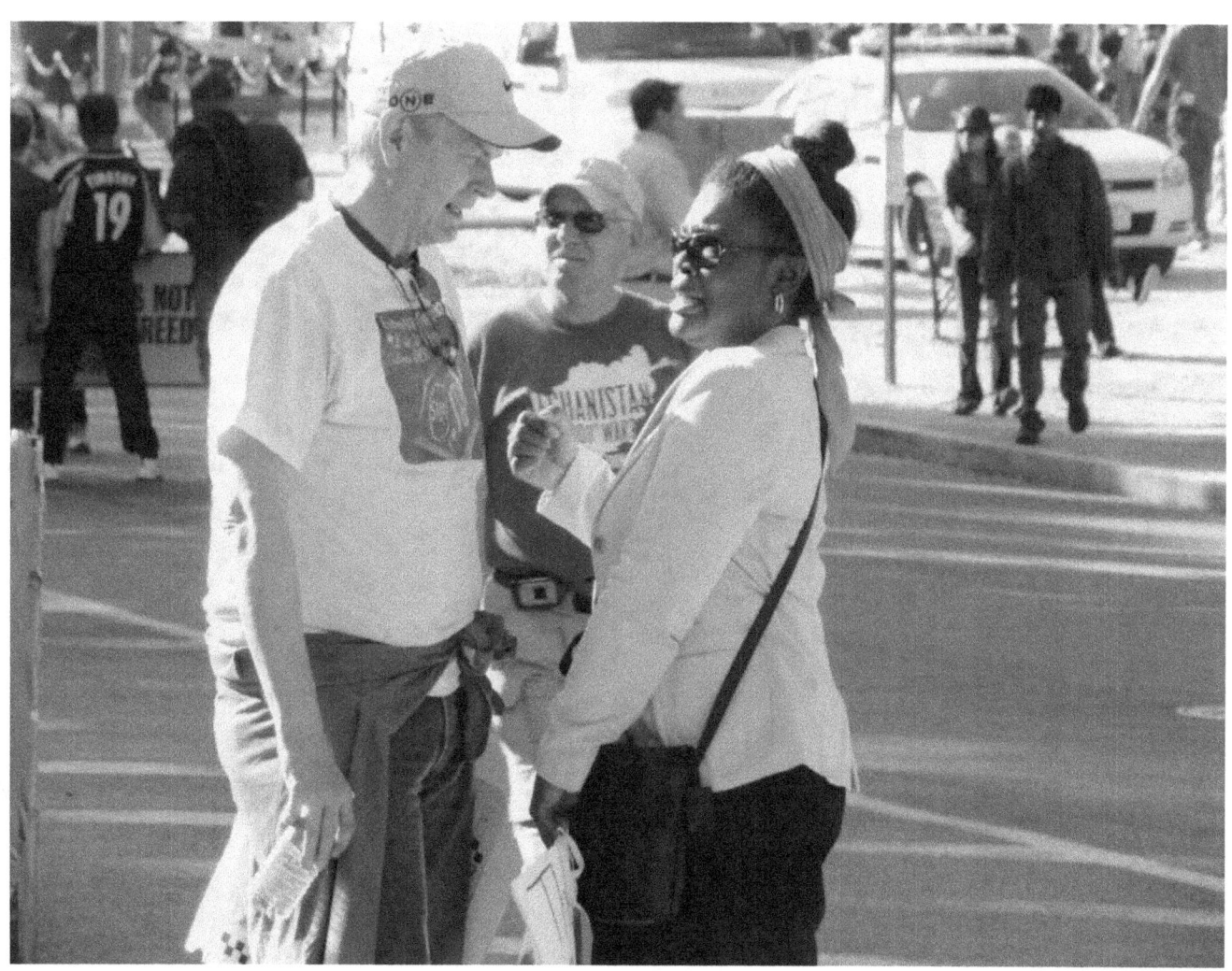

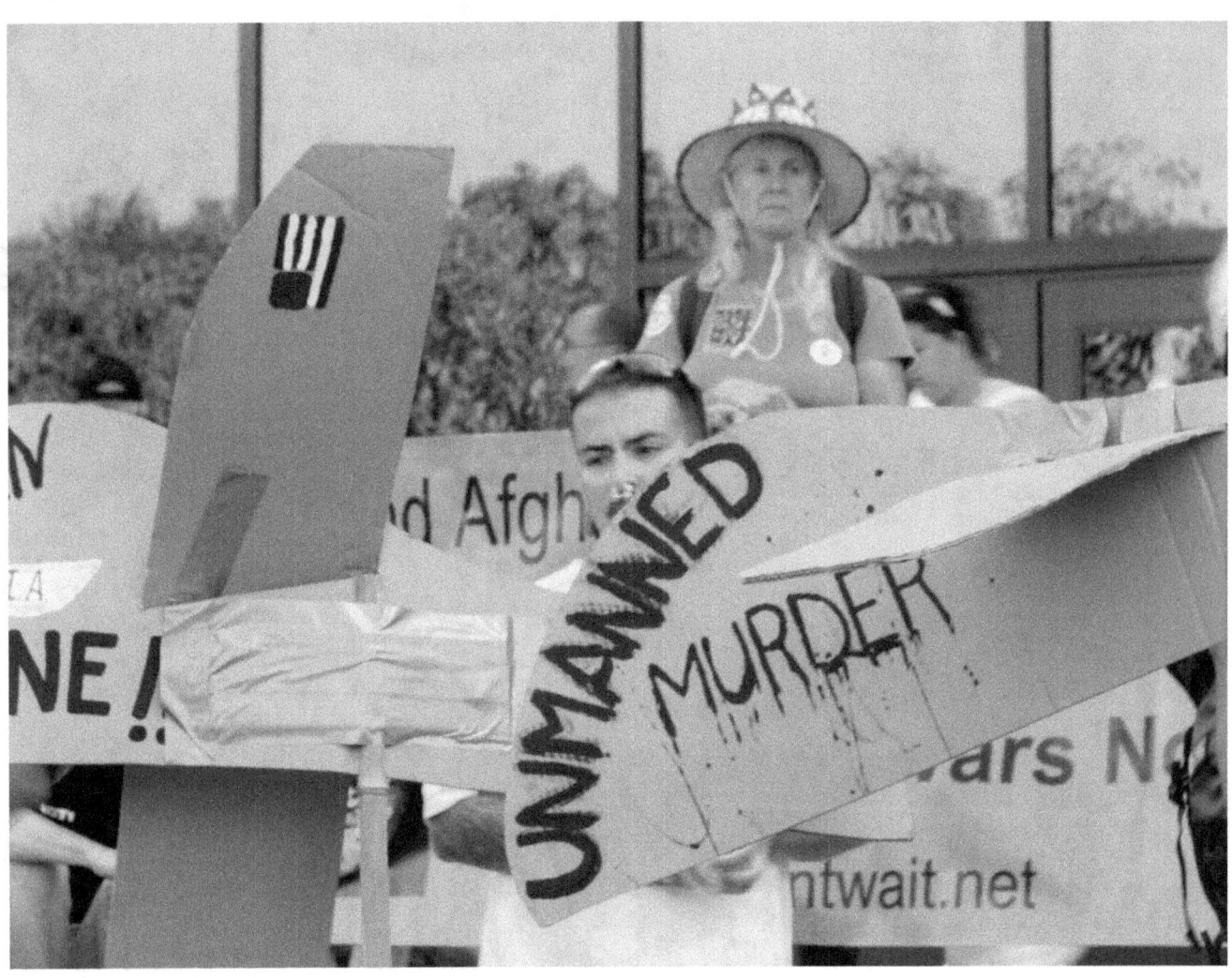

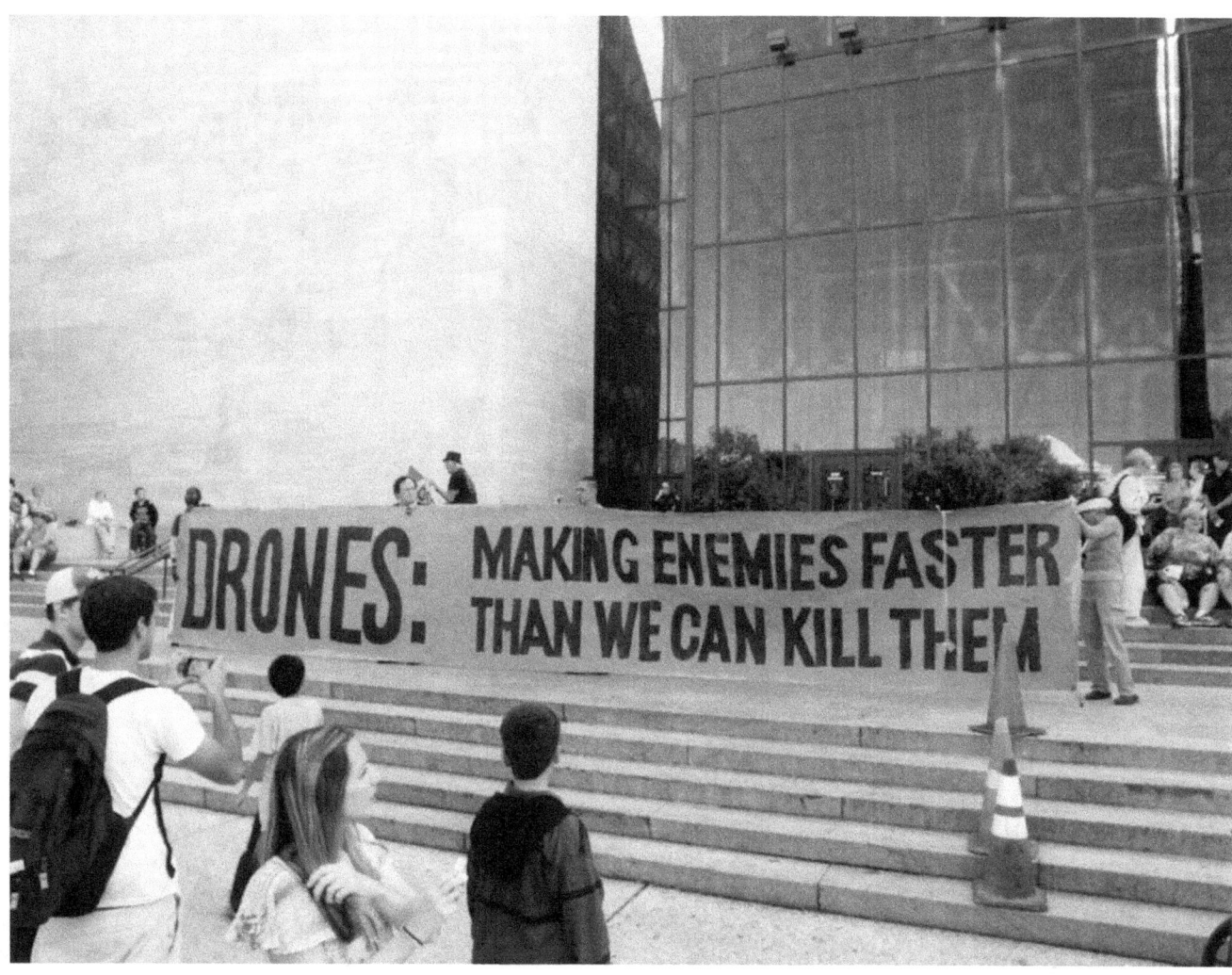

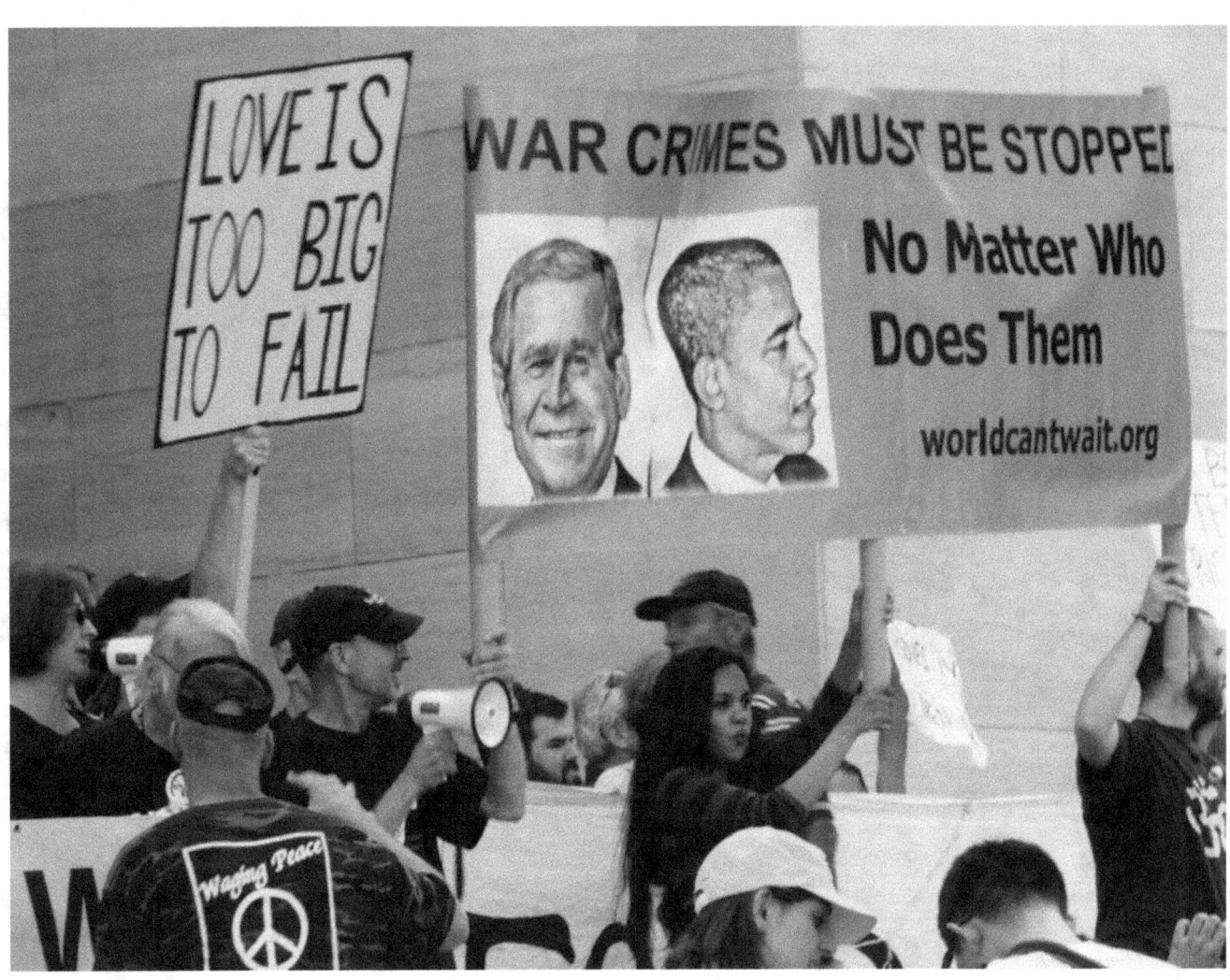

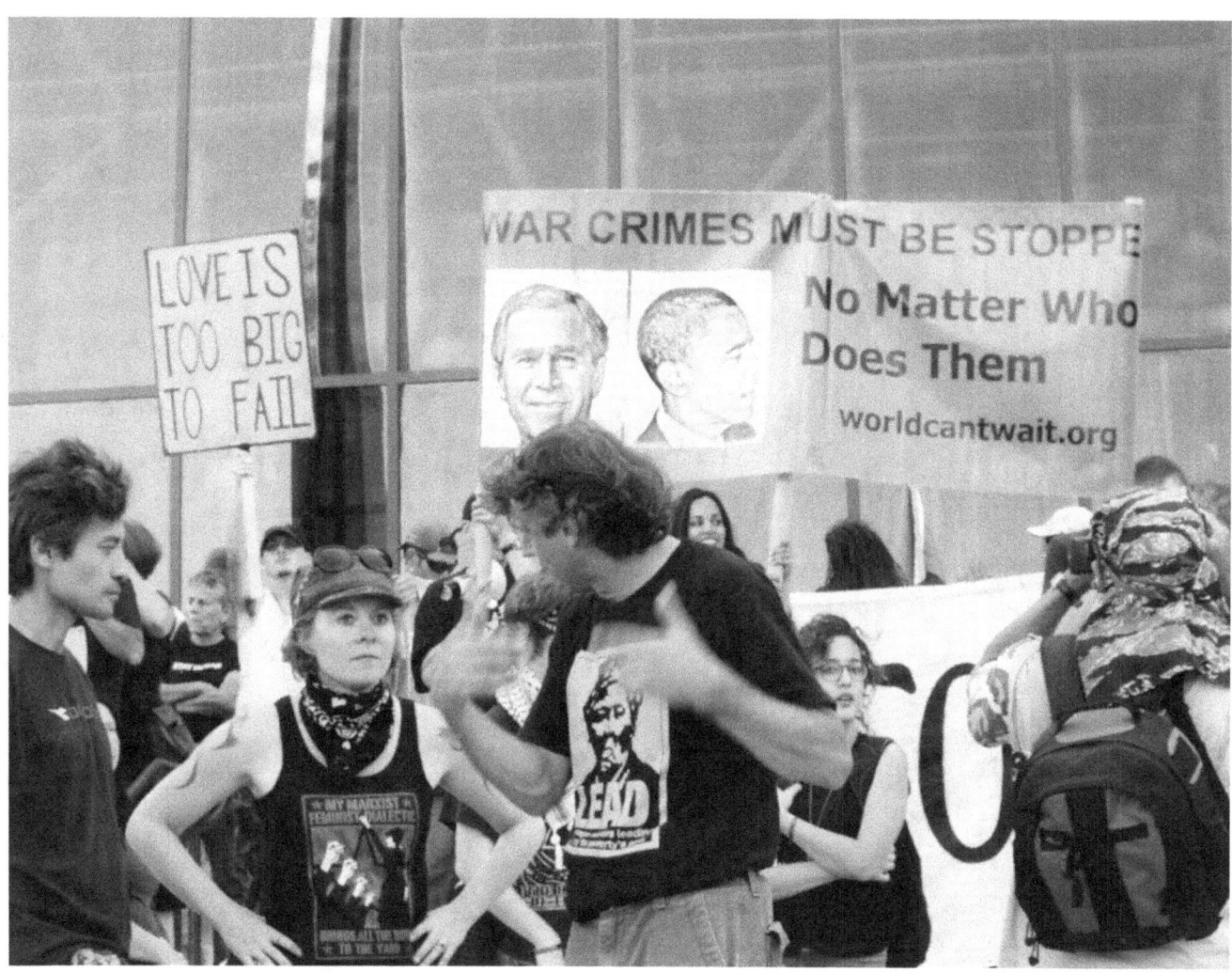

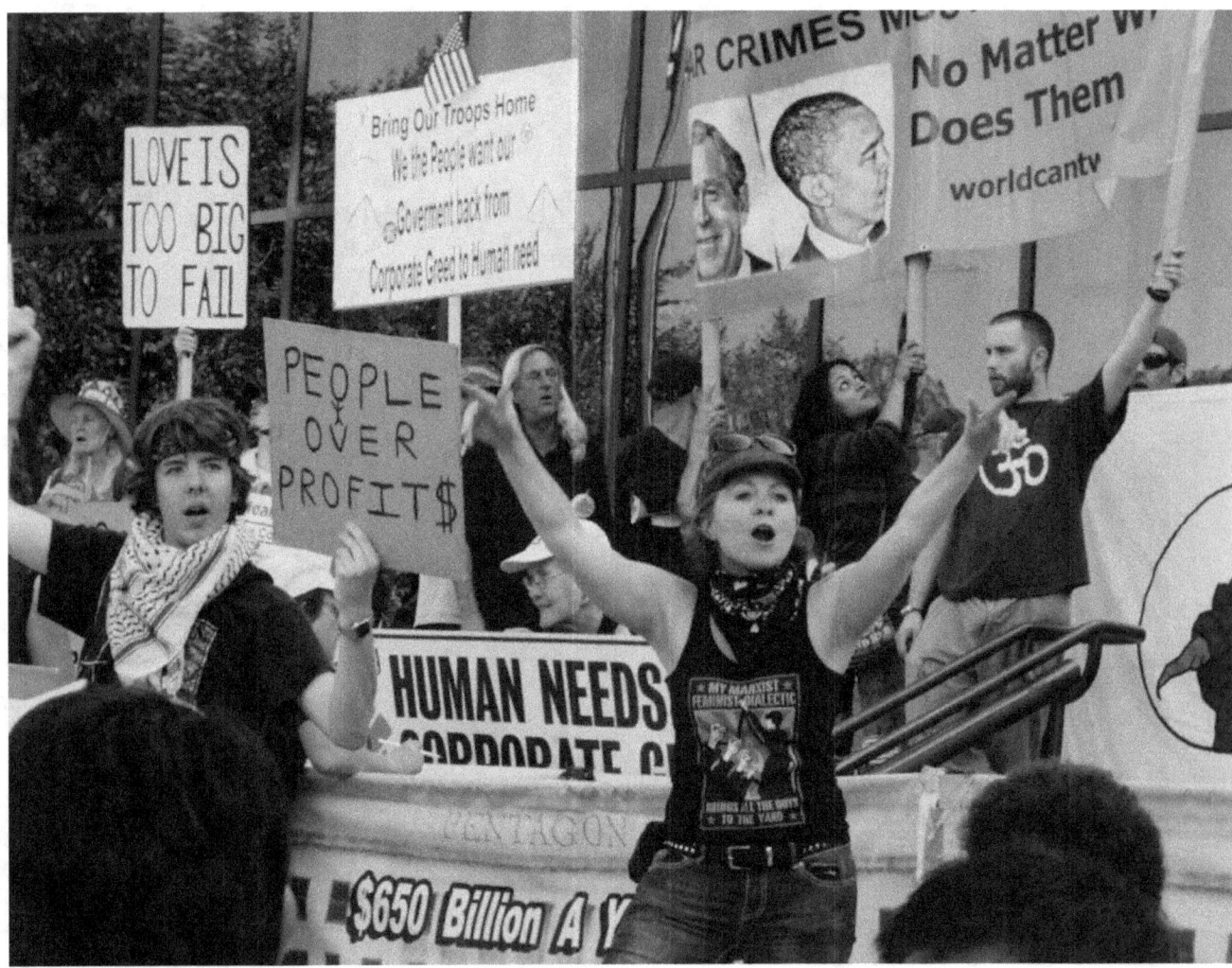

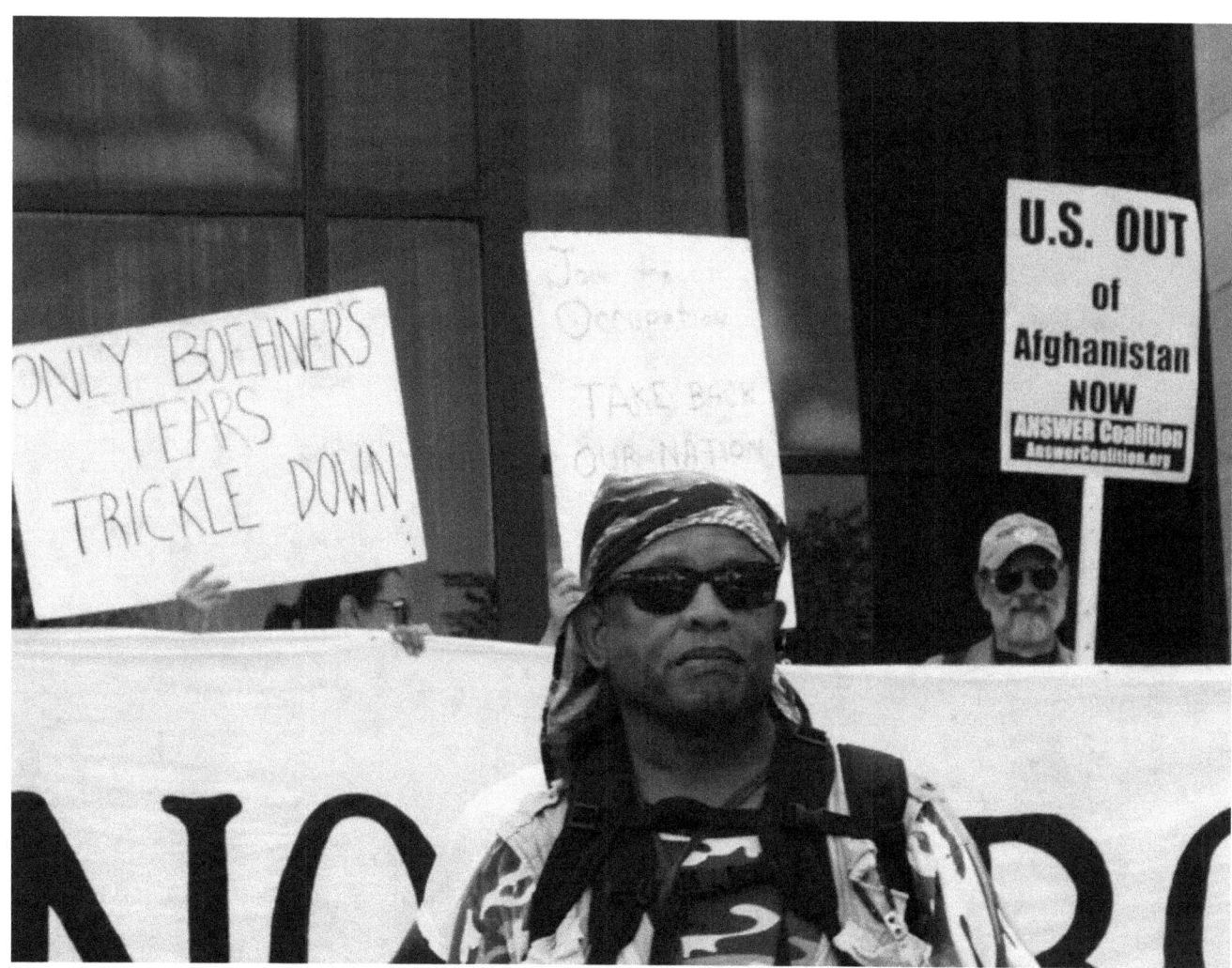

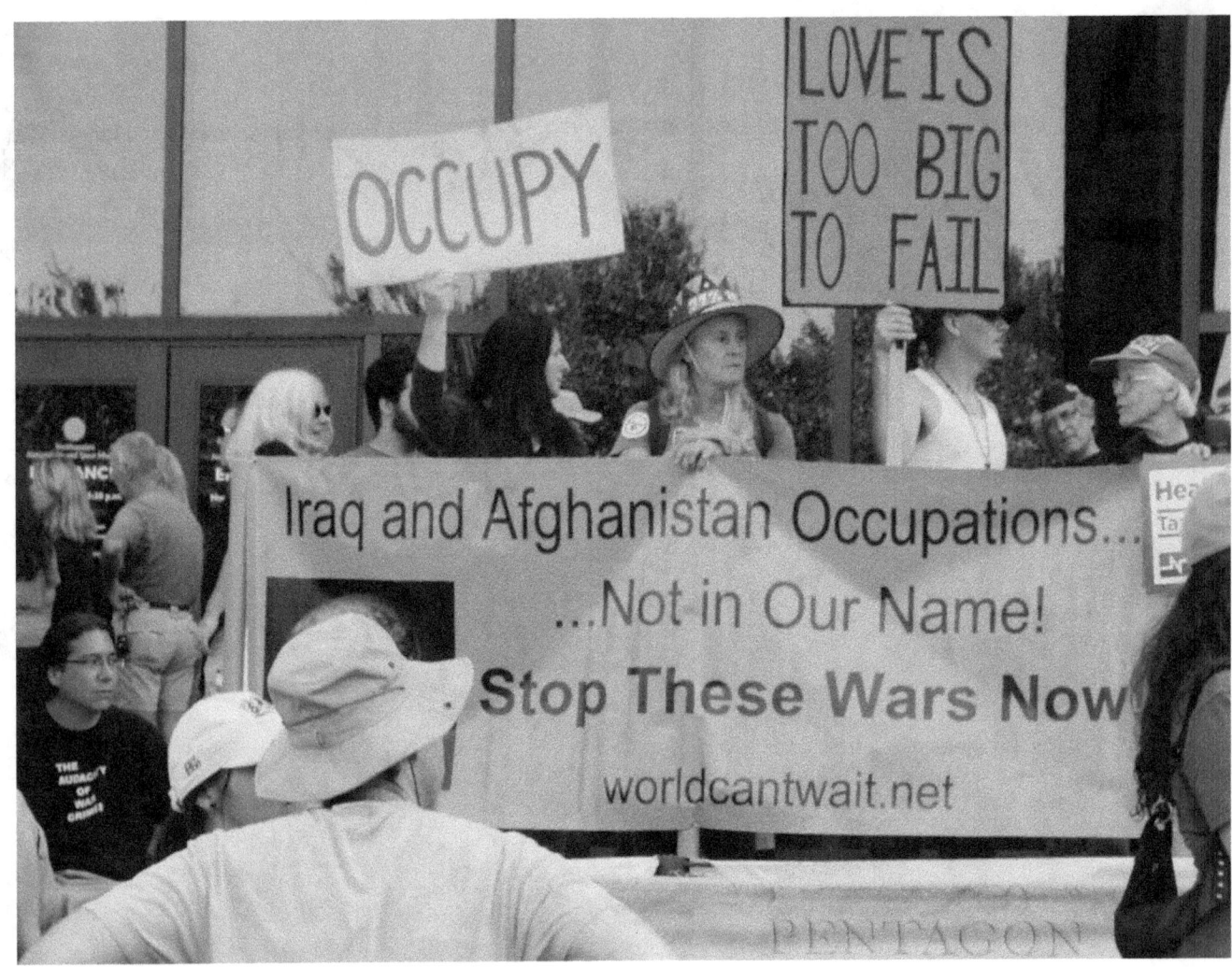

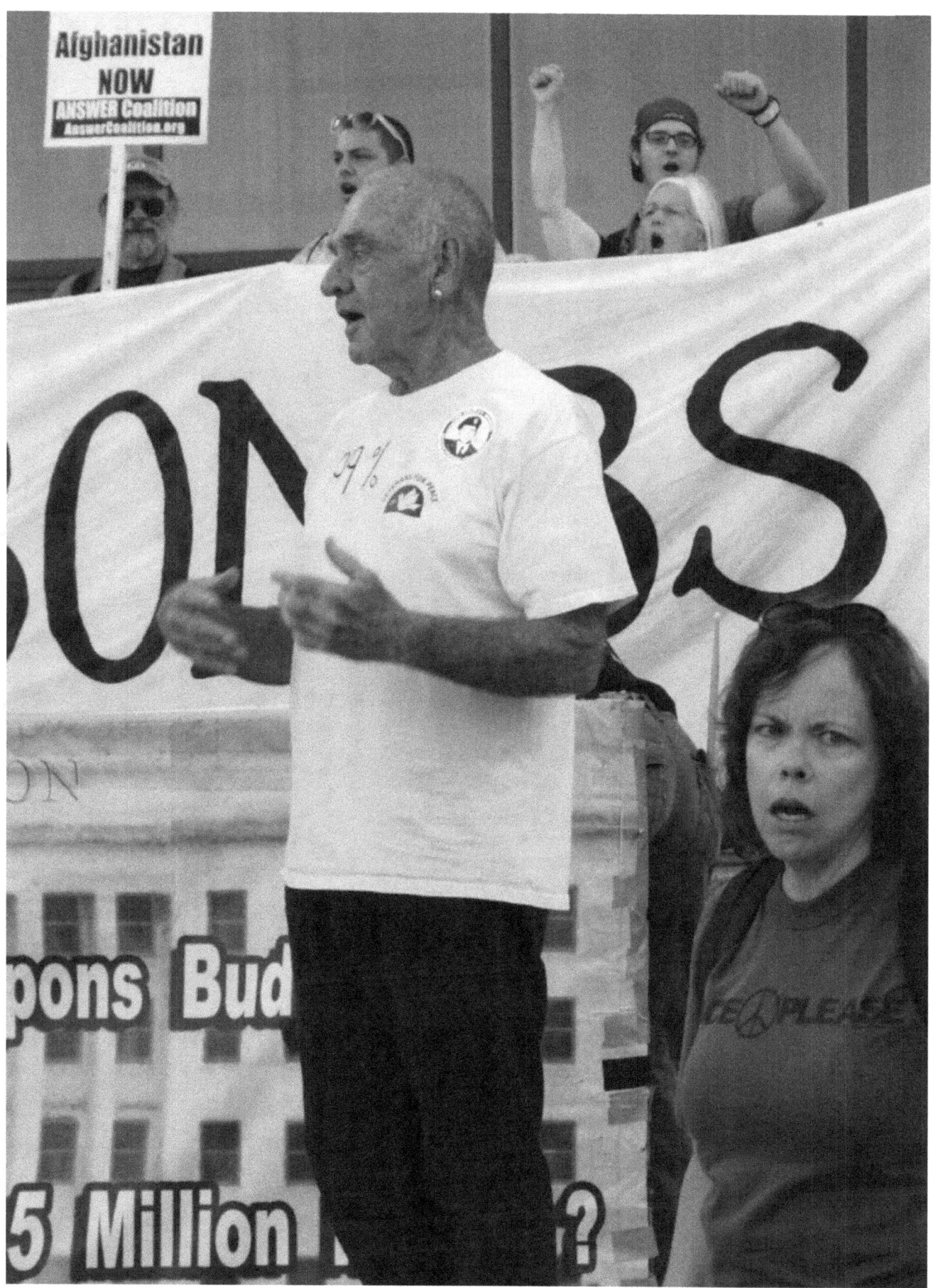

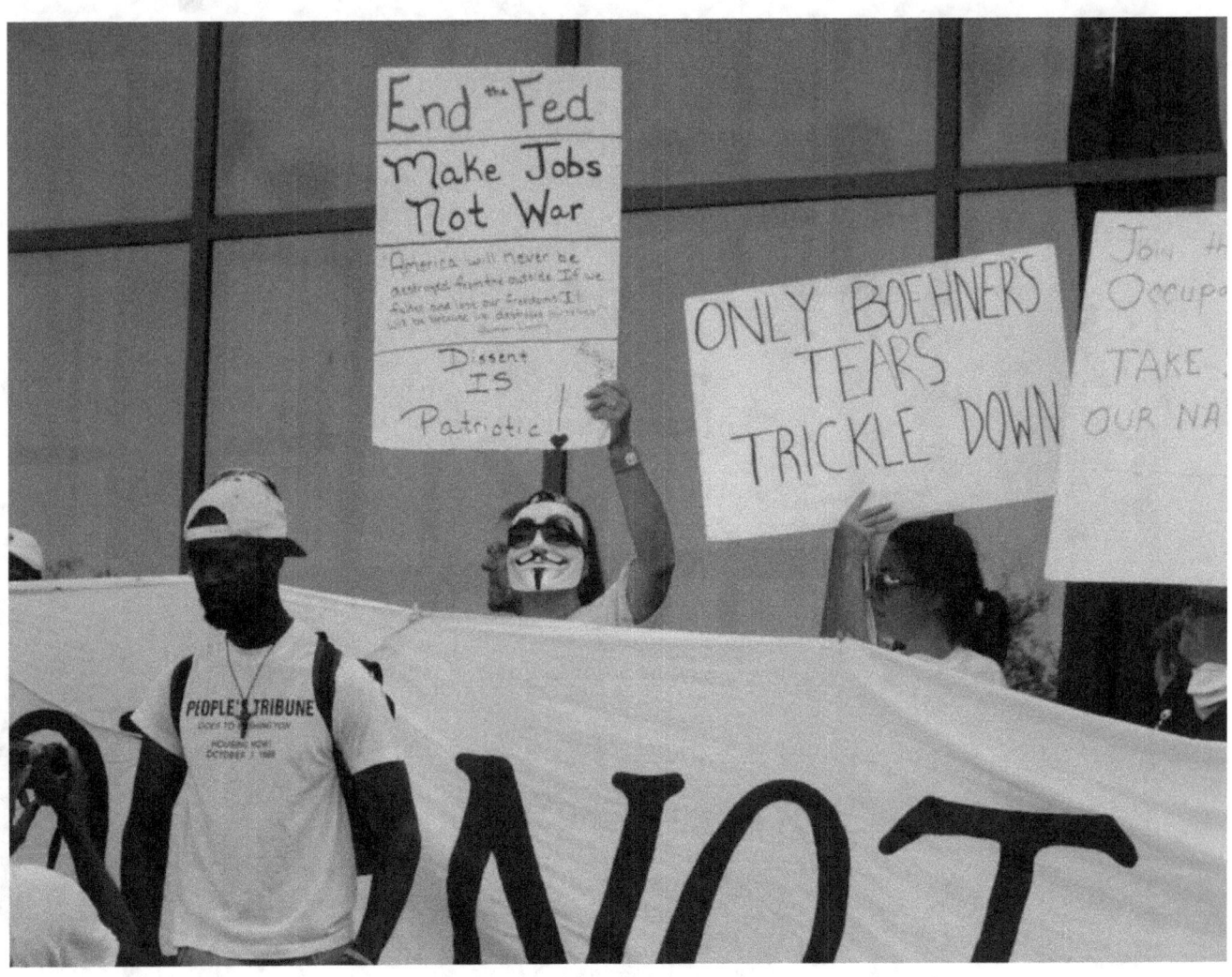

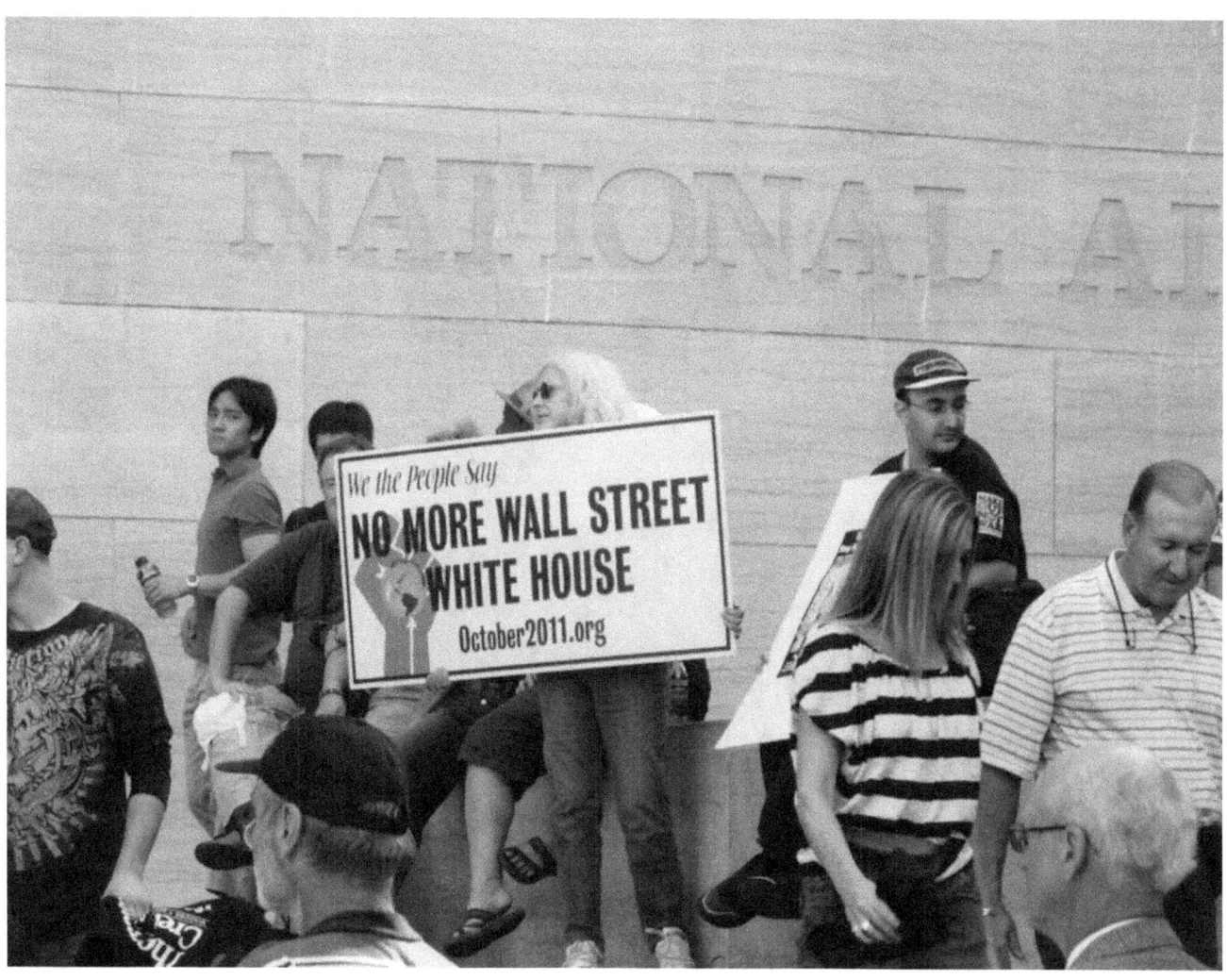

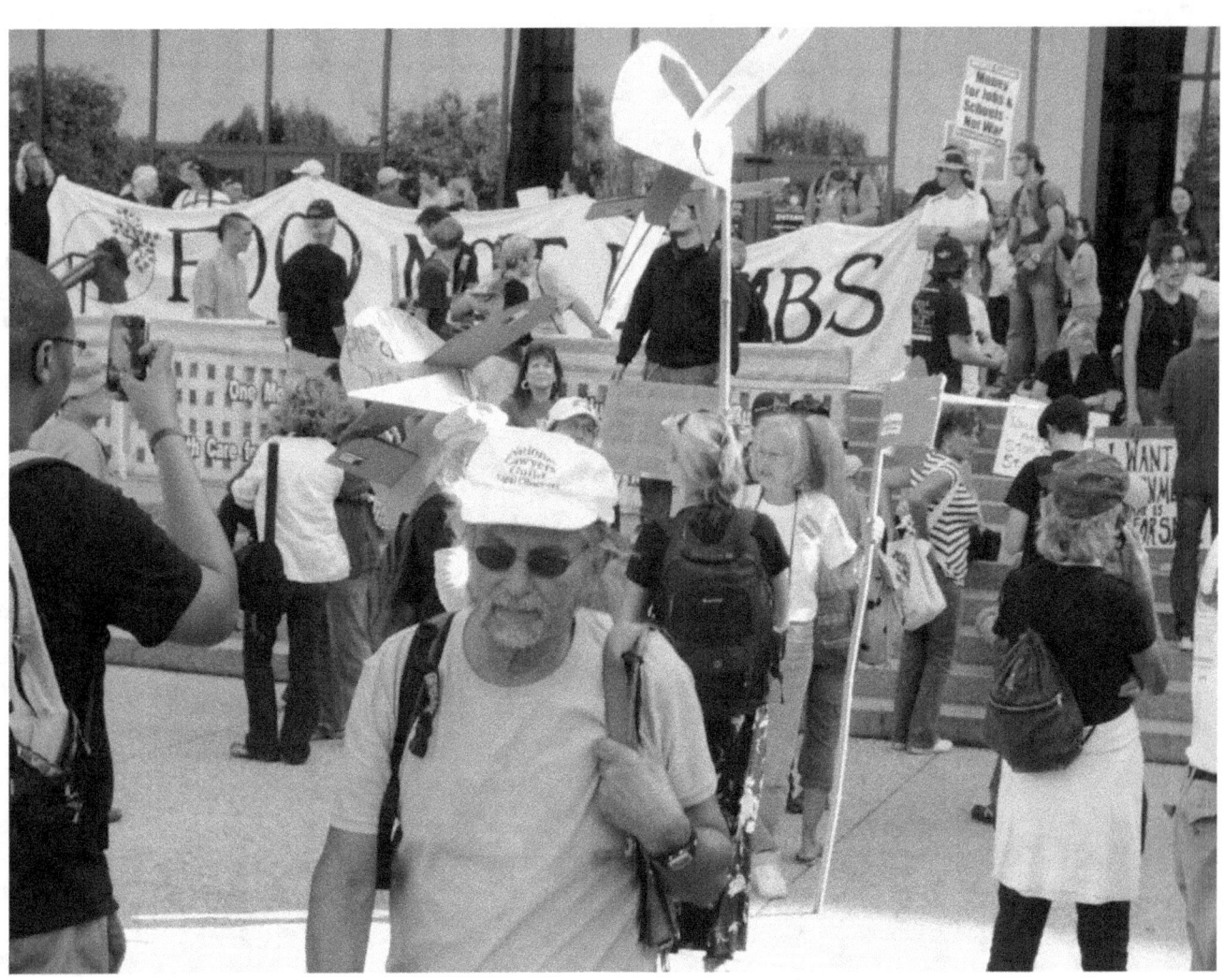

Remnant of the Occupy D.C. encampment at Freedom Plaza, June 17, 2012.

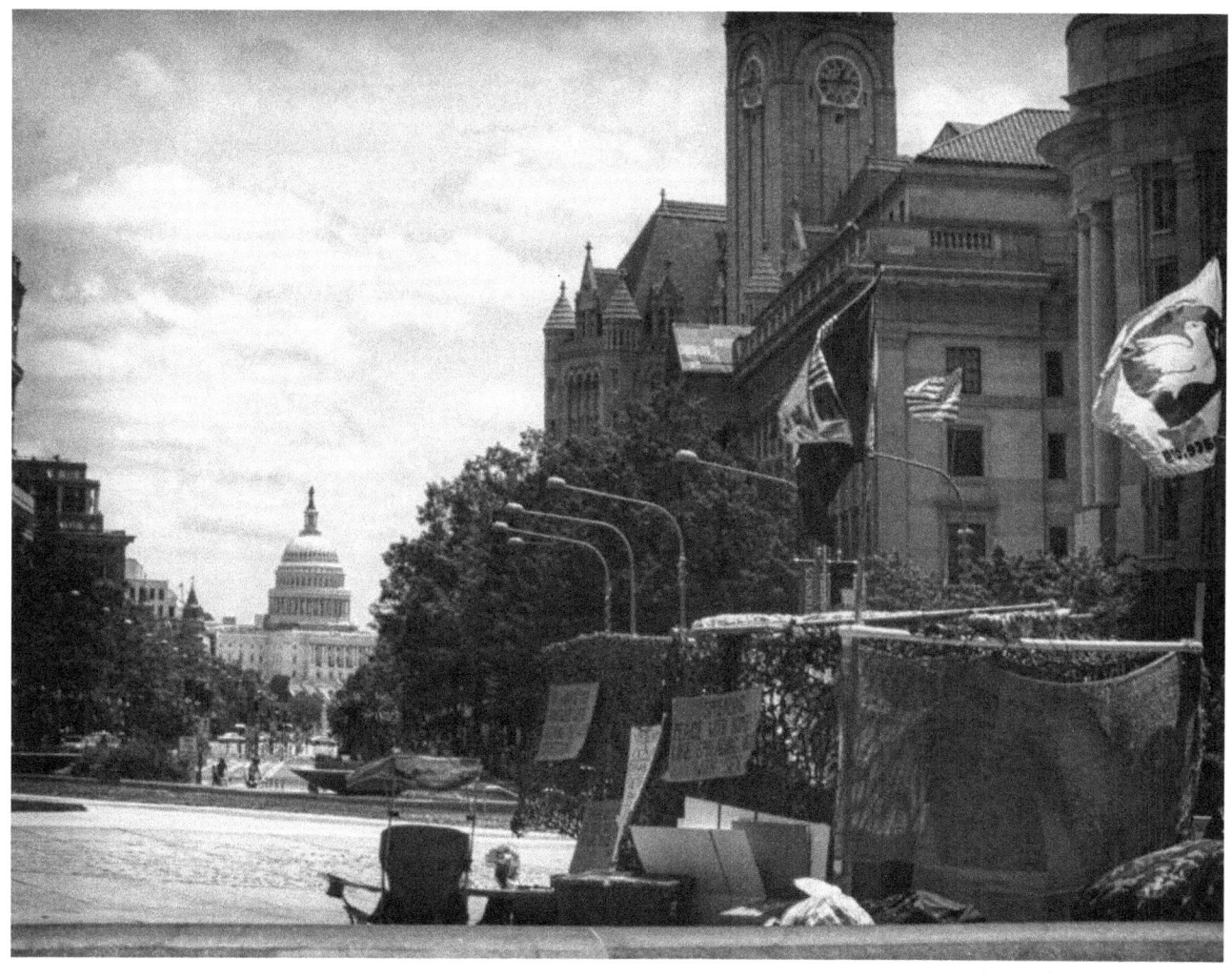

END

www.ingramcontent.com/pod-product-compliance
Lightning Source LLC
Chambersburg PA
CBHW081458170526
45166CB00008B/2467